INTERACTIVE JAPANESE

❶

Takako Tomoda and Brian May

INTERACTIVE JAPANESE 1

An Introductory Course

KODANSHA INTERNATIONAL
Tokyo • New York • London

Illustrations by Mitsuru Takahashi.

Distributed in the United States by Kodansha America, Inc., 114 Fifth Avenue,
New York, New York, 10011, and in the United Kingdom and continental Europe
by Kodansha Europe Ltd., 95, Aldwych, London WC2B 4JF.

Published by Kodansha International Ltd., 17-14 Otowa 1-chome,
Bunkyo-ku, Tokyo 112, and Kodansha America, Inc.

Printed in Japan.

ISBN 4-7700-2050-3

First edition, 1996

96 97 98 99 00 10 9 8 7 6 5 4 3 2 1

CONTENTS　もくじ　目次

Sociocultural Points

Writing

New Structures and Expressions

おはようございます。こんにちは。こんばんは。(noun)ですか。AはBです。
はい、そう です。いいえ、ちがいます。Use of particle の. Use of わたし.
おげんきですか。すみません。おねがいします。

LESSON 3   33

Functions and Situations

Sociocultural Points

Writing

New Structures and Expressions

これは なん ですか。これ / それは noun です／ではありません。
どうも ありがとう。ありがとうございます。いいえ（reply to ありがとう）。
いただきます。ごちそうさまでした。おそまつさまでした。use of ね。
さようなら。しつれいします。じゃ、また。おやすみなさい。

Functions and Situations

Sociocultural Points

Writing

New Structures and Expressions

わたしは／も place に／へ いきます／いきません。
いきました／いきませんでした。どこにいきますか。
きょうと へも／にも いきますか。ここ／そこ。
にほん の どこ ですか。A と B へ いきました。
いつ いきますか。Use and non-use of particle に
in time expressions. いってきます。いってらっしゃい。
ただいま。おかえりなさい。でした。ではありませんでした。

Functions and Situations

Sociocultural Points

Writing

New Structures and Expressions

なんじ ですか。ふん、ぷん、はん。から／まで。
ごぜん／ごご。つぎの。 time に つきます。time に でます。
place に つきます。place を でます。なんばんせん。
destination ゆきの でんしゃ。どういたしまして。

LESSON 8   111

Functions and Situations

Sociocultural Points

Writing

New Structures and Expressions

name でございます。もしもし、（なまえ）ですが。
name さん、おねがいします。
ぼく。しょうしょう おまちください。また、でんわ します。
から／まで with place。きます、かえります。use of ごろ。
いい ですか。いい ですよ。ごしょうかい します。
こちらは nameさんです。こちらこそ どうぞよろしく。
にほんご がおじょうずですね。まだまだ です。さあ、まあ、やあ。

LESSON 9   125

Functions and Situations

Sociocultural Points

LESSON 10   141

LESSON 11   156

LESSON 12   173

LESSON 13   188

New Structures and Expressions

Particle を。 Transitive and intransitive verbs.
Conjunctions: そして、それから、または。
Use of で with actions. Frequency adverbs:
まいにち、まいばん、まいあさ、まいしゅう、
いつも、よく、ときどき、あまり、ぜんぜん。
Use of まだ.

LESSON 14 206

New Structures and Expressions

なん人 ですか。きょうだい が いますか。
あに が 一人 と いもうと が 二人 います。
ごしゅみ は。しつれい ですが。けん、く、ちょうめ、ばんち。

LESSON 15 225

Writing

New Structures and Expressions

いくつ ですか。nounを number ください。なんまい。
なん本。ほかに は。それ だけ です。colors.
どっち、こちら、そちら、あちら、あなた。
なん才 ですか。おさきに しつれい します。生年月日。

LESSON 16   242

Functions and Situations

Sociocultural Points

New Structures and Expressions

placeに thingが あります。が／は。conjunction や。
ございます／でございます。もうしわけ ありません。
なんぱく。 thingは どこ に ありますか。

LESSON 17   257

Functions and Situations

Sociocultural Points

せったい　　　　　　　　　　　　　　　　　　　　　　　　　　**17.7**
Japanese holidays, Children's Day　　　　　　　　　　　　**17.8–9**

New Structures and Expressions
どこに すんでいますか。 じかん／よていが ありますか。
おととし、 きょねん、 ことし、 らいねん、 さらいねん。
ちょっとまってください。 (time) はちょっと。 だいじょうぶ。
(time)に(event)があります。 ほんとう。 なんの。 しりません。

Preface

To you as a student

While the long-term goals of language learners are many and various, all must start with the basics. When these basics have clear practical applications in everyday life their mastery is all the more pleasurable. *Interactive Japanese 1* focuses upon the key communication skills you require when visiting Japan or interacting with Japanese people in your own country. Once you can successfully convey basic information and deal with commonly encountered situations you have established the basis for further social interaction in the Japanese language and have opened the doors which lead to competence in many more specialized areas.

The process of understanding and conveying information in a foreign language is crucial to the development of the confidence you require to continue along the path to fluency. The principle purposes of this textbook are to provide you with the experience of meaningful interaction in Japanese, an insight into Japanese society and culture, and a step by step introduction to the reading and writing of Japanese.

The *Interactive Japanese* series has been many years in the making. This first volume contains material which has been tested and revised many times with the aim of discovering a method of presentation which allows the language to unfold smoothly and evenly. By presenting the material in small chunks, each of which is applied to a practical purpose, we demonstrate the relevance of each new point to real-life communication and avoid overloading you with too much material too soon. In this way you learn Japanese conversation at the same time as acquiring a firm basis in the structure of the Japanese language.

Although this text is designed for classroom use it is equally suitable for self study. Each section contains sufficient explanation for you to use it, and the cassette tape (available separately), for your own private study or to catch up on any lessons you may not have been able to fit in to your busy schedule.

To you as a teacher

Interactive Japanese 1 has been designed to provide you with an easy to use, well referenced text for upper secondary students and adult learners who are beginning the study of the Japanese language. This text is interactive in the sense that it stresses active classroom use with its numerous pair-work activities and dialogues which lend themselves to role-play and adaption. Listening, reading, and writing are included both as separate and integrated skills activities.

You will find this text contains all you need to conduct successful student-centered classes since each subsection flows onto the next and key structural and sociocultural points are all explained. The moderate pace of the text coupled with the mix of speaking, listening, reading and writing activities keep classes stimulating and promote interaction between students. Sections on writing hiragana and kanji and homework provide reinforcement between lessons and encourage self-directed learning.

Years of classroom testing and feedback has shown that *Interactive Japanese 1* is easily understood by all types of learners and provides busy teachers with an interesting and relevant course which requires a minimum of preparation and support materials.

Upon completion of this text students will:

- be able to use basic spoken Japanese to interact with Japanese people while traveling in Japan and in contact with Japanese people abroad.

- have a basic understanding of the structure of the Japanese language.

- have acquired sociocultural knowledge relevant to the topics covered.

- be able to read and write hiragana and twenty-four kanji.

- be able to use a Japanese-English dictionary.

- have been exposed to katakana and a large number of kanji.

Acknowledgments

We would like to thank the following people for their support in the preparation of this text and the accompanying cassette: Nakatani Takayuki, Matsui Takaaki, Matsui Tamiko, Nagasawa Hiroko, Takahashi Mitsuko; Tomoda Mutsuko, Andrew Pratt, Belinda Fleming, Michael Brase, and our editor Paul Hulbert.

Introduction

1. How can *Interactive Japanese 1* help you learn Japanese?

Whether you are an absolute beginner at Japanese or whether you have a smattering of the language, *Interactive Japanese 1* can set you firmly and confidently on the path to fluency in Japanese. By introducing the language step by step, with no huge leaps and each step explained and illustrated in a realistic and usable fashion, this text guides you through the fundamentals of the Japanese language. In addition, the numerous notes on social and cultural aspects of Japan help you use the language you have learned in an appropriate fashion while providing you with some of the background information you need when interacting with Japanese people.

The writing practice sections and charts set you on the road to Japanese literacy and the instructions on dictionary usage provide you with the keys to self-study. The comprehensive referencing system and many notes ensure you will find this textbook a useful reference even after you have mastered the material contained within.

2. What does *Interactive Japanese 1* cover?

Interactive Japanese 1 and its cassette tapes (available separately) teaches you basic Japanese conversation with a focus on commonly used daily expressions, question and answer techniques, and the conversational strategies you need when interacting with Japanese people either as a visitor to Japan or as a host to Japanese people in your own country.

We have limited the complexity of the language to simple single-verb sentences which have wide application in everyday conversation. By using these basic structures in over sixty frequently encountered situations you will learn how to communicate your needs and make social contact with Japanese people.

Besides being an introduction to Japanese conversation, *Interactive Japanese 1* teaches you the basics of the Japanese writing system. You learn to read and write all the hiragana, twenty-four kanji, as well as dictionary skills. This text also exposes you to katakana and a considerable number of kanji without requiring their mastery. Romanization is included for all Japanese script in the first three lessons. From Lesson 4 this romanization is progressively removed for hiragana and the kanji covered in the textbook. This step by step introduction of Japanese script steadily raises your reading and writing level throughout the text in line with the improvement in your speaking and listening.
Each lesson is followed by a homework section that provides you with the means to check your understanding of the language you have covered. At the back of the text are charts for hiragana and katakana, instructions for using a Japanese-English dictionary, a

comprehensive vocabulary list, a list of all grammatical points and key expressions, and homework answers.

3. What *Interactive Japanese 1* does not include.

While katakana script is included throughout *Interactive Japanese 1* there is no practice section for learning katakana. We assume that you will first learn hiragana before progressing to katakana and that katakana study would commence in Lesson 16. However, this does not mean that your study of katakana cannot begin earlier.

Twenty-four kanji are introduced in the writing practice sections of *Interactive Japanese 1* but these do not appear in dialogues until the lesson in which they are introduced. Lessons 15, 16, and 17 contain all twenty-four kanji. However, lists of new vocabulary and subsection titles give words written in both hiragana and kanji in later lessons to provide you with exposure to more kanji than are required to comprehend the passages in the textbook.

There are no English translations of dialogues or other passages because you are able to work out the meanings of the Japanese passages by consulting the notes which precede and follow them. The inclusion of such comprehensive notes makes translations superfluous. Moreover, translations can have a negative effect by encouraging you to translate everything into English rather than concentrate on understanding the Japanese directly.

4. The structure of *Interactive Japanese 1*.

The textbook is divided into seventeen lessons each of which should require about three hours of class time to complete. The lessons themselves are divided into subsections which deal with new language points, conversation, oral practice, sociocultural notes, grammatical explanations, listening, reading, or writing. The language sections typically comprise:

- an introduction in which the new point is explained.

- a conversation which illustrates the point functionally using a situation likely to be encountered by students when interacting with Japanese people.

- a practice section which often involves an information gap activity requiring oral pair-work.

Throughout each lesson are notes on language usage, Japanese culture and society, and summaries of the key language patterns which need to be mastered.
The last sections of Lessons 1-15 cover the writing of hiragana and twenty four kanji with an emphasis on stroke order and proportion.

From an educational standpoint *Interactive Japanese 1* includes both structural/functional and communicative features. Its explicit focus is upon communicating information in realistic situations with the implicit introduction and reinforcement of basic grammatical structures. Language points are introduced systematically according to a spiral structure which continues in subsequent volumes. When a new grammatical point is first introduced only its key features are practiced. Further details are introduced when the structure is again encountered in a different situation. Rather than explaining each grammatical point in exhaustive detail before moving on to the next, this spiral structure allows each grammatical structure to be revised and extended each time it is encountered. This has a positive effect on student learning and motivation because new material is not made overly complex. Since a new point often involves aspects of previously encountered material it can be speedily assimilated and used giving students a sense of achievement and allowing class time to be used for activities which involve students rather than extensive explanation. The practice of new structures is through pair-work which requires the exchange of information by repeatedly using the target language pattern within a meaningful context. This obviates the need for mechanical drills and focuses students' attention on the process of information exchange.

Since each lesson comprises a number of subsections, each relating to a new point, classes can be structured flexibly. Breaks can be made at a number of points in each lesson so it is not necessary to cover a complete lesson in each class. The sectional structure allows classes to be more stimulating for students and less demanding for teachers because the focus of the lesson shifts from teacher to tape player to student pair to textbook and back to teacher a number of times during a lesson. The result is a more student-centered class and reduced teacher talking time which allows the teacher time to monitor the progress of the class and individual students. This structure also makes reference to the tape and indexes quick and convenient.

5. Using *Interactive Japanese 1* for self-study.

Since *Interactive Japanese 1* provides complete explanations of all the language introduced along with a comprehensive vocabulary index and charts of Japanese script, it can be used for independent self study or revision at home.
To use this textbook effectively we recommend you follow variations on the following procedure:

1. Listen to the tape and practice saying the Japanese syllables. Reading the notes in sections 1.6, 1.9, and 1.10 will assist you. To ensure your pronunciation is good, it is worth recording yourself on another tape and playing it back until you get it right.

2. Approach each lesson section by section, first reading the notes and then the new language material.

3. Play the conversation (*kaiwa*) section right through a few times so that you get used to the sound of the language. Then do it again using the pause button so you can repeat it sentence by sentence. The aim is to copy the sound and rhythm of the tape as best you can.

4. Using the tape you can practice taking one role in the conversation by using the volume control. If you are taking part B, play the first part of the conversation (part A) then turn down the volume while you say part B, then back up again so you hear the next part A and so on throughout the conversation. Once you have done this a few times you

will find you can easily judge when to change the volume so you can have a smooth conversation with the voice on the tape.

5. Imagine yourself in the same situation as in the conversation and work out how to substitute appropriate words for those underlined in the conversation to make it relevant to you. Using a blank tape record one part (part A) of the modified version of the conversation leaving pauses where the B parts should be. Compare your pronunciation and rhythm with that on the *Interactive Japanese 1* tapes and re-record any errors.

6. Play back what you have just recorded and fill in the other role (part B). This way you can practice the modified conversation with yourself. You can also record the B part in the same fashion so you will be able to practice both parts of the conversation.

You can keep this recording so you can practice it again later. Soon you will be able to memorize and adapt both parts of the conversation and will be well on the way to fluency in Japanese.

When you are at home washing dishes or in the car it is a good idea to play the *Interactive Japanese 1* tapes right through. It doesn't matter whether you have covered all the lessons, the aim is to get used to the sound of Japanese. At first it will all sound like gobbledygook but gradually you will be able to pick out words and then sentences. The more you listen the faster you will progress.

7. The practice sections (*renshuu*) aim to practice specific points and expand your vocabulary. These are designed for use with a partner but you can also use them in the following fashion. First, listen to the new vocabulary on the tape and repeat the words till you get the pronunciation right. Look at part A of the *renshuu* and work out what information you need and the questions you need to ask in order to get it. Say each question aloud then turn to table B and say the answer. Finally you should complete both parts A and B by writing the answers in the blanks using as much Japanese script as you have learned.

8. In some lessons there are listening comprehension exercises (*kikitori renshuu*). To use these effectively you should first read the introduction and imagine the situation. Then read the comprehension questions so you know what information to listen for. After this, play the tape a number of times until you can answer the questions. Then read through the passage and check that you understand it. Finally, check the answers (*kotae*) at the end of the lesson.

9. *Interactive Japanese 1* will teach you to write all of the hiragana script as well as some kanji. It is important that you put effort into learning the writing system as it will also aid your understanding of the language. A few new characters are introduced in each lesson so by Lesson 15 you will be able to both read and write hiragana. This is a major step towards the mastery of Japanese.

6. Using _Interactive Japanese 1_ in the classroom (notes for teachers).

This text is designed to allow you to make your class active and student-centered. Since both language and sociocultural points are explained in the text students can be encouraged to read these prior to class so valuable class time can be spent on meaningful activities.

The following is a typical class structure:

1. Briefly introduce the new topic and direct students' attention to the material in the textbook. Once you have convinced your students of the value of previewing the lesson this will take very little class time.

2. Go over the new vocabulary or structures which are introduced paying attention to pronunciation and intonation. The tapes can assist you in this.

3. Set the scene for the dialogue. This is done briefly in the textbook but experienced teachers may wish to extend this by introducing props.

4. Ask the class some simple comprehension questions relating to the dialogue to focus them on the content.

5. Play the tape a couple of times using "pause" if necessary.

6. Check comprehension and direct students' attention to the main points of the dialogue.

7. Have the students practice the dialogue in pairs. At first they can read it verbatim, then substitute different words for those underlined. Finally, have them use their creativity to extend and modify the dialogue. Encourage students to switch partners and roles. In some cases you may wish the students to memorize the dialogue and perform it. Some students are willing to do this for the whole class but others are not. Having all student pairs perform at the same time while you monitor their progress is one way of overcoming this problem and using class time more effectively.

8. Explain the pair-work practice activity and the proper use of the A and B sections. The first time you do this kind of activity you need to make things very clear and also check that each pair is doing the right thing. Once students understand that the point of these activities is to use spoken language to convey information and written language to record it, the set up time for these activities will be greatly reduced.

   Since some pair-work practice sections focus upon vocabulary learning the pronunciation of new items may need to be covered prior to commencing the activity. This can be found on the cassette.

9. Allow the students to do the pair-work practice until most have finished. The faster students can swap roles or swap partners.

10. Experienced teachers can now add a freer activity. This could be:

    • working in pairs or small groups to construct a dialogue which they then perform, or record and self correct with minimal assistance from the teacher.

- writing a short paragraph, postcards or diary entry, relating to the topic which they exchange with other students or groups then self correct and discuss.
- an extended listening activity aimed at listening for specific information using a tape or video.
- a group discussion activity pertaining to sociocultural points covered in the lesson.
- bring authentic materials, such as food packets, containing hiragana and have students work out what is written on them.

The above is a general model which is not applicable to all sections and requires adaptation to the individual topic, the experience of the teacher, and the ability of the student group.

We suggest that teachers use as much spoken Japanese in the classroom as possible and the gradual introduction of classroom commands in Japanese is a good way to do this. The number and form of such commands is highly dependent upon the teacher and the student group so we have not included them in this textbook.

The writing practice sections are placed at the end of the lessons but this does not mean that this section should be practiced last. It may be advantageous to begin with this section so the new characters learned can be practiced throughout the lesson. In classes in which latecomers are common we have found that encouraging students, as a group, to practice their writing on the board while assisting them with their writing style is a good way to begin the class. We have also found that introducing the new characters at a natural break point during the lesson is a good way of adding variety to the class. It is also quite possible to accelerate the rate of introduction of Japanese script. In the textbook it takes fifteen lessons to cover all the hiragana based upon the allocation of about 10 minutes per lesson to the learning of script and the assumption that students will do some homework. Although there is a two-lesson lag in the removal of romanization for learned characters from the text, in our own teaching we use all learned characters when writing on the board and encourage students to acquire the hiragana as fast as possible. From Lesson 16 there is no writing section since we would expect katakana to be introduced at this point if not earlier.

The textbook assumes students will do some homework and a homework section is included after each lesson. These not only revise the structures given in the lesson but also introduce new vocabulary items relevant to the characters learned to date.

7. Future publications in the series.

Subsequent volumes of *Interactive Japanese* are currently in preparation as are texts on learning katakana and kanji.

第一課

1.1 Meeting someone for the first time

When two people meet for the first time they greet each other, give their names, and bow.
This is a situation you will often encounter and the following is the easiest way to manage it.

■Conversation 1.1　かいわ　　会話

Introducing yourself

Tanaka and Suzuki have never met before. They introduce themselves and bow.

たなか : はじめまして、たなか です。	どうぞ よろしく。
Ta na ka:　Ha ji me ma shi te,　Ta na ka　de su.	*Doo　zo　yo　ro shi ku*
すずき : はじめまして、すずき です。	どうぞ よろしく。
Su zu ki:　Ha ji me ma shi te,　Su zu ki　de su.	*Doo　zo　yo ro shi ku.*

はじめまして
たなかです。
どうぞよろしく

はじめまして
すずきです。
どうぞよろしく

Practice the above greeting by substituting your name in the underlined position.

Notes: We can break this short conversation up into three parts:

1. は じ め ま し て
ha ji me ma shi te

This is the greeting you use when you first meet someone. It means something like "Hello, (it's the) first time" and is used like the English "How do you do?"

2. た な か で す
Ta na ka de su.

"Tanaka" is the man's family name and **desu** (です) is a word which can mean "am," "is," or "are" depending on circumstance. This part is like "(I) am Tanaka" but notice that there is no word for "I" in this sentence. This is because the "I" is understood from the context, that is, it is obvious that Tanaka is referring to himself. You will find that unnecessary words are usually left out in Japanese. Also, the **desu** (です) comes at the end of the sentence so, in English this would be "Tanaka am."

The word **desu** (です) can be pronounced just as it is written i.e. **de su** or with the **u** of **su** silent so that it becomes **des**. We will use the second shortened version as it is the most common but the silent **u** is still always written.

3. ど う ぞ よ ろ し く
Doo   zo yo ro shi ku.

It is very difficult to give an English equivalent for this part. It means something like: "please (regard me and our future relations) favorably."

Note the way the "o" sound in **doozo** (どうぞ) is lengthened without its pronunciation changing. When saying these expressions try to pronounce each syllable with equal stress and time. All new expressions in the notes for this lesson are broken up into syllables to help you do this.

As you can see it is not possible to translate Japanese into English word for word. Instead you learn phrases and sentences which are appropriate in various situations. Trying to make up sentences by matching an English word for each Japanese word just won't work. For one thing, as we saw with **desu**, word order is different in Japanese sentences. Also, words that are are necessary in English are often left out in Japanese. Once you get the hang of learning groups of words and learn to resist the urge to find out what each bit means in English, learning Japanese will seem much easier. In fact this goes for any foreign language.

In the box below is a summary of the language pattern (called **bunkei** in Japanese) that you have just learned.

はじめまして、	（なまえ）です。	どうぞ よろしく。
Ha ji memashi te,	*(family name) de su.*	*Doo zo yo ro shi ku.*
How do you do.	I'm (family name).	Pleased to meet you.

1.2 The bow   おじぎ   お辞儀

Japanese people bow (do **ojigi**) rather a lot and it takes a while to get used to. In general people do **ojigi** (おじぎ) when they meet, part, say thank you, or say sorry. In the first conversation you will do **ojigi** on the "*Doozo yoroshiku*" part. When doing **ojigi**, you bend at the waist with your back straight looking at the ground. Don't look up at the other person. **Ojigi** (おじぎ) is a little different for men and women. Women place their hands on the front of their legs and men keep their arms straight at their sides (see picture above).

1.3 Asking for information—Country   くに   国

Once you have met someone and learned their name, the next thing is to find out a little more information about them. You could ask them their country (**kuni**). Here is a list of countries. Can you work out which they are? Write the English in the blanks.

📼 　　　　Kuni くに	Kuni くに
nihon にほん ＿＿＿＿＿＿	amerika アメリカ ＿＿＿＿＿＿
oosutoraria オーストラリア ＿＿＿＿＿＿	kankoku かんこく ＿＿＿＿＿＿
chuugoku ちゅうごく ＿＿＿＿＿＿	itaria イタリア ＿＿＿＿＿＿
furansu フランス ＿＿＿＿＿＿	taiwan たいわん ＿＿＿＿＿＿
doitsu ドイツ ＿＿＿＿＿＿	indoneshia インドネシア ＿＿＿＿＿＿

kanada カナダ _____	nyuujiirando ニュージーランド _____
igirisu イギリス _____	mareeshia マレーシア _____
indo インド _____	tai タイ _____

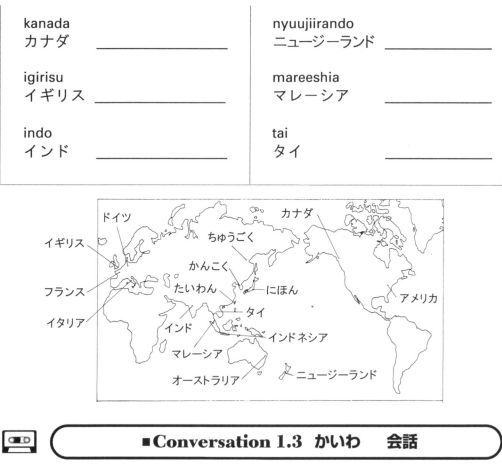

■**Conversation 1.3 かいわ   会話**

Asking what country someone is from

The following conversation is set at an international gathering in Japan. Mr. Matsui (who is obviously Japanese) meets Mr. Smith and they introduce themselves. Mr. Matsui is curious as to where Mr. Smith (**Sumisu**) is from.

まつい：はじめまして、まつい です。 どうぞ よろしく。
Matsu i   Ha ji memashi te,   Ma tsu i de su.   Doo zo yo ro shi ku.

スミス：はじめまして、スミス です。 どうぞ よろしく。
Su mi su: Ha ji me ma shi te,   Smith   de su.   Doo   zo yo ro shi ku.

まつい：スミス さん、おくに は。
Ma tsu i: Su mi su   sa n,   o ku ni wa?

スミス：<u>アメリカ</u> です。
Su mi su: A me ri ka de su.

まつい：ああ そう です か。
Ma tsu i: Aa   soo   de su ka.

Practice this conversation substituting the underlined words for different names and countries.

Notes: There are three new expressions in this conversation:

1. おく に は。
o ku ni wa?

Kuni くに means "country." An o お is put in front of a word to make it more polite. This o お is called an honorific and has no equivalent in English. It can be placed in front of many (but not all) nouns. In this situation it also shows that the kuni くに being referred to is the other person's kuni くに and not the speaker's. This is because you do not use honorifics when referring to things associated with yourself. In this sentence there is no need for a Japanese word for "your" because o kuni おくに can only refer to your country.
—When one Japanese person asks another this question the meaning of kuni くに changes slightly. In such cases it refers to the person's home town in Japan.
—This sentence is actually incomplete. It is like asking "Your country…?" Although there is no question mark in Japanese, we have used one here to indicate that a questioning tone is necessary for an unfinished question such as this to make sense.
—The wa は is a grammatical feature which is untranslatable. It will be explained later.

2. スミス さん
Su mi su sa n

When Mr. Matsui talks to Mr. Smith he addresses him as "Sumisu san." This san さん is placed **after** a person's name and can mean Mr., Mrs., Miss, or Ms. You should always put san さん after another person's name when talking to them or about them. San さん can come after the family name or the given name. You do not use san さん after your own name or the names of family members or very close friends.

3. ああ そう です か。
aa   soo   de su ka.

This is an expression used to show interest in what the other person has just told you. You will use this expression a lot. It is said with an even intonation and an expression of felt interest. It translates literally as "Oh, is that so?" but it is more like "Oh really" in the way it is used. In Japanese this kind of expression, called aizuchi あいづち, is used by the listener a great deal in conversation. It shows that you are interested in what you are hearing. People will feel uncomfortable if you just listen silently when someone is talking to you. You should, therefore, repeatedly use some kind of aizuchi あいづち.

1.4 Asking for information–Occupation しごと　仕事

Another thing you are likely to be asked by someone you have just met is your job or occupation (shigoto). Look up a dictionary or the vocabulary index at the back of this textbook and write the English in the blanks for the following shigoto しごと.

Shigoto しごと		**Shigoto しごと**	
isha いしゃ	_____	kyooshi きょうし	_____
kangofu かんごふ	_____	bengoshi べんごし	_____
kaishain かいしゃいん	_____	gakusei がくせい	_____
hisho ひしょ	_____	koomuin こうむいん	_____

■Conversation 1.4　かいわ　会話

Asking someone's occupation

Continuing the previous conversation between Matsui and Smith, Mr. Matsui asks Smith's occupation. Smith replies and then asks the same question of Matsui.

まつい：おしごと は。	Matsu i:　O shi go to　wa …?
スミス：<u>こうむいん</u> です。<u>まつい</u> さん は。	Su mi su:　Koo mu i　n　desu.　<u>Ma tsu i</u>　sa　n　wa?
まつい：<u>かいしゃいん</u> です。	Matsu i:　Ka i　sha i　n　de su.
スミス：ああ そう です か。	Su mi su:　Aa　soo　de su　ka.

Practice this conversation substituting different names and jobs in the underlined parts. Then start with conversation 1.3 and continue with this one.

Note: There are two new expressions in this part:

1. おしごとは。
o shi go to wa …?

This is another unfinished question just like **o kuni wa**…? It is like asking "Your job …?" Unfinished sentences are often used in Japanese conversation.

2. まついさんは。
Ma tsu i sa n wa …?

This is a very convenient way of asking a question back. In the conversation, instead of asking Matsui's job by saying **"o shigoto wa…?"** Smith just said "And you Mr. Matsui…?" Since Matsui's previous question was about **shigoto** しごと, he can understand from the context what Smith is asking. This method can be used to ask any question back to the other person.

■Language pattern 1.4　ぶんけい　　文型

おくには。 *o ku ni wa …?*	Your country…?
おしごとは。 *o shi go to wa …?*	Your job…?
(なまえ)さんは。 *(name) sa n wa …?*	And you Mr / Ms (name)…?

1.5 Names　　なまえ　　名前

In Japan people usually introduce themselves using their family name only or their full name. When someone says their full name, the family name comes first and the given name second (people only have one given name). For example, if a woman's given name is "Yoshiko" and her family is "Suzuki," her full name will be "Suzuki Yoshiko." In general, people are referred to by their family names unless they are close friends. Here is a list of some common Japanese **namae** なまえ.

📼 Family Names		Women's Names		Men's Names	
Tanaka	たなか	Hanako	はなこ	Taroo	たろう
Yamada	やまだ	Tomoko	ともこ	Ichiroo	いちろう

Ishida	いしだ	Yukiko	ゆきこ	Yukio	ゆきお
Yamamoto	やまもと	Michiko	みちこ	Michio	みちお
Suzuki	すずき	Miyuki	みゆき	Daisuke	だいすけ
Honda	ほんだ	Emi	えみ	Akira	あきら
Ishizaki	いしざき	Yumi	ゆみ	Jun	じゅん
Ueda	うえだ	Rie	りえ	Hiroshi	ひろし
Katoo	かとう	Masako	まさこ	Kenji	けんじ

1.6 Some comments on pronunciation　はつおん

In Japanese there are only five vowel sounds. These are always pronounced the same way. In Japanese these are written in **hiragana**, which is a kind of alphabet.

At first we will use the Roman letters **a, i, u, e,** and **o** to represent these sounds. These Roman letters are called **roomaji** ローマじ in Japanese. One of the difficulties with **roomaji** is that, unlike **hiragana** ひらがな, a letter in English can be pronounced a number of ways. As each **hiragana** ひらがな has a fixed sound, Japanese is easy to spell.

Since these vowels have more than one pronunciation in English, you need to make sure you keep to the correct pronunciation when reading in **roomaji**.

The following is a rough guide to Japanese pronunciation, but since English vowels vary with accent you should pay careful attention to the tape.

a	あ	as in: father, above, soya, collar	not as in: ant, cake, car
i	い	as in: police, hockey, icky, ink	not as in: binary, iron
u	う	as in: Malibu, sue, flu	not as in: under, up, surface
e	え	as in: enemy, egg, air	not as in: the, see, even
o	お	as in: ox, origin, okker, comic	not as in: order, to, soot

Japanese vowels can be short and clipped or long depending on the word. It is only the length that varies and not the sound. Therefore, **aa, ii, uu, ee, oo,** have the same pronunciation as above, only with a longer sound.

1.7 Doozo and Doomo　どうぞ　どうも

In any interpersonal interaction in nihon にほん you will use these two useful little words again and again. They have no simple English equivalents but once you understand their function you will find them easy to use.

doozo　どうぞ is used by the person offering something. We have learned doozo yoroshiku, in this case you are offering a good relationship. However, in other cases the offer is more basic.

doomo　どうも is used by the person receiving something. It is a short way of acknowledging thanks.

Although these expressions are often attached to other phrases, we will just consider some common situations in which they are used independently.

1. Handing someone an object

2. Offering something

1.8 The Japanese archipelago　にほんれっとう　日本列島

Japan is a string of mountainous volcanic islands stretching some 3000 km from north to south. There are four large islands and numerous smaller ones. The most northerly island is called Hokkaido. Compared to the rest of Japan, it is sparsely settled and has long cold winters. The largest island is Honshu. It contains the bulk of the population and the capital city Tokyo. South of Honshu is Kyushu. Kyushu is also heavily populated and has a mild almost sub-tropical climate. Next to Honshu and Kyushu is Shikoku, the smallest of the four main islands. From Kyushu a line of small islands stretches south. The largest and best known of these is Okinawa.

The area of water between Honshu, Kyushu, and Shikoku is known as the Inland Sea in English and **Setonaikai** in Japanese. The sea to the west of Japan and between Japan and Korea (**Kankoku**) is the Sea of Japan (**Nihonkai**) and to the east of Japan is the Pacific Ocean (**Taiheiyo**). To the north of Hokkaido is the Sea of Okhotsk (**Ohootsukukai**).

Locate the following features on the map (chizu) **of nihon にほん below.**

Hokkaido	ほっかいどう	北海道
Honshuu	ほんしゅう	本州
Shikoku	しこく	四国
Kyuushuu	きゅうしゅう	九州
Okinawa	おきなわ	沖縄
Setonaikai	せとないかい	瀬戸内海
Nihonkai	にほんかい	日本海
Taiheiyoo	たいへいよう	太平洋
Ohootsukukai	オホーツクかい	オホーツク海
Tookyoo	とうきょう	東京
Kankoku	かんこく	韓国
Chuugoku	ちゅうごく	中国

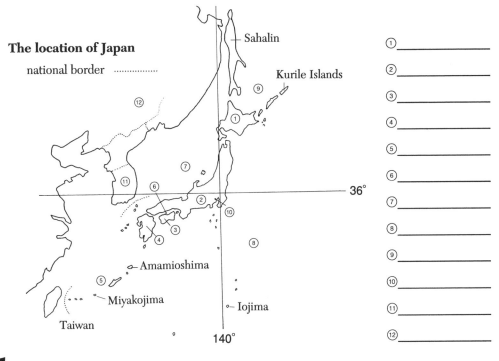

The location of Japan

national border ················

Sahalin

Kurile Islands

Amamioshima

Miyakojima

Taiwan

Iojima

36°

140°

① _____
② _____
③ _____
④ _____
⑤ _____
⑥ _____
⑦ _____
⑧ _____
⑨ _____
⑩ _____
⑪ _____
⑫ _____

1.9 General notes on Japanese and this text

1. In Japanese there are no equivalents to **a** or **the** in English. "A job" and "the job" are both just "job" i.e. **shigoto**.

2. **Plurals** are not often used in Japanese. Both "job" and "jobs" are **shigoto**. Plural forms can be made for a number of words when necessary, but on the whole they are avoided.

3. **Capitals**: There are no upper and lower case letters in Japanese. Names and new sentences are not marked by a different form of the letter as they are in English. In the early part of this text we will use upper case letters for names and new sentences but we will phase this out later.

4. **Punctuation**: The end of a Japanese sentence is marked by a small circle which is referred to as **maru** まる i.e. 。. This has the same function as a period in English. We only use this **maru** まる when writing in Japanese script, not when writing in romanized script. In Japanese script, pauses are marked by a kind of comma which is referred to as **ten** てん i.e. 、. The rules for the use of this **ten** てん are rather unclear. It can be used whenever a pause makes the meaning clearer or the sentence more like speech. Quotation marks are somewhat different. Quotes start with 「 and end with 」.

5. **Spacing**: In Japanese script there are no spaces between words, only between sentences. This may seem strange but actually it doesn't present any problem once you get used to it. However, in this text we leave a space between words and particles to make things clear for you.

6. When writing Japanese in romanized script, in the notes we have used a different font to indicate that the word is spelt as it is said in Japanese. For example, the city Tokyo is written as **Tookyoo** in the text because both the "o" sounds are long. When Tokyo is spelt as it is in English, there is no font change.

7. **Direction**: Japanese can be written either in lines from left to right just as in English, or in columns from right to left. In Japan books, magazines, and newspapers often use the second method. This textbook, however, adopts the first method since it is more familiar to English speakers.

1.10 The Japanese writing system

Japanese is not usually written in roman letters (**roomaji**). They are only used in textbooks for foreigners or on signs for the assistance of visitors to Japan. Japanese books, newspapers, magazines, and other publications use a combination of three scripts as follows:

1. **hiragana** ひらがな is a regular syllabary in which each symbol corresponds to the sound of each syllable used in Japanese. The grammatical features of Japanese are always written in **hiragana**, as are quite a number of words. You will learn the forty-six **hiragana** in this text. **Hiragana** can be easily recognized by their rounded shape e.g.
あ か さ た な は ま や ら わ の ん お こ る ゆ ぬ ね す ふ そ み ち も め

2. **kanji** かんじ are ideographic characters which originated in China. Each character has a particular meaning, but its pronunciation varies with the way it is used according to certain principles. **Kanji** are used extensively to write nouns, verbs, numbers, and names. There are thousands of **kanji** and you will learn to write a few common ones in this text. They can be recognized by their complexity, variety, and fairly square shape, e.g.
国 仕 事 名 前 日 月 火 水 木 金 土 円 一 二 三 四 五 六 七 八 九 十 本 雨 気

3. **katakana** カタカナ is a syllabary just like **hiragana**. It is mostly used to write words borrowed from foreign languages, but it is also used for brand names, exclamations, onomatpoea, slang, and botanical and zoological names. Its use can be compared to italics in English. **Katakana** can be recognized by its simple, square form, e.g.
コ オ ソ フ ム ル イ ウ ノ ミ ア カ サ タ ナ ロ キ セ ニ ネ ク ラ レ テ チ ト

Answers こたえ 答

1.3 Japan; Australia; China; France; Germany; Canada; England; India; America (U.S.A.); South Korea; Italy; Taiwan; Indonesia; New Zealand; Malaysia; Thailand.

1.4 medical doctor; nurse; company employee; secretary; teacher/instructor; lawyer; student; public servant.

Writing Japanese script 1.11

When writing **hiragana** be sure to pay attention to the direction and order of the strokes. Irrespective of complexity, all **hiragana** characters are written the same size. To practice, first trace the character with your finger paying attention to the stroke numbers and direction arrows. You can also place some translucent paper over the example and trace it a few times. Then practice writing the character by yourself in the boxes. Use an HB or B pencil.

Note: If you are using a Japanese word processer or a Japanese word processing program on your computer you can type a word in using roman letters and have it appear on the screen in **hiragana**, **katakana**, or **kanji**. You can use the system of romanization used in this text to type **hiragana** into your computer. However, there are some modifications you have to make and also some alternative ways. We have noted these for each **hiragana**.

kuni く に is the Japanese word for "country." This word comprises two syllables **ku** く and **ni** に. These syllables are each made up of one consonant sound and one vowel sound, i.e. k + u = **ku** く ; n + i = **ni** に. く is written in one stroke and に in three.

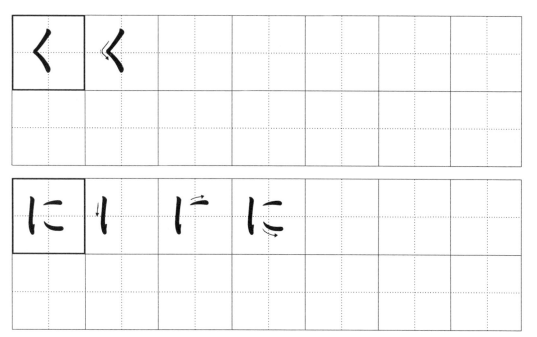

One of the five vowels is **o** お. We have seen this **hiragana** used as an honorific in front of various words, e.g. **okuni** おくに. It is written in three strokes.

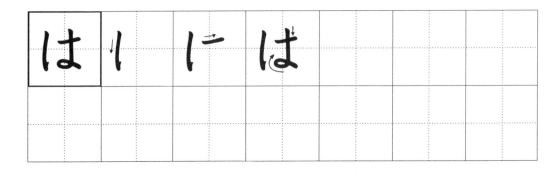

The next **hiragana** is the particle **wa** は. It indicates that what precedes it is the topic of the sentence. This **hiragana** is pronounced "ha" when it is not used as a particle. When you type it into a word processor using a standard alphabetical keyboard you always type "ha."

LESSON

1

第一課

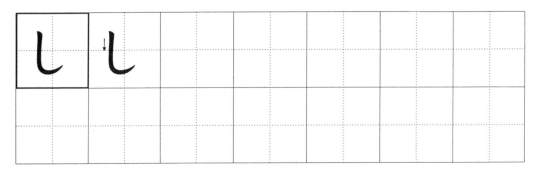

The first syllable of the word for "job" i.e. **shigoto** is **shi** し. It is written with just one stroke. It can also be typed into most word processors as "si."

See if you can read these words: おくに は..., おしgoto は..., はjimemaして,お namae.

1. Fill in the blanks to complete the dialogues (use as much hiragana as you can).

1) A: たなかさん、(　　　　　　　　) は…
    Ta na ka sa n   *wa…*

  B: いしゃ です。
    i sha   de su.

2) A: スミスさん、(　　　　　　　　) は…
    Su mi su sa n   *wa.*

  B: ドイツです。
    Do i tsu de su.

  A: ああ、(　　　　　　　　) か。
    aa   *ka.*

2. Answer the following questions. (Write in Japanese where appropriate.)

1) What do you say when you meet someone for the first time ?
(Use your own name.)

_____

2) When you give your name in the Japanese way, which name comes first, the given name or the family name ?

_____

3) What do you say when you offer something to someone ?

_____

3. Write the correct word in each blank to complete the sentences.

Japan consists of four major islands. The largest island is (　　　　　　　),
the northern most island is (　　　　　　　　), the southern island is
(　　　　　　　　) and the smallest of the four main islands is
(　　　　　　　　). The capital city of Japan is (　　　　　　　).

4. ✍ Let's write in Japanese ! Write a HIRAGANA in each ___.

_____ _____ means "country." "_____ _____ _____ は。 " is used to ask another person's country.

Let's write new words using the **HIRAGANA** that you've learned. Write one **HIRAGANA** in each box.

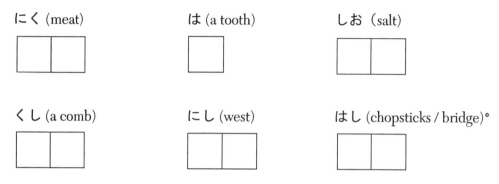

にく (meat)

は (a tooth)

しお （salt)

くし (a comb)

にし (west)

はし (chopsticks / bridge)゜

゜When the は is stressed it means "chopsticks." When the し is stressed it means "bridge."

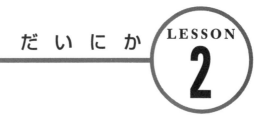
第二課

2.1 Greeting someone you know

When you meet someone you have met before, it is not appropriate to say **"hajimemashite"** はじめまして. In such situations the greeting you use depends on the time of day.

おはようございます
o ha yoo go za i ma su

こんにちは
ko n ni chi wa

こんばんは
ko n ba n wa

Notes:

There are a few things to take note of when using these greetings:

1. Ohayoogozaimasu おはよう ございます is used until about 11 a.m. Between friends and family it is often shortened to **ohayoo** おはよう.

2. Konnichi wa こんにち は is used during the daytime from about 11 a.m. till about 6 p.m. It is not used between members of the same family.

3. Konban wa こんばん は is used in the evening after about 6 p.m. It is not used between members of the same family.

4. All of these greetings are used when meeting but never when parting.

5. Although these expressions are the Japanese equivalents of "Good morning," "Good day," and "Good evening," they do not contain any word meaning "good." The actual meanings of these greetings are as follows:

—ohayoo gozaimasu is an archaic way of saying "It's early."
—konnichi wa is an unfinished question similar to **"okuni wa…"** It literally means "Today…?" with the implied question "How is it?"
—konban wa is similar to the above. It means "This evening…(how is it ?)"

2.2 Asking how someone is

After greeting someone you haven't seen for a while you can ask how they are.

You'll say:	おげんき です か。 *o ge n ki de su ka.*
the reply is:	はい、 げんき です。 *ha i, ge n ki de su.*

Notes:

1. Genki げんき means "in good health" or "full of vitality," however, in this situation it is simply a greeting, so you are not expected to reply with an accurate description of your state of health.
Unless you are feeling particularly bad the reply will be the positive **"hai, genki desu."**

2. The honorific o お is attached to genki げんき to indicate that it is the listener who is being referred to.

3. The ka か after desu です is the equivalent of a question mark.

4. In the reply, you first say hai はい which means "yes." Since you are talking about yourself there is no o お in front of genki げんき, and since this is an answer there is no question mark ka か.

5. Ogenki desu ka shouldn't be used when greeting people whom you know to be sick.

6. This greeting is often shortened to **"genki…?"** between close friends.

7. It is never used when greeting family members. Nor is it used when greeting people you see often. Although it is often given as the Japanese equivalent of "How are you?" its meaning is more like "How have you been?"

Meeting by chance

In the following conversation **(kaiwa)** the two people, Honda (A) and Suzuki (B), have met before but don't see each other very often. They are not close friends, since close friends would speak less formally.

A: あ、 <u>すずき</u> さん、 <u>こんにち は</u>。
　 a,　 Su zu ki　 sa n,　 ko n ni chi wa.

B: <u>こんにち は</u>。
　 ko n　 ni chi wa.

A: おげんき です か。
　 o ge n ki de su ka.

B: はい、 げんき です。　 <u>ほんだ</u> さん は……。
　 ha i,　 _____ de su.　 Ho n da sa n　 wa...?

A: はい、 げんき です。
　 _____, ge n ki de su.

Fill in the blanks and then practice the above **kaiwa** with your partner. Change the names and greetings (underlined parts).

Note: a あ is just a noise that expresses surprise. It is similar to " Oh ! " in English.

2.3 Nationality and language こくせき と ことば　国籍と言葉

In the last lesson we learned the names of a number of countries (kuni). Since Japanese is a very regular and logical language it is quite easy to convert the name of the kuni くに into the name of the people who live there. All you do is add jin (person or people) to the country name. The kuni くに Japan is nihon にほん, so the nationality (kokuseki) is nihonjin にほんじん (literally "Japan person").

The same method is used to make the language (kotoba) of the kuni くに. Just add go ご (which means "language") to the name of the kuni くに. So if the kuni くに is China (chuugoku), the kotoba ことば is chuugokugo ちゅうごくご (Chinese language).

Use the clues to fill in the chart below. Think carefully about the last column!

■Practice 2.3　れんしゅう　　練習

Kuni くに 国	Kokuseki こくせき 国籍	Kotoba ことば 言葉
nihon にほん	nihonjin にほんじん	＿＿＿＿＿ にほんご
chuugoku ちゅうごく	＿＿＿＿＿ ちゅうごくじん	chuugokugo ちゅうごくご
＿＿＿＿＿ フランス	furansujin フランスじん	＿＿＿＿＿ フランスご
doitsu ドイツ	＿＿＿＿＿ ドイツじん	＿＿＿＿＿ ドイツご
＿＿＿＿＿ かんこく	kankokujin かんこくじん	＿＿＿＿＿ かんこくご
igirisu イギリス	＿＿＿＿＿ イギリスじん	eigo えいご
oosutoraria オーストラリア	＿＿＿＿＿ オーストラリアじん	えいご
＿＿＿＿＿ アメリカ	amerikajin アメリカじん	えいご

2.4 Asking questions しつもん

So far we have learned how to find out a person's **kuni** くに by asking the open question
o kuni wa…? However, there may be a situation when we want to know if a person
comes from a particular country or not. For example, you may wish to practice your
Japanese by first asking someone "Are you Japanese?"

To make such a question, all you do is add the question words **desu ka** ですか to the
kokuseki こくせき, i.e. **nihonjin desu ka.**　にほんじん です か。Are you Japanese?
The answers to such a question could only be YES—**hai** はい or NO—**iie** いいえ
(pronounced "ee eh").
If the person is Japanese, their reply would most likely be: **hai, soo desu** はい、そう で
す which means "yes, (that) is so."

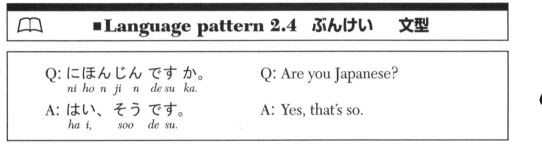

■Language pattern 2.4 ぶんけい　　文型

> Q: にほんじん です か。　　　Q: Are you Japanese?
> *ni ho n ji n de su ka.*
>
> A: はい、そう です。　　　　A: Yes, that's so.
> *ha i,　soo　de su.*

You can ask the same type of question about someone's **shigoto** しごと. For instance, if
you wanted to know if someone were a student (**gakusei**).

> Q: がくせい です か。　　　　Q: Are you a student?
> *ga ku se i de su ka.*
>
> A: はい、そう です。　　　　A: Yes, that's so.
> *ha i,　soo　de su*

However, if the person were not a student the **kaiwa** かいわ would go this way:

> Q: がくせい です か。　　　　Q: Are you a student?
> *ga ku se i de su ka.*
>
> A: いいえ、ちがいます。　　　A: No, that's not so.
> *i　i　e,　chi ga i ma su.*

As we have seen **iie** いいえ means "no." The word **chigaimasu** literally means "It's
different" or "That's not the case." It is the general negative reply to questions of this type.

■Conversation 2.4 かいわ　会話

Meeting someone at the airport.

This same language pattern can also be used when asking a person's なまえ.

In the following **kaiwa** かいわ Mary is waiting at the airport for Ms. Tanaka to come through. However there are many **nihonjin** にほんじん at the airport and Mary has only seen a photo of Ms. Tanaka. The first person she approaches turns out not to be Ms. Tanaka.

Mary:	すみません、<u>たなか</u> さん です か。 *Su mi ma se n,　Ta na ka　sa n　de su　ka.*
Nihonjin:	いいえ、ちがいます。 *i i e,　chiga i ma su.*
Mary:	すみません。 *Su mi ma se n.*

(tries another person)

Mary:	すみません、<u>たなか</u> さん です か。 *Su mi ma se n,　Ta na ka　sa n　de su　ka.*
Tanaka:	はい、そう です。<u>メリー</u>さん です か。 *ha i,　soo　de su.　Me rii　sa n　de su　ka.*
Mary:	はい、そう です。はじめまして。 *ha i,　soo　de su.　Ha ji me ma shi te.*
Tanaka:	はじめまして、<u>たなか ゆみこ</u> です。 *ha ji me ma shi te,　Ta na ka　Yu mi ko　de su.* どうぞ よろしくおねがいします。 *doo　zo　yo ro shi ku　o ne ga i shi ma su.*
Mary:	どうぞ よろしく。 *Doo　zo　yo ro shi ku.*

Practice this **kaiwa** かいわ substituting the names (underlined).

Notes: There are two new expressions which come up in this **kaiwa** かいわ:

1. すみません **sumimasen** is what you say when you go up to someone to ask a question or attract attention. It is like "excuse me." You can also use the same expression to mean "sorry" when you have interrupted someone or taken up their time.

2. The longer form of **doozo yoroshiku** どうぞ よろしく is **doozo yoroshiku onegaishimasu.** This last word **onegaishimasu** おねがいします is like "please," it makes the expression more polite. For the moment it is sufficient for you to learn the short version, but you should be able to recognize the longer version when you hear it.

2.5 Asking about people

In **nihongo** にほんご when you are talking to someone and asking a question such as "Are you a teacher ?" there is no need for a word meaning "you" because it is obvious who is being asked. The Japanese sentence **kyooshi desu ka** きょうしですか translated directly into **eigo** えいご is just "teacher are ?" However when talking about a person who isn't there, it is necessary to indicate who is being referred to, usually by name.

For example: When you tell someone "John is a teacher" you might say:

ジョン さん は きょうし です。
Jon   sa n wa kyoo shi de su.

2.6 The particle は

In this sentence there is a grammar word **wa** は which is called a particle. It cannot be translated into **eigo** えいご as it has a function rather than a meaning. Its function is to indicate that **Jon san** is the **topic** we are talking about. That is, は indicates who or what is the topic of a sentence. は comes immediately after the topic.

Examples れい　例 ————————————————————

Read the following example (**rei** れい) and translate them into **eigo** えいご.

1. メリーさん は べんごし です。
   Me rii   sa n wa be n go shi de su.

2. ゆみこさん は ひしょ です。
   Yu mi ko sa n wa hi sho   de su.

3. たなかさん は にほんじん です。
   Tana ka sa n wa ni ho n ji n de su.

4. チャックさん は アメリカじん です。
   Cha kku   sa n wa a me ri ka ji n de su.

These sentences can be transformed into questions by just adding **ka** か.

e.g. やまだ さん は いしゃ です か。
Yamada sa n wa i sha de su ka.

Is Yamada a doctor?

タスマニア は くに です か。
Ta su ma ni a wa ku ni de su ka.

Is Tasmania a country ?

2.7 The particle of possession の

So far we know the words **kyooshi** (teacher) and **eigo** (English language). If a person's **shigoto** しごと is an English language teacher they can say this in **nihongo** にほんご by using another particle, **no** の, to join the two words as follows: **eigo no kyooshi.**

i) This particle is like the **eigo** えいご "of " except that the word order is reversed.

i.e. にほんご **の** きょうし
ni ho n go no kyoo shi

teacher **of** Japanese language

ii) **No** の can also show possession. This time it is like 's in **eigo** えいご.

i.e. たなか さん **の** しごと
ta na ka sa n no shi go to

Mr. Tanaka's job

2.8 せんせい　先生

Sensei is a title similar to **san** さん. It is used after the names of teachers, doctors, esteemed professionals and artists, even politicians. Unlike **san** さん it can be used to replace the person's **namae** なまえ. So students can address their teacher just as"**sensei**" in class. The teacher's **namae** なまえ isn't necessary when it is obvious who is being referred to. **Sensei** せんせい is also used when referring to a teacher, e.g. **Yoshikosan no eigo no sensei**, instead of using **kyooshi** きょうし. However you cannot use **sensei** せんせい when referring to yourself.

■Conversation 2.8　かいわ　会話

Greeting your teacher

When greeting your teachers you should address them simply as **sensei** せんせい or use their family name followed by the title **sensei** せんせい.

がくせい：<u>たなか</u> せんせい、<u>こんばん は</u>。
ga ku se i:　ta na ka se n se i,　ko n ba n wa.

たなか：　<u>こんばん は</u>。
Ta na ka:　ko n ba n wa.

Practice by substituting different Japanese family names and the three daily greetings you have already learned.

2.9 Talking about yourself—わたし　私

When referring to yourself you may need a word for "I." There are a number of these in nihongo にほんご but the most universal is watashi わたし. When it is yourself that is the topic watashi わたし will be followed by は. Here is some basic information about me:

わたし は ブライアン メイ です。
wa ta shi wa Bura i a n Me i de su.

わたし は オーストラリアじん です。
wa ta shi wa oo su to ra ri a ji n de su.

わたし は にほんご の きょうし です。
wa ta shi wa ni ho n go no kyoo shi de su.

Write similar sentences about yourself in nihongo にほんご.

Note:

In normal conversation when it is obvious that you are referring to yourself, i.e. that you are the topic, the watashi wa わたし は part is usually left out.

By simply adding the particle no の to watashi わたし we get a word for "my" or "mine" which is: watashi no わたし の.

わたし の しごと　　　　　My job.
wa ta shi no shi go to

わたし の くに　　　　　　My country.
wa ta shi no ku ni

わたし の です。　　　　　(It) is mine.
wa ta shi no de su.

Examples れい　例 —————————————————————

1. わたし の くに は イギリスです。　　　　My country is England.
   Wa ta shi no ku ni wa i gi ri su de su.

2. すずき さん は わたし の がくせい です。　　Ms. Suzuki is my student.
   Su zu ki sa n wa wa ta shi no ga ku se i de su.

A. What do the following sentences mean ? Write English translations.

1. やまだ さん の いしゃ は ドイツじん です。
   Yama da sa n no i sha wa do i tsu ji n de su.

   _____

2. ビル さん の にほんご の きょうし の なまえ は やまもと です。
   Bi ru sa n no ni ho n go no kyoo shi no na ma e wa Ya ma mo to de su.

   _____

3. オーストラリア の ことば は えいご です。
   Oo su to ra ri a no ko to ba wa e i go de su.

   _____

4. ヒルダ さん は すずき さん の ドイツご の きょうし です。
   Hi ru da san wa Su zu ki sa n no do i tsu go no kyoo shi de su.

   _____

5. すずき さん は わたし の べんごし です。
   Su zu ki sa n wa wa ta shi no be n go shi de su.

   _____

B. Write the particles は or の in the blanks to make meaningful sentences.

1. にほん_____ことば_____にほんご です。

   Nihon _____ kotoba _____ nihongo desu.

2. やまださん _____ちゅうごくじん ですか。

   Yamada san _____ chuugokujin desu ka.

3. マリーンさん_____フランスご_____きょうし です。

   Marlene san _____ furansugo _____ kyooshi desu.

4. ジム さん_____べんごし_____なまえ_____ジュディー です か。

   Jim san _____ bengoshi _____ namae _____ Judy desu ka.

5. わたし_____にほんご_____きょうし_____いしだ せんせい です。

   Watashi _____ nihongo _____ kyooshi _____ Ishida sensei desu.

2.10 The Japanese flag にほんの はた　日本の旗

The national flag of Japan is a red circle on a white background. The flag (**hata** はた) represents the rising sun and is called **"hi no maru"** (日の丸) which means literally "sun circle" or **"nisshooki"** (日章旗) which means "Sun emblem flag." The origin of the flag is unclear since the design has been used for centuries. It became the national flag used by merchant shipping in 1870.

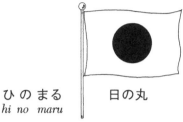

ひ の まる
hi no maru　　日の丸

2.11 The country name—にほん (にっぽん)　日本

The name of the country Japan is written with two characters, 日 which means "sun" and 本 which means "origin." It is pronounced **nihon** にほん or more formally as **nippon** にっぽん. The origin of the name is unclear but it probably dates from the seventh century. One explanation of its origin is that it was chosen to designate the country which lies to the east of China and is therefore located where the sun rises. If this is the case then the name can be translated literally as "origin of the sun."

2.12 National symbols: Chrysanthemum and cherry blossom

There is no official national emblem but the crest of the imperial family (**tennooke**) is often used in this way. It is a circular sixteen-petalled chrysanthemum (**juuroku ben no kiku no hana**). Another flower which is often used to symbolize Japan is the cherry blossom (**sakura** さくら). This flower has long been admired for its beauty and has taken on a considerable amount of symbolism.

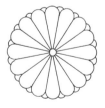

じゅうろくべん の きく の はな
(十六弁 の 菊 の 花)
juuroku ben no kiku no hana

さくら
(桜)
sakura

2.13 The national anthem—きみがよ　君が代

The national anthem of Japan is called **kimigayo** きみがよ. It is an ancient poem written by an unknown author over a thousand years ago which was set to music last century. The words translate into English as:

"May the reign of the Emperor continue for a thousand, nay, eight thousand generations and for the eternity that it takes for small pebbles to grow into a great rock and become covered with moss."

きみがよは ちよに やちよに さざれ いしの いわおとなりて こけの むすまで。
ki mi ga yowa chiyo ni   yachi yoni   sa za re   i shino   i wa o to na ri te   ko ke no musu ma de.

君が代は　千代に 八千代に さざれ 石の　巌となりて　　苔のむすまで。

Answers　こたえ　答え

Conversation 2.2　genki; hai.

Practice 2.3　nihongo; chuugoku; furansu; furansugo; doitsugo; kankoku; kankokugo; igirisujin; oosutorariajin; eigo; amerika; eigo.

Practice 2.9

A.　1. Mr./Ms. Yamada's doctor is German.
　　2. Bill's Japanese language teacher's name is Yamamoto.
　　3. The language of Australia is English.
　　4. Hilda is Suzuki's German language teacher.
　　5. Mr./Ms. Suzuki is my lawyer.

B.　1. の, は;　　2. は;　　3. は, の;　　4. の, の, は;　　5. の, の, は.

The next two **hiragana** will allow us to write the words for "yes" and "no." These are **hai** and **iie**. The word **hai** comprises two **hiragana**, **ha** は and **i** い. We have already seen the **hiragana** は used as the particle which marks the topic **wa**. However, when は is not used as a particle it is pronounced "ha." In general, each **hiragana** has only one pronunciation with no variations, so は is something of an exception. The new **hiragana** い is written with two strokes.

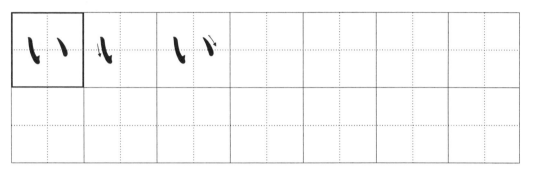

The word for "no" **iie** comprises three **hiragana**: **i**, **i**, and **e**. It is written いいえ. The new **hiragana** **e** え is written with two strokes.

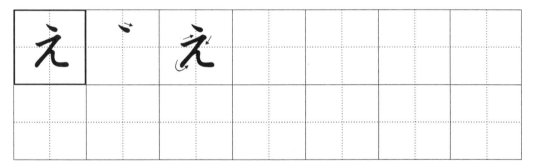

When two **hiragana** are written together the sound is just lengthened. A less emphatic version of "yes" is **ee**, it is written ええ.

The next **hiragana** is **ho** ほ. Be careful not to confuse it with は.

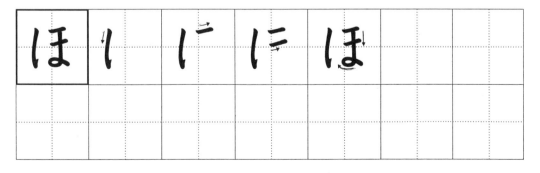

The next one is n ん. It is the only **hiragana** that doesn't contain a vowel sound and cannot begin a word. When typing it into a word processor "nn" is usually required.

ん　ん

The particle which indicates possession is no の. It is a bit like 's in English. の is also used in spelling words.

の　の

See if you can work out the following words. You've had them all in class.

い sha	くに	be ん go し	ta い wa ん
ko んに chi は	かん ko く	ga く se い	に ほ ん
かい sha いん	wa ta し の	ko o mu いん	にほん ji ん

1. Fill in the blanks to complete the following sentences.
（**Use as much** hiragana **as possible.**）

1) やまだ さん （   ） ひしょ です。 (Ms. Yamada is a secretary.)
   Ya mada sa n   *hi sho   desu.*

2) わたしは にほんご （   ） きょうし です。
   wa ta shi wa ni ho n go   *kyoo shi de su.*

3) A: お げんき です （   ）。
   o   ge n ki de su

   B: （   ）、 げんき です。
                ge n ki de su.

4) A: たなか さん は がくせい です か。
   Ta na ka sa n wa ga ku se i   de su ka.

   B: いいえ、（   ）。
   i i   e,

5) A: チン せんせい は たいわんじん ですか。
   Chin se n se i wa ta i wa n ji n   de su ka.

   B: はい、（   ）。
   ha i

2. Answer the following questions and write the answers in Japanese.

1) What is the Japanese word for Chinese language？

_____

2) What title do you use after a teacher's name instead of **san** さん？

_____

3) What is the name of the Japanese national anthem？

_____

3. Translate the following sentences into nihongo.

1) Excuse me. Are you Hanako ? _____

2) I am Australian. _____

3) Good morning ! _____

4) My English teacher's name is Bill. _____

_____

5) Good evening ! _____

4. ✍ Let's write in Japanese ! Write a HIRAGANA in each ___.

The name of the country "Japan" in Japanese is: ____ ____ ____.

"No" in Japanese is: ____ ____ ____. "Yes" in Japanese is: ____ ____.

Let's write some new words using the HIRAGANA that you've learned. Write one HIRAGANA in each box.

いえ (a house)

ほん (a book)

はえ (a fly)

第三課

3.1 The parts of the day

あさ（朝）
a sa

ひる（昼）
hi ru

ばん（晩）
ba n

あさ **asa**	is till about 11 a.m.
ひる **hiru**	is from about midday till sunset.
ばん **ban**	is from sundown till late. (Night is also called yoru よる.)

3.2 Meals ごはん　ご飯

In each of these parts of the day we usually have a meal. In nihongo にほんご the word for "meal" is **gohan** ごはん. **Gohan** also means "cooked rice" and this is a major part of most meals in **nihon** にほん. In a day the three **gohan** ごはん are as follows:

あさ ごはん
a sa go ha n

ひる ごはん
hi ru go ha n

ばん ごはん
ba n go ha n

3.3 Accommodation　しゅくはく　宿泊

When you travel to nihon にほん there are a number of types of accommodation (shukuhaku) to choose from depending on your budget and taste. Most tourists stay in the international hotels (hoteru). These are rather expensive and just like similar hoteru the world over. Equally expensive, but more culturally interesting, are the Japanese-style (nihonshiki) hotels called ryokan りょかん. Ryokan りょかん are usually large establishments with nihonshiki にほんしき rooms, baths, and gohan ごはん.

Smaller and less expensive are the nihonshiki にほんしき guest houses called minshuku みんしゅく. These are usually family businesses and can be found all over nihon にほん. Both asagohan あさごはん and bangohan ばんごはん are often included in the price of a night's accommodation.

3.4 Breakfast at a minshuku みんしゅく の あさごはん 民宿の朝ご飯

The gohan ごはん you will be served in a minshuku みんしゅく will be nihonshiki にほんしき. If you are not used to Japanese food there may be a number of foods you won't recognize. The following is a picture of a fairly typical asagohan あさごはん in a minshuku みんしゅく.

みんしゅく の あさごはん　　民宿の朝ご飯
min shu ku no a sa goha n

■Conversation 3.4 かいわ　会話

The first minshuku breakfast

In the following **kaiwa** the foreign guest (G) is sitting down to **asagohan** あさごはん in a **minshuku** みんしゅく. This **asagohan** あさごはん is quite different to what he is used to so he asks the lady (L) in the **minshuku** about some of the things.

すいません、
これは なん
ですか。

L: おはよう ございます。
o ha yoo　go za i ma su.

G: おはよう ございます。
o ha yoo　go za i ma su.

L: あさごはん を どうぞ。
a sa go ha n　o doo　zo.

G: はい、どうも ありがとう。（すわります）いただきます。
ha i,　doo mo a ri ga too.　(he sits down)　i ta da ki ma su.

L: どうぞ。
do o　zo.

G: すみません、これ は なん です か。
su m ma se n,　ko re wa na n　de su ka.

L: それ は さかな です。
so re wa sa ka na de su.

G: これ は...
ko re wa...?

L: のり です。
no ri de su.

G: これ は チーズ です か。　(Pointing at the white pieces floating in the soup.)
ko re wa chi i zu de su ka.

L: いいえ、それ は チーズ で は ありません。それ は とうふ です。
i i e,　so re wa chi i zu de wa a ri ma se n.　so re wa to o fu de su.

G: ああ、そう です か。
aa,　soo　de su ka.

LESSON **3** 第三課

35

Notes:

1. これ(kore) and それ(sore) are used like "this" and "that" in English. **Kore** (this) refers to a thing nearer the speaker while **sore** (that) refers to a thing nearer the person being spoken to.

2. どうもありがとう doomoarigatoo means "thank you." The shortest form of "thank you" is simply **doomo** which is rather like "thanks." This is lengthened to **doomo arigatoo** and then further to **doomo arigatoo gozaimasu**.

3. いただきます itadakimasu is an expression said by a person who is about to eat a meal. You should always say this before starting to eat with other people. It has no religious overtones, in fact, it is just a polite way of saying "I am going to eat."

■Practice 3.4 れんしゅう 練習

First find out the **eigo** えいご for the various items on the tray (**obon**) (See 3.9). Look at the picture of the tray (**obon** おぼん) of food and practice this **kaiwa** かいわ by substituting different foods in the underlined parts.

ごはん *go ha n*	_____	みそしる *mi soshi ru*	_____
しょうゆ *shoo yu*	_____	おちゃ *o cha*	_____
つけもの *tsu ke mo no*	_____	のり *no ri*	_____
さかな *sa ka na*	_____	とうふ *too fu*	_____
たまご *ta ma go*	_____	はし *ha shi*	_____

1. This is an open question using "what" nan なん, so the answer will be some information.

Q: これ は なん です か。
  ko re wa na n de su ka.

A: それ は (name of thing) です。
  so re wa   *de su.*

Q: What is this?

A: That is (name of thing).

2. This question is closed. The answer is either "yes" or "no." In this case it is "no."

Q: これ は (name of thing) です か。
  ko re wa   *de su ka.*

A: いいえ、それ は (name of thing) ではありません。
  i i e, so re wa   *de wa a ri ma se n.*

Q: Is this (name of thing)?

A: No, that's not (name of thing).

で は ありません de wa arimasen is the negative from of です desu. It means "is not" "are not," etc. The other negative answer: iie chigaimasu いいえ、ちがいます could have been used here, but then the name of the thing could not have been put into the answer.

3.5 Finishing a meal

When you finish a meal you thank whoever provided it by saying:
gochisoo sama deshita ごちそう さま でした or the shorter version gochisoo sama. It means something like "That was a feast."

The standard response from the person who prepared the meal is:
o somatsu sama deshita おそまつ さま でした. It means something like "It wasn't much of a meal."

In nihon にほん it is customary to deny any praise you receive. When people compliment you or your family you should deny the compliments and so show appropriate modesty. Always find something good to say to others but don't tell them how good you or your family members are. Let them find out !

■Conversation 3.5　かいわ　　会話

Finishing Breakfast

In this **kaiwa** かいわ the guest is talking to the lady in the **minshuku** みんしゅく as he finishes **asagohan** あさ ごはん.

> G: ごちそう さま でした。
> *go chi soo　sa ma　de shi ta.*
>
> L: お そまつ さま でした。
> *o　so ma tsu　sa ma　de shi ta.*

3.6 Starting a conversation—The weather　てんき　　天気

A common way to initiate a conversation is to comment on the weather (**tenki**). After greeting someone you could comment on the temperature or whether the **tenki** てんき was pleasant or unpleasant. To do this we need words for:

hot	あつい *a tsu i*	pleasant weather	いい てんき *i i　te n ki*
cold	さむい *samu i*	unpleasant weather	いやな てんき *i ya na　te n ki*

■Conversation 3.6　かいわ　　会話

Talking about the weather

Yamada (Y) and Tanaka (T) meet and exchange greetings. It is a cold morning.

> Y: ああ、たなかさん、おはよう ございます。
> *a a,　ta na ka sa n,　o ha yoo　go za i ma su.*
>
> T: おはよう ございます。
> *o ha yoo　go za i ma su.*
>
> Y: さむい です ね。
> *sa mu i　de su　ne.*
>
> T: そう です ね。とても さむい です ね。
> *soo　de su　ne.　to te mo　sa mu i　de su　ne.*
>
> Y: ええ。
> *e e.*

Practice this **kaiwa** かいわ with a partner (**aite**) by substituting the underlined words.

Notes

1. aa ああ is a less surprised version of "oh."

2. ee ええ is a softer, less emphatic form of **hai** はい. It is pronounced like "air" without the "ah."

3. soo desu ne そう です ね is the reply to any statement that ends in **ne** ね. **Ne** is like the English "isn't it?" or "aren't we?" or "won't it?" and many other such tag questions. It is used when the information being talked about is shared by both speaker and listener, and the speaker expects agreement from the listener. **Ee, soo desu ne** translates literally as "yes, (that) is so, isn't it." However, the following Australian vernacular expresses it better:

Y: it's hot eh!
T: yeah, sure is, eh.

4. totemo とても is like the English "very."

3.7 Finishing a conversation

When parting you generally say one of the following:

📼

1. **sayoonara** さようなら is equivalent to "goodbye." However, it is not appropriate in business situations. In such cases **shitsurei shimasu** しつれい します is generally used.

2. **ja, mata** じゃ、また translates as "Well, (see you) again." It is a less formal expression used between friends and colleagues.

3. **oyasuminasai** おやすみなさい can be used when parting late at night to go home, as well as when actually going to bed. It translates as "Have a sleep." It can be shortened to おやすみ among friends and family.

📼 **■Conversation 3.7 かいわ　会話**

Saying goodbye

Two acquaintances are on a train. One is getting off at the next station which is **Shinjuku** しんじゅく, a huge station in Tokyo.

A: あ、 しんじゅく です ね。 では、 さようなら。
   a,   shi n ju ku de su ne. de wa, sa yoo na ra.

B: じゃ、 また。
   ja ,   ma ta.

Note: **ja** じゃ is the contracted form of **dewa** では. They both mean 'well' in this context.

3.8 Listening practice　きき とり れんしゅう　聞き取り練習

On a plane ひこうき で 飛行機で

Two strangers are sitting together on a plane (hikooki) ひこうき on the way to or from Australia. One of them (B) appears to be a nihonjin にほんじん so the other (A), who can speak some nihongo にほんご, starts up a conversation.

Fill in the blanks and then answer the questions below

A: すみません、にほんじん です か。
　su mi ma se n, ＿＿＿＿＿＿ de su ka.

B: はい、そう です。
　ha i, soo de su.

A: わたし は ブライアン です。どうぞ よろしく。
　＿＿＿＿ wa Bu ra i a n de su. doo zo yo ro shi ku.

B: ともだ です。どうぞ よろしく。
　To mo da ＿＿＿ doo zo yo ro shi ku.

　ブライアン さん は オーストラリアじん です か。
　Bu ra i a n sa n wa oo su to ra ri a ji n de su ka.

A: いいえ、ちがいます。イギリスじん です。
　ii e, chi ga i ma su. i gi ri su ji n de su.

B: ああ そう です か。がくせい です か。
　aa soo de su ka. ＿＿＿＿＿ de su ka.

A: はい、そう です。ともだ さん は…。
　＿＿＿, soo ＿＿＿. To mo da sa n wa…?

B: かいしゃいん です。わたし の めいし です。どうぞ。
　＿＿＿＿＿＿＿ de su. wa ta shi no me i shi de su. doo zo.

A: ありがとう ございます。
　a ri ga too go za i ma su.

B: いいえ。
　i i e.

Questions しつもん 質問

1. What are their names?
2. Is the man Australian?
3. What does he do?
4 What is her job?
5. What does she give him?

Notes

1. Meishi めいし（名刺）is a name card or business card. All nihonjin にほんじん white collar workers will have one of these.

2. The reply to arigatoo ありがとう is iie いいえ. The reply to "thank you" is always negative. Here, the short form iie いいえ (no) is used. This is similar to the English "not at all."

3.9 Japanese food　　にほん の たべもの　日本 の 食べ物

There is a wide variety of food available in Japan. This includes many kinds of traditional foods and a large number of foods from overseas. Nevertheless, the main elements of Japanese cooking are rice; noodles; many kinds of fish (sakana) and other seafood including sea vegetable such as nori; eggs (tamago); soya products such as bean curd (toofu) and soy sauce (shooyu) and a bean paste called miso which is an ingredient in many dishes including the popular soup (miso shiru); vegetables such as spinach, daikon, egg plant, cucumber, capsicum; sweet potato, burdock roots, shallots, and carrots which can be cooked, used in salads, or made into pickles (tsukemono); and fruits such as mandarins, peaches, nashi pears, persimmons; loquats, and melons.

These days meat, bread, and dairy products are quite popular and the range of common vegetables and fruits has broadened to include cabbages, potatoes, tomatoes, onions, bananas, apples, oranges, grapes, kiwi fruit, and mangoes to name a few.

The most common eating implement is hashi (chopsticks) but spoons and sometimes knives and forks are also used. Green tea (ocha) is usually served with Japanese meals.

Japanese traditional food is very regional with each area having its own particular dishes. In fact, one of the reasons Japanese people travel within Japan is to sample the local specialties.

In the cities there are restaurants from all over the world but in the countryside the main kinds of cooking, available to visitors are Japanese, Chinese, and Korean, although pasta and curry rice are available almost anywhere.

LESSON 3 第三課

Answers こたえ 答え
3.8. nihonjin; watashi; desu; gakusei; hai; desu; kaishain.
Questions 1. Brian, Ms. Tomoda. 2. No, he isn't. 3. He is a student.
4. She is a company employee. 5. Her business card.

41

Writing Japanese script 3.10

A word which we have used a number of times is **desu**. It can mean "is," "are," "am," or "will be" depending on the context. It is only found at the end of a sentence. **Desu** comprises two hiragana, **de** で and **su** す. The hiragana **de** で is actually a modified symbol consisting of two parts: the hiragana **te** て and two ditto marks, known in Japanese as "ten ten." By adding **ten ten** (てん てん) to the hiragana **te** て, its pronunciation changes to **de** で. Many other hiragana can also be modified in a similar way. First practice **te** て which is written in one stroke and then **de** で which is three strokes.

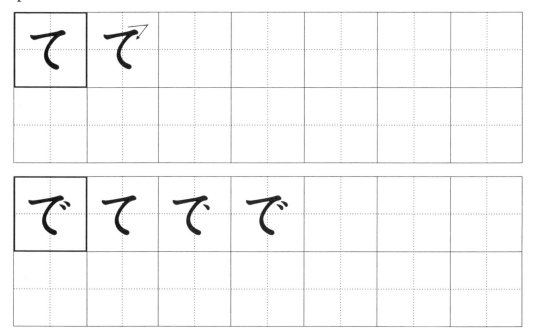

The next hiragana is **su** す. At the end of sentences the **u** sound in **su** is often left off. So **desu** です is usually, but not always, pronounced "des." At the beginning or in the middle of words **su** is not shortened. The **hiragana** す is written with two strokes. When "ten ten" is added this **hiragana** is pronounced **zu** ず.

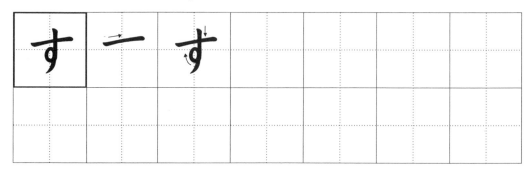

LESSON **3** 第三課

ず

This "ten ten" can be added to other, but not all, **hiragana**. When added to は it becomes **ba** ば; ほ becomes **bo** ぼ; く becomes **gu** ぐ; and し becomes **ji** じ.

ば

ぼ

ぐ

じ

A very useful **hiragana** is the vowel sound **u** う because this **hiragana** is also used to lengthen other vowel sounds. Till now you have seen these written in **roomaji** by doubling the vowel. In **hiragana** the vowel sounds u and o are lengthened by adding う. Here are some examples: **hoo** ほう, **noo** のう, **oo** おう, **kuu** くう, **suu** すう, **guu** ぐう. Even though the **roomaji** usually doubles the vowel, when typing into the word processor you must key in "u."

う゛う

Try reading these words: おはし, doうmo, おはyoうgozaいますす, すmimaseん, ばんgoはん, koんばんは, はい,soうです.

1. Match the Japanese words with their English meanings by joining them with a line.

めいし
me i shi   morning

ひこうき
hi koo ki   weather

あさ
as a   tea

ばんごはん
ba n go ha n   business card

てんき
te n ki   midday

おちゃ
o cha   aeroplane

ひる
hi ru   egg

たまご
ta ma go   dinner

2. Fill in the blanks to complete the following sentences.

1) Q: これ は （   ） ですか。
　　ko re wa　　　　　　　　　　　　 *de su ka.*

　　A: それ は のり です。
　　　so re wa no ri de su.

2) Q: これ は さかな です か。
　　ko re wa sa ka na de su ka.

　　A: いいえ、 それ は さかな （   ）。
　　　i i e　　so re wa sa kana

3) A: あつい です ね。
　　a tsu i de su ne.

　　B: ええ、 （   ） ですね。 とても あつい です ね。
　　　e e,　　　　　　　 *de su ne.*　 *to te mo a tsu i de su ne.*

LESSON

3

第三課

3. Answer the following questions and write the answers in Japanese.

1) When you want to know what a thing nearer the person you are speaking to is, what do you say? _____

2) What do you say before you start eating a meal?

_____

3) What do you say to your host after you finish eating a meal?

_____

4. Translate the following into nihongo にほんご.

1) It is pleasant weather, isn' it? _____

2) A: Thank you. B: Not at all. A: _____

　　　　　　　　　　　　　　　　 B: _____

3) Goodbye. _____

5. ✍ Let's write in Japanese! Write a HIRAGANA in each ___ .

"A Japanese person" in Japanese is: ____ ____ ____ ____ ____

"Evening" in Japanese is: ____ ____

"Good" in Japanese is: ____ ____

Let's write new words using the HIRAGANA that you've learned. Write one HIRAGANA in each box.

すいえい (swimming)

ぼうし (a hat/cap)

うし (cow, ox)

てんいん (salesclerk)

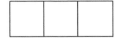

じしん (earthquake)

すし (sushi)

第四課

Note: The roomaji for the hiragana: く に お は し, introduced in Lesson 1, has been removed from Lesson 4 and subsequent lessons.

4.1 Talking about someone vs talking to someone

What – なん (nan)

In Lesson 1 when we asked someone their く に (kuni) or their しごと (shigoto), we just said おくには…(okuni wa…?) or おしごとは….(oshigoto wa…?) By simply putting the honorific お(o) in front of く に (kuni) and しごと (shigoto) we made these words more polite and indicated that we were referring to the other person's country or job. We also used an incomplete question by just ending in は (wa–the topic marker), leaving the rest of the question to be assumed. However, when referring to someone who is not there, we need to make a complete question in order to avoid confusion. For example, if I were asking about Ishida san's job, I would have to first indicate that Ishida san's しごと (shigoto) was the topic and then ask the question "what is it?" In にほんご (nihongo) this question would be as follows:

いしだ さん の しごと は なん です か。
i   da sa n no   go to   na n de su ka.
Ishida san's job **WA** what is **KA**.

Where–どこ (doko)

In the case of a person's く に, in Lesson 1 we simply asked the person directly おくには… But, if we were talking about Maria's country, we would have to use her なまえ (namae) and the word for country (く に) joined by の (no) to form the topic: マリアさ ん の く に (maria san no kuni). Then add the question "where is it?" In にほんご (nihongo) a country is a place so the appropriate question word is "where"–どこ (doko).

マリアさん の く に は どこ です か。
ma ri a sa n no   do ko de su ka
Maria san's country **WA** where is **KA**.

📖 ■Language pattern 4.1 ぶんけい   文型

A. Talking to someone

Incomplete questions can be used when the context is clear.

Complete question	Incomplete question
お しごと は なん です か。 *go to na n de su ka.* お くに は どこ です か。 *do ko de su ka.*	お しごと は... *go to* お くに は...

B. Talking about someone e.g. Maria マリア

When the context is not clear, complete questions are preferable.

マリアさん の しごと は なん です か。 *mari a sa n no go to na n de su ka.*	What is Maria's Job?
マリアさん の くに は どこ です か。 *ma ri a sa n no do ko de su ka.*	Where is Maria's country?

Note: these questions could also be used when talking with Maria since in Japanese the person's name is often used instead of a word for "you."

■Conversation 4.1 かいわ   会話

Filling in details

This かいわ (kaiwa) is set in a Japanese language school にほんご がっこう (nihongo gakkoo) in Tokyo. Two にほんご の きょうし (nihongo no kyooshi), Suzuki and Tanaka, are talking about their students who come from various くに and have various しごと (shigoto). Although each student's details are recorded in the roll book, some information is missing. They ask about Carter カーター (kaataa) and Lopez ロペス (ropesu).

すずき せんせい：<u>カーター</u> さん の しごと は なん です か。
Su zu ki se n se i   Kaa taa   sa n no   go to   na n de su ka.

たなか せんせい：<u>かんごふ</u> です。
Tana ka se n se i   ka n go fu de su.

すずき せんせい：ああ、そう です か。
Su zu ki se n se i   aa,   soo   de su ka.

たなか せんせい：<u>ロペス</u> さん の くに は どこ です か。
Tanaka se   n se i   Ro pe su sa n no   do ko de su ka.

LESSON **4** 第四課

47

すずき せんせい：<u>ブラジル</u>です。
Su zu ki se n se i   Bu ra ji ru de su.

たなか せんせい：ああ、そう です か。
Ta na ka se n se i   aa   soo de su ka.

■Practice 4.1 れんしゅう　練習

Table A below is a list of students' names, jobs, and countries. Some of the information is missing. For each student details about either their しごと (**shigoto**) or くに have been left out. You can find the missing data in Table B at the end of this lesson. Table B, however, does not list the information in Table A.

Three new しごと (**shigoto**) and two new くに appear the tables:

ぎんこういん *gi n koo i n*	bank employee	**ブラジル** *bu ra ji ru*	Brazil
てんいん *te n i n*	shop assistant	**フィリピン** *fi ri pi n*	The Philippines
がいこうかん *ga i koo ka n*	diplomat, person in the diplomatic service		

Some of the students' family names (がくせいのなまえ) may not be that obvious. They are all written in **katakana**.

チェン *che n*	Chen	**ライ** *ra i*	Lai	**マテロ** *ma te ro*	Matello
ホール *hoo ru*	Hall	**ロレン** *ro re n*	Loren	**ジャクソン** *ja ku so n*	Jackson
スミス *su mi su*	Smith	**ヘラ** *he ra*	Heller	**ウイリアムス** *u i ri a mu su*	Williams
カストロ *ka su to ro*	Castro	**キン** *ki n*	Kim	**ブラウン** *bu ra u n*	Brown

Work with your partner to fill in the blanks in the tables. One of you will look at Table A while the other will use Table B. This way you will each have access to the information that the other lacks. Ask each other the questions in **kaiwa** 4.1 to fill in the blanks on your table. The answers are also written under each blank in **hiragana** or **katakana**.

🔊 Table A

なまえ *na ma e*	しごと *go to*	くに	なまえ *na ma e*	しごと *go to*	くに
チェン *Che n*	いしゃ *i sha*	_____ ちゅうごく	ヘラ *He ra*	_____ こうむいん	ドイツ *do i tsu*

ホール *Ho o ru*	**かんごふ**	ニュージーランド *nyuu jii ran do*	キン *Ki n*	てんいん *te n i n*	**かんこく**
スミス *Sumisu*	べんごし *be n go*	**アメリカ**	マテロ *Mate ro*	**がいこうかん**	イタリア *i ta ri a*
カストロ *Kasu toro*	**かいしゃいん**	フィリピン *fi ri pi n*	ジャクソン *Ja ku so n*	がくせい *ga se i*	**オーストラリア**
ライ *Ra i*	ぎんこういん *gi n koo i n*	**たいわん**	ウイリアムス *U i ri a m su*	**ひしょ**	イギリス *i gi ri su*
ロレン *Rore n*	**フランスご の きょうし**	フランス *fu ra n su*	ブラウン *Bu ra u n*	えいご の *e i go no* きょうし *kyoo*	**カナダ**

4.2 Finding places

When traveling in にほん (nihon) you will probably need to find out how to get to all kinds of places. Here are some typical examples.

Look up the vocabulary list at the back of this textbook and write the えいご (eigo) in the blanks. The かんじ (kanji) are also given.

えき *e ki*	_____	駅
おてあらい *te a ra i*	_____	お手洗い
トイレ *to i re*	_____	
ゆうびんきょく *yuu bi n kyo*	_____	郵便局
でんわ *de n wa*	_____	電話
ぎんこう *gi n koo*	_____	銀行
こうばん *koo ba n*	_____	交番
バスてい *ba su te i*	_____	バス停

Note:
こうばん (kooban) is like a small police station. They are common in Japan and can often be found near えき (eki) and large intersections.

■Conversation 4.2　かいわ　　会話

Looking for a toilet

You (A) are trying to find a toilet so you approach someone (B) and ask. They point and tell you it is "over there" あそこ (**asoko**) but you can't work out exactly where they mean. They realize that you haven't understood, わかりません (**wakarimasen**), and take you to the toilet.

A: すみません、<u>おてあらい</u> は どこ です か。
　　su mi ma se n,　　te a ra i　　do ko de su ka.

B: あそこ です。
　　a so ko de su.

A: え、どこ です か。
　　e,　　do ko de su ka.

B: あ、わかりません か。じゃ、きて ください。
　　a,　　wa ka ri ma se n　ka.　ja,　ki te　da sa i.

A: どうも すみません。
　　doo　mo　su mi ma se n.

Practice the above **kaiwa** かいわ using the vocabulary given in 4.2.

Notes:

1. あそこ (**asoko**) refers to a place in the distance. It is like "over there" in English.

2. え (**e**) said with rising intonation is one way of indicating that you either you didn't understand or didn't quite catch what was said to you. It is only used in informal conversation. In formal situations は (**ha**) with rising intonation is used.

3. わかりません (**wakarimasen**) is the negative of the verb "understand" わかります (**wakarimasu**). The ません (**masen**) ending indicates that it is negative, so it is like "not understand." In the かいわ (**kaiwa**) the question mark か (**ka**) is added, so it literally means, "don't you understand?"
   As you will recall, the negative of です (**desu**) is で は ありません (**de wa arimasen**). This also ends in ません (**masen**) and means "isn't," "are not," or "am not."

4. じゃ (**ja**) is something like "well" or "in that case" in えいご (**eigo**). It is used when deciding something or when changing the topic.

5. ください (**kudasai**) is equivalent to "please." In this かいわ (**kaiwa**) it is attached to the verb "come" to make "please come (this way)" きて ください (**kite kudasai**).

4.3 What's this in Japanese?

We already know that the Japanese language is called にほんご (nihongo). We also know how to ask the question "what's this?" これ は なん です か (kore wa nan desu ka). We can combine these by adding the particle で (de). で is the particle that indicates the method or way of doing something. In this case the method of saying is nihongo. Since particles always follow what they refer to, we get the phrase にほんご で (nihongo de). This is equivalent to "in Japanese" in えいご (eigo). The particle で (de) is similar in usage to the English prepositions "by," "with," and "in" when they refer to a way of doing something.

■Language pattern 4.3　ぶんけい　文型

When you are in にほん (nihon) and are trying to learn new words you can always point to some object that you don't know the name of and ask a にほんじん (nihonjin) the following:
Literal Pattern: this **WA** Japanese **DE** what is **KA**.

Q: これ は にほんご で なん です か。
　 ko re　　　ho n go de na n de su ka.
A: それ は いす です。
　 so re　　 i su　de su.

Q: What is this (called) in Japanese?

A: That is a "chair."

Alternatively, when you want to find the にほんご (nihongo) for a word in えいご (eigo), you can ask a にほんじん (nihonjin) who knows some えいご (eigo) :
Literal Pattern: "station" **WA** Japanese **DE** what is **KA**.

Q: station は にほんご で なん です か。
　 "station"　　　 *ho n go de na n de su ka.*
A: えきです。
　 ki de su

Q: What is "station" in Japanese

A: It's "eki."

■Conversation 4.3　かいわ　会話

Asking the Japanese name of something

You (A) want to know the names of various things in the room. You point to things and ask a にほんじん (B) who, in turn wants to know the names of them in えいご. Sometimes you don't get the word at first so you have to ask them to repeat.

LESSON

4

第四課

51

A: <u>これ</u> は にほんご で なん です か。
<small>ko re ／ ho n go de na n de su ka</small>

B: <u>それ</u> です か。
<small>so re de su ka</small>

A: はい、 そう です。
<small>i soo de su</small>

B: <u>それ</u> は <u>いす</u> です。
<small>so re i su de su</small>

A: すみません、 もう いちど いって ください。
<small>sumi ma se n moo i chi do i tte da sa i</small>

B: <u>いす</u> です。
<small>i su de su</small>

A: <u>いす</u>。
<small>i su</small>

B: ええ、 そう です。 <u>いす</u> は えいご で なん です か。
<small>e e, soo de su. i su e i go de na n de su ka.</small>

A: <u>"chair"</u> です。
<small>de su.</small>

B: <u>"cair"</u> です か。
<small>de su ka.</small>

A: ちがいます、 <u>"chair"</u> です。
<small>chi ga i ma su de su</small>

B: <u>"chair"</u>。

A: ええ、 そう です。
<small>e e, soo de su</small>

Notes:

1. After you (A) asked the question "What's this in Japanese?," the にほんじん (B) replied with それ です か (**sore desu ka**) — literally, "is it that?" This will seem a strange question until you realize that it is just a way of confirming your question. It is like "Do you mean that?" In にほんご (**nihongo**) people often repeat what was just said to them as a question in order to check that they heard correctly and to show that they are listening. Such questions are not really questions and the reply is simply ええ (**ee**) or はい (**hai**) with or without the そう です (**soo desu**) part.

2. もう いちど いって ください (**moo ichido itte kudasai**) is what you say when you want the other person to repeat what they have just said. もう (**moo**) is like "again," いちど (**ichido**) is "one time," and いって (**itte**) is a form of the verb "say." We learned ください (**kudasai**: please) earlier.

4.4 This, that, and that これ それ あれ

As you have already learned, things near you (the speaker) are referred to as これ (kore) while things near the other person (the listener) are referred to as それ (sore). This is just like the difference between "this" and "that" in English.

However, another situation exists. There are things which are neither near the speaker nor the listener. In えいご (eigo) these are also referred to as "that" but this is not the case in にほんご (nihongo). Such objects are referred to as あれ (are) by both the speaker and listener.

■Conversation 4.4 かいわ 会話

A person sees a strange thing hanging in the window and points to it.

A: あれ は なん ですか。
　　a re　na n de su ka

B: てるてるぼうず です。
　　te ru te ru boo zu de su

A: え、もう いちど いって ください。
　　e　moo　i chi do　itte　da sa i

B: てるてるぼうず です。
　　te ru te ru boo zu de su

Note: てるてるぼうず (teruteruboozu): This is one of the many things you will encounter in Japan for which an English word cannot be found. It is a simple paper doll which children make and hang from the eaves of the house when they want the weather to be good for the next day because they are going somewhere special. Literally, the word means "shine, shine boy."

4.5 Classroom きょうしつ 教室

In the following table are a number of things commonly found in a classroom (kyooshitsu). Since you don't know the English (eigo) for a number of these words you can find out by using the following question.

Q: つくえ は えいご で なん ですか。
　　tsu e　e i go de na n　de su ka.

A: "desk" です。
　　de su

■Practice 4.5　れんしゅう　　練習

In the following practice, Table A has half the information you need, the other half is in Table B at the end of the lesson. With a partner first find out the えいご (eigo) by asking the question above and writing the えいご (eigo) in the blanks.

Table A

いす *i su*	chair	椅子	ほん *ho n*	book	本
つくえ *tsu e*	_____	机	ペン *pe n*		_____
まど *ma do*	window	窓	ドア *do a*	door	
ゆか *yu ka*	_____	床	こくばん *ko ba n*	_____	黒板
かべ *ka be*	wall	壁	はくばん *ba n*	whiteboard	白板
てんじょう *te n joo*	_____	天井	かばん *ka ba n*	_____	鞄

Next, practice かいわ (kaiwa) 4.3 using the names of the objects in the picture. In your classroom there are some things which are near you, others which are near your partner, while others are not particularly near either of you. Use これ (kore), それ (sore), or あれ (are) depending on the relative location of the thing to which you are referring in your きょうしつ (kyooshitsu).

4.6 The geography of Japan　　にほんのちり　　日本の地理

The land area of Japan is almost 378,000 sq. kms which is slightly larger than Malaysia, about the same size as California, and about half the size of New South Wales in Australia. About 70% of the land is mountainous, most of which is covered with forest. Agriculture is practiced on about 15% of the land and about 3% is residential. Only 0.4% of land is industrial. This means that the population density is very high and agriculture is intensive on the flat land that is available.

The highest mountain is Mt. Fuji ふじさん (fujisan) at 3,776 m. It is a dormant volcano which is just visible from Tokyo on a clear day. The next highest mountain is きただけ (kita dake) at 3,192 m. Two well known active volcanos are Mt. Aso あそさん (aso san) which has a huge caldera and Sakura Jima さくらじま which sometimes showers the city of Kagoshima with ash. Both of these are on the island of Kyushu but all of the islands are thermally active with hot springs おんせん (onsen) abundant.

Most of the rivers of Japan are fairly short. The longest two are the Tone River とねがわ (**tone gawa**) in Honshu at 322 km and the Ishikari River いしかりがわ (**ishikari gawa**) in Hokkaido at 268 km. Tokyo is located on the Sumida River すみだがわ (**sumida gawa**) and the river which flows through Kyoto is the Kamo River かもがわ (**kamo gawa**).

There are many lakes in Japan, the largest is Lake Biwa びわこ (**biwa ko**) north of Osaka. It has a surface area of 670 sq. km. Around Mt. Fuji are five small lakes called ふじごこ(**fuji go ko**) and one larger one called あしのこ (**ashi no ko**) which are very popular sightseeing destinations. The deepest lake in にほん (**nihon**) is くっしゃろこ (**kussharo ko**) in Hokkaido with a depth of 117.5 m.

4.1 Table B

なまえ *nama e*	しごと *go to*	くに	なまえ *nama e*	しごと *go to*	くに
チェン *Che n*	いしゃ	ちゅうごく *chu go*	ヘラ *He ra*	こうむいん *koo mu i n*	ドイツ
ホール *Ho o ru*	かんごふ *ka n go fu*	ニュージーランド	キン *Ki n*	てんいん	かんこく *ka n ko*
スミス *Sumisu*	べんごし	アメリカ *a me ri ka*	マテロ *Mate ro*	がいこうかん *ga i koo ka n*	イタリア
カストロ *Kasu toro*	かいしゃいん *ka i sha i n*	フィリピン	ジャクソン *Ja ku so n*	がくせい	オーストラリア *oo su toraria*

ライ *Ra i*	<u>ぎんこういん</u>	たいわん *ta i wa n*	ウイリアムス *U i ri a m su*	ひしょ *hi sho*	<u>イギリス</u>
ロレン *Ro re n*	フランスご *fu ra n su go* の きょうし *no kyoo*	<u>フランス</u>	ブラウン *Bu ra u n*	<u>えいご の きょうし</u>	カナダ *ka na da*

4.5 Table B

いす *i su*	chair	椅子	ほん *ho n*	book	本
つくえ *tsu e*	desk	机	ペン *pe n*	pen	
まど *ma do*	＿＿＿	窓	ドア *do a*	＿＿＿	
ゆか *yu ka*	floor	床	こくばん *ko ba n*	blackboard	黒板
かべ *ka be*	＿＿＿	壁	はくばん *ba n*	＿＿＿	白板
てんじょう *te n joo*	ceiling	天井	かばん *ka ba n*	bag	鞄

Answer こたえ 答
4.2 train station; toilet; toilet; post office; telephone; bank; police box; bus stop.

The question word for "where" is **doko** どこ. It comprises the **hiragana do** ど and **ko** こ. The first **hiragana** is a syllable modified in the same way as **de** で is. The basic character is **to** と to which **ten ten** てんてん is added to change it to **do** ど. First practice と and then ど.

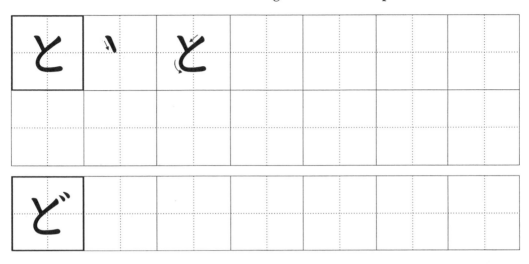

The second syllable of **doko** どこ is **ko** こ. When てんてん is added to **ko** こ it becomes **go** ご.

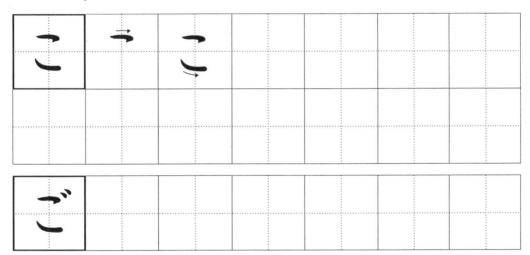

The question word for "what" is either **nan** なん or **nani** なに depending on the context. We've covered **n** ん and **ni** に already so you need **na** な. **Na** な is written with four strokes. Be careful to get the stroke order right.

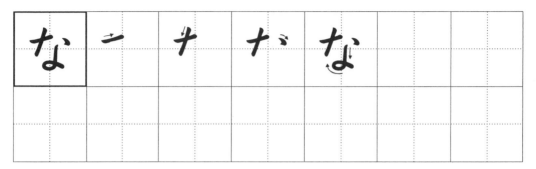

The **hiragana yo** よ is written with two strokes. Be careful not to curl the tail back upwards.

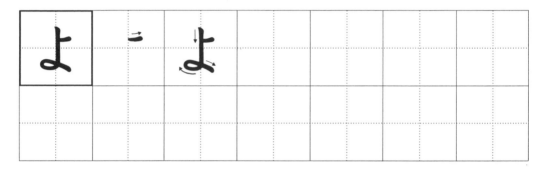

When written smaller this **hiragana** is used to make combined syllables such as **sho** しょ. When う is added the sound is lengthened to **shoo** しょう. Note: when you input しょう into a word processor you type "shou."

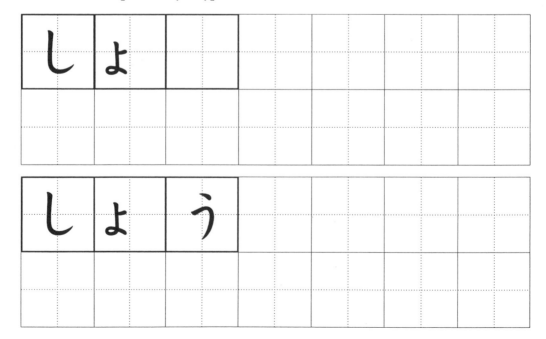

Try reading the following short dialogues:

A: おくに は どこ です **ka**。
B: にほん です。

A: おしごと は なん です **ka**。
B: てんいん です。

A: "book" は にほんご で なん です **ka**。
B: ほん です。

HOMEWORK 4 しゅくだい 宿題

1. Match the Japanese words with their English meanings by joining them with a line.

でんわ	denwa	book
いす	isu	bag
かばん	kaban	window
まど	mado	secretary
ほん	hon	chair
ちゅうごく	chuugoku	student
ひしょ	hisho	train station
がくせい	gakusei	China
えき	eki	telephone

2. Fill in the blanks to complete the following sentences.

1) Q:ほんださん（　　　　　）しごと（　　　　　）なんですか。
　　 ho n da sa n　　　　　*go to*　　　　　*na n de su ka*
　A: かんごふ です。
　　 ka n go fu de su.

2) Q: "Desk" は にほんご(　　　　　)なん です か。
　　　　　　　　　ho n go　　　*na n   de su ka.*
　A: つくえ です。
　　 tsu ku e de su.

3) Q: おてあらい は （　　　　　）です か。
　　　　　　 te a ra i　　　　　*de su ka.*
　A: あそこ です。
　　 a so ko de su.

3. Translate the following sentences into nihongo にほんご.

1) Where is Ms Smith's country? _____

2) Please come (this way).   _____

3) *"Ginkoo"* is "bank" in English. _____

4) Please say it again.   _____

5) I don't understand.   _____

4. Choose the correct one.

1) The highest mountain in Japan is (Aso san,　Fuji san,　Sakurajima).

2) The longest river in Japan is (Sumidagawa,　Ishikarigawa,　Tonegawa).

3) About (70%,　50%,　90%) of Japan is mountainous.

5. ✍ Let's write in Japanese ! Write a HIRAGANA in each ___.

The question word "where" in Japanese is ____ ____ , and "what" is ____ ____ .

"Job" in Japanese is ____ ____ ____ .

"Police box" in Japanese is ____ ____ ____ ____ .

Let's write some words using the HIRAGANA that you've learned. Write one HIRAGANA in each box.
(When you write a small よ it goes in a separate square and takes up the bottom two thirds of the square. All small hiragana are written this way. The large hiragana should fill most of the square.)

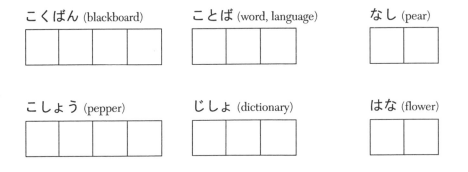

こくばん (blackboard)

ことば (word, language)

なし (pear)

こしょう (pepper)

じしょ (dictionary)

はな (flower)

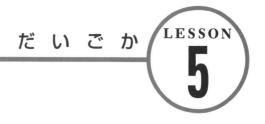

第五課

Note: In this lesson the **roomaji** for く に お は し い え ほ ん の has been removed.

5.1 Numbers   かず   数

The following are the numbers one to thirteen にほんご で (nihongo de). They are written both ひらがな で (hiragana de) and かんじ で (kanji de).

1	いち *chi*	一	8	はち *chi*	八
2	に	二	9	く	九
3	さん *sa*	三	10	じゅう *juu*	十
4	し	四	11	じゅういち *juu chi*	十一
5	ご *go*	五	12	じゅうに *juu*	十二
6	ろく *ro*	六	13	じゅうさん *juu sa*	十三
7	しち *chi*	七			

5.2 Months   つき   月

To get the months (つき tsuki) of the year にほんご で (nihongo de), all you do is add the suffix がつ (gatsu) to the number of the month. This がつ (gatsu) means "month" but it is only used as part of the name of the month. The name of the first month of the year is made up of the word for "one" (いち ichi) with the suffix がつ (gatsu) attached, so "January" is いちがつ (ichigatsu). **Note:** this is the name of the month and does not mean "one month."

いちがつ *chi ga tsu*	一月	しちがつ *chi ga tsu*	七月
にがつ *ga tsu*	二月	はちがつ *chi ga tsu*	八月
さんがつ *sa ga tsu*	三月	くがつ *ga tsu*	九月
しがつ *ga tsu*	四月	じゅうがつ *juu ga tsu*	十月
ごがつ *go ga tsu*	五月	じゅういちがつ *juu chi ga tsu*	十一月
ろくがつ *ro ga tsu*	六月	じゅうにがつ *juu ga tsu*	十二月

Note: Gatsu is written with the same かんじ (kanji) as つき (tsuki) which is the general word for month, this is because they both have the same meaning. Kanji かんじ can be pronounced differently depending on context so both tsuki 月 and ichigatsu 一月 share the same kanji i.e. 月.

■Practice 5.2　れんしゅう　練習

To memorize the months, work with a partner and point to the various つき (tsuki) which are written below かんじ で (kanji de), just as they are on a Japanese calendar nihon no karendaa にほん の カレンダー.

Person A: 　　(points and asks) なん月 です か。
　　　　　　　　　　　　　　　　　na gatsu de su ka

Person B: 　　(answers) さん月 です。
　　　　　　　　　　　　　sa gatsu de su

一月	二月	三月	四月	五月	六月
七月	八月	九月	十月	十一月	十二月

■Language pattern 5.2　ぶんけい　文型

To ask the question "what month is it?" take the word nan なん (what) and attach the suffix がつ (gatsu) to get the following:

Q: なんがつ です か。 or なん月 です か。　　Q: What month is it?
　na gatsu de su ka

A: にがつ です。　　　or 二月 です。　　　A: It's February.
　ga tsu de su

5.3 Seasons　　きせつ　季節

In にほん the seasons きせつ (kisetsu) are particularly distinctive and the change in きせつ (kisetsu) is quite marked.

はる	なつ	あき	ふゆ
ru	*na tsu*	*a ki*	*fu yu*
春	夏	秋	冬

In にほん there is also a wet season called つゆ (tsuyu) 梅雨. This is part of なつ (natsu) and is characterized by drizzle and high levels of humidity. つゆ (tsuyu) varies from year to year but it generally starts in the middle of ろくがつ (roku gatsu) and finishes in early しちがつ (shichi gatsu) .

■Practice 5.3　れんしゅう　練習

With a partner practice the つき (tsuki) and きせつ (kisetsu) by imagining person A is a にほんじん (nihonjin) who doesn't know about the seasons in your part of the world.
Ask and answer questions like: "Is June winter?" or "Is June summer?" Substitute the underlined words and make sure your replies are appropriate.

A: 六月 は ふゆ です か。
　　rokugatsu　fu yu　de su　ka

B: はい、そう です。
　　　　　 soo　　de su

Or

A: 六月 は なつ です か。
　　rokugatsu　na tsu de su ka

B: いいえ、なつ では ありません。ふゆ です。
　　　　　 na tsu　de　　a ri ma se n　　fu yu　de su

5.4 When? – いつ

If you were planning a trip to にほん you would probably want to know when each きせつ (kisetsu) was. You could ask "When is summer in Japan?" like this:

> Q:にほん の なつ は いつ です か。　(literally) Japan's summer when is?
> 　　　　　*na tsu*　　　　　*tsu de su ka*

Since なつ (natsu) covers three months, the reply would be a period of time. In えいご (eigo) periods of time can be expressed using words such as "from" and "to" or "till." にほんご で(nihongo de) the words used are から (kara) and まで (made). So "from June to August" would be:

> A: 六 月 から 八 月 まで です。　(literally) June from August till is.
> 　*rokugatsu ka ra　hachigatsu ma de de　su*

Note: Both から (kara) and まで (made) follow the words they refer to. Also, 八月まで (hachigatsu made) includes 八月 (hachigatsu).

 ▰**Conversation 5.4 かいわ　会話**

Talking about seasonal differences

The きせつ (kisetsu) in にほん and オーストラリア (oosutoraria) occur in quite different months. In fact they are virtually opposite because Japan is in the northern hemisphere **(kita hankyuu)** and Australia is in the southern hemisphere **(minami hankyuu)**. This intrigues many にほんじん **(nihonjin)** and often gives rise to conversations similar to the following:

> A: オーストラリア の なつ は いつ です か。
> 　*oo　su to ra ri a　　na tsu　　　tsu de su ka*
>
> B: 十二月 から 二月 まで です。
> 　*juunigatsu ka ra nigatsu ma de de su*
>
> A: ああ、そう です か。 にほん と ちがいます ね。
> 　*a　a　　soo　de su ka　　　　　　to chi ga　ma su ne*
>
> B: ええ、そう です ね。
> 　　　　　*soo　　de su　ne*

Notes:

1. We have seen ちがいます chigaimasu used as a negative reply as in "iie, chigaimasu." but you may recall that ちがいます (chigaimasu) actually means "is different." In the above かいわ (kaiwa) it is used with this meaning. にほん と ちがいます ね nihon to chigaimasu ne means "different from Japan, isn't it."

2. The ね (ne) on the end is the "isn't it" part, it indicates we both know that the summer months are different in Japan.

3. If we were talking about another northern hemisphere きたはんきゅう (kitahankyuu) country such as アメリカ (amerika) or イギリス (igirisu), the seasons would be the same おなじ (onaji) as in にほん. So, the following comment would be appropriate:

にほん と おなじ です ね。　　　(That) is the same as Japan, isn't it.
　　　to　　na ji　de su　ne

 ■**Practice 5.4　れんしゅう　練習**

Practice the above **kaiwa** かいわ using the following information about the seasons in Australia and Japan. Substitute the underlined parts.

オーストラリア の きせつ　　(oosutoraria no kisetsu)
o o su to ra ri a　　ki se tsu

はる *ru*	九月 *ku gatsu*	～ 十一月 *juuichigatsu*
なつ *na tsu*	十二月 *juunigatsu*	～ 二月 *ni gatsu*
あき *a ki*	三月 *sangatsu*	～ 五月 *gogatsu*
ふゆ *fu yu*	六月 *rokugatsu*	～ 八月 *hachigatsu*

にほん の きせつ　　(nihon no kisetsu)
ki se tsu

はる *ru*	三月 *sangatsu*	～ 五月 *gogatsu*
なつ *na tsu*	六月 *rokugatsu*	～ 八月 *hachigatsu*
あき *a ki*	九月 *kugatsu*	～ 十一月 *juuichigatsu*
ふゆ *fu yu*	十二月 *juunigatsu*	～ 二月 *nigatsu*

A は B と ちがいます。 　　　　*to chi ga ma su.*	A is different from B.
A は B と おなじ です。 　　　　*to na ji de su*	A is the same as B.

The full form of this pattern is used to contrast two things, A and B (A と B). The と (to) is equivalent to "and."

Examples れい 例

1.　オーストラリア の なつ は にほん の なつ と ちがいます。
　　o o su to ra ri a   na tsu   na tsu to chi ga   ma su.

2.　にほん の あさ ごはん は イギリス の あさ ごはん と ちがいます。
　　　　　　a sa go   i gi ri su   a sa go   to chi ga   ma su.

3.　オーストラリア の えいご は アメリカ の えいご と ちがいます。
　　o o   su to ra ri a   go   a me ri ka   go to chi ga   ma su.

4.　みなみはんきゅう の きせつ は きたはんきゅう の きせつ と ちがいます。
　　mi na mi   kyuu   ki se tsu   ki ta   kyuu   ki se tsu to chi ga   ma su.

5.5 Telephone number　　でんわ ばんごう　電話番号

1. When saying a telephone number でんわ ばんごう (denwa bangoo) we need to use the numbers we learned for the months plus zero. にほんご で (nihongo de) "zero" is れい (rei), but ゼロ (zero) is also often used these days.

2. The number four is usually given as よん (yon) rather than し when saying でんわ ばんごう (denwa bangoo). The longer form of nine, きゅう (kyuu) is prefered over く, as is the alternative form of seven, なな (nana).

3. でんわ ばんごう (denwa bangoo) typically comprise two sections e.g. 344–8093. The dash is said as の, so the number is: さん よん よん の はち れい きゅう さん (san yon yon no hachi rei kyuu san).

4. To make the question "What is your telephone number?" you add ばん (ban) (number) to なん (nan) (what), you can also attach the honorific お to でんわ ばんごう (denwa bangoo) to get the question:

お でんわ ばんごう は なんばん です か。
de   wa ba   goo   na   ba   de su ka.

Note: The お is optional. By making the word more polite it clearly refers to the listener's number.

Asking someone's phone number

When someone asks your でんわ ばんごう (denwa bangoo) they may want your home number うち の でんわばんごう (uchi no denwa bango) or your number at the company かいしゃ (kaisha).

A: おでんわばんごう は なんばん です か。
    de wa ba goo   na ba de su ka.

B: わたしの うち の です か。
    wa ta   u chi   de su ka.

A: いいえ、<u>かいしゃ</u> の です。
    ka sha   de su.

B: <u>かいしゃ</u> の は <u>823</u> の <u>4519</u> です。
    ka sha   de su.

A: ありがとう ございます。
    a ri ga too go za   ma su.

Note: In the かいわ (kaiwa), B's reply わたしの うち の です か (watashi no uchi no desu ka) is a shortened form of the sentence わたしの うち の でんわばんごう です か (watashi no uchi no denwabangoo desu ka). Since we know we are talking about でんわばんごう (denwabangoo), this word can be left out.

Practice the above かいわ (kaiwa) with different でんわばんごう (denwabangoo). You can also substitute the following words in place of かいしゃ (kaisha):

がっこう *ga kkoo*	school	学校
だいがく *da ga*	university	大学
つとめさき *tsu to me sa ki*	business, place of work	勤め先

Sometimes an area code しがいきょくばん (shigaikyokuban) (市外局番) is also needed. This is simply joined with の, e.g.

(03) 889-3046   れい さん の はち はち きゅう の さん れい よん ろく
                    re sa   chi chi kyuu   sa re   yo ro

LESSON **5** 第五課

▪Language pattern 5.5　ぶんけい　　文型

Q:お でんわ ばんごう は なんばん です か。
　　de　wa ba　goo　　na　ba　　de su ka.

Q: What is your phone number?

A:さん ご はち の きゅう なな ご よん です。
　sa　go chi　　kyu u na na go　yo　de su.

A: It's 358-9754.

5.6 Important numbers　　たいせつな でんわ ばんごう

When asking the でんわばんごう (denwabangoo) of a place such as the American embassy アメリカ たいしかん (amerika taishikan), just attach the name of the place to the front of the question by dropping the お and adding の:

Q:　アメリカ たいしかん の でんわ ばんごう は なんばん です か。
　　a me ri ka ta　　　ka　　de wa ba　goo　　　na　ba　　de su ka.
　　What's the phone number of the American embassy?

▪Practice 5.6　れんしゅう　　練習

When you are in Tokyo とうきょう (tookyoo) there are a number of たいせつな でんわ ばんごう (taisetsuna denwabangoo) which you should know. Using Tables A and B below, practice asking and giving でんわ ばんごう (denwabangoo) with a partner.

Table A

Place ばしょ 場所	でんわばんごう 電話番号	
アメリカ たいしかん *a me ri ka ta　　ka*	＿＿＿＿＿	American embassy 米国大使館
イギリス たいしかん *i gi ri su ta　　ka*	3265 - 5511	British embassy 英国大使館
オーストラリア たいしかん *o o sutora ri a ta　　ka*	＿＿＿＿＿	Australian embassy 豪州大使館
けいさつ *ke　sa tsu*	110	police 警察
しょうぼうしょ *shoo　boo sho*	＿＿＿＿＿	fire(and ambulance) 消防署

LESSON 5 第五課

68

カンタス こうくう *ka n ta su koo u*	3593 - 7000	Qantas Airlines カンタス航空	
ばんごう あんない *ba goo a na*	_____	directory assistance 番号案内	
にほん こうくう *koo u*	3457 - 1111	Japan Airlines 日本航空	
いみんきょく *mi kyo*	_____	immigration office 移民局	
かんこう あんない *ka koo a na*	3502 - 1461	tourist information 観光案内	

Note: The police number is usually read in a different fashion as: *"hyakutoo ban"* ひゃく とお ばん literally, "number one hundred ten." Once you've studied Lessons 9 and 15 the reason for this reading will become apparent.

5.7 The climate of Japan   にほんのきこう   日本の気候

Since Japan stretches from north to south its climate ranges from sub-frigid in Hokkaido to sub-tropical in Okinawa. However, the climate of the main islands is temperate, with the main difference being between the Pacific coast, which has hot humid summers and dry winters, and the Japan Sea coast which has very heavy snow falls in winter. In Niigata there can be 4–5 meters of snow making it one of the snowiest places in the world.

In general, Japan is rather wet with precipitation ranging from 1,000 to 2,500 mm per year. On the Pacific coast much of this falls in the rainy season in June and July, and in the typhoon たいふう (taifuu 台風) season in August and October. Typhoons cause considerable damage through flooding and landslides.

The climate of Tokyo is fairly mild. The average temperature ranges from 6.6°C in January to 27.4°C in August. In winter the days are often clear and dry, there are some light snow falls but the temperature seldom drops below minus 5°C. Inland from Tokyo, the mountains catch enough snow for skiing to be popular. Summer is hot and muggy with the maximum temperature reaching 40°C on rare occasions. Since there are few good beachs this is perhaps the most unpleasant season. The wettest month is October and the driest is December. The average annual precipitation is 1,503 mm.

The most popular seasons are spring and autumn. In spring the spectacle of cherry blossoms さくら (sakura 桜) attracts sightseers who go to view the blossoms and sit beneath them in the parks eating, drinking, and enjoying themselves. Such parties are called はなみ (hanami).

In autumn it is popular to go to the mountains where the autumn leaves こうよう (kooyoo 紅葉) put on a spectacular display. The change of the seasons is quite marked in Japan and has been a source of inspiration for art and culture over the centuries.

Place ばしょ 場所	でんわ ばんごう 電話番号	
アメリカ たいしかん *a me ri ka ta ka*	3224 - 5000	American embassy 米国大使館
イギリス たいしかん *i gi ri su ta ka*	＿＿＿＿＿	British embassy 英国大使館
オーストラリア たいしかん *o o su to ra ri a ta ka*	5232 - 4111	Australian embassy 豪州大使館
けいさつ *ke sa tsu*	＿＿＿＿＿	police 警察
しょうぼうしょ *sho o boo sho*	119	fire (and ambulance) 消防署
カンタス こうくう *ka n ta su koo u*	＿＿＿＿＿	Qantas Airlines カンタス航空
ばんごう あんない *ba goo a na*	104	directory assistance 番号案内
にほん こうくう *koo u*	＿＿＿＿＿	Japan Airlines 日本航空
いみんきょく *mi kyo*	3580 - 4111	immigration office 移民局
かんこう あんない *ka koo a na*	＿＿＿＿＿	tourist information 観光案内

Writing Japanese script 5.8

The next hiragana is ka か.When used at the end of a sentence it makes the sentence into a question. It is rather like a question mark when used this way. When ten ten てんてん is added ka か becomes ga が.

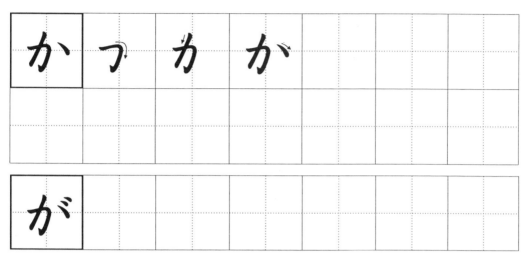

The next hiragana, tsu つ is quite special in that it has a particular function, as well as a sound. When written full size it has the sound "tsu" as in natsu なつ (summer), itsu い つ (when). However, when it is written smaller it is not sounded at all. Rather, it functions as a filler for a syllable which is skipped over. So far we have seen this phenomenon in roomaji as doubled letters e.g. gakkoo. This is just a spelling convention used in roomaji. The skipped syllable in gakkoo is actually indicated by a small tsu (known as "chiisai tsu") as follows: がっこう. When てんてん is added, it is pronounced zu づ, but it is far less common than the other zu ず. When you type these into a word processor, "tu" can be used for つ and "du" is usually used for づ. In the case of chiisai つ, you key in the doubled consonant, so がっこう is typed in as "gakkou."

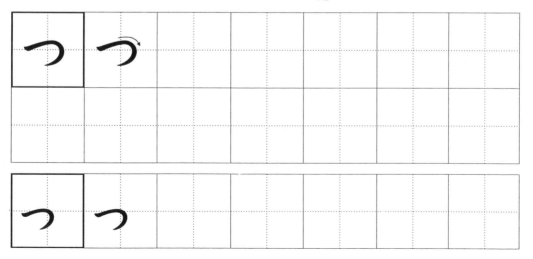

71

So far all the symbols we have learned have been hiragana. Each of these has a particular sound value but no particular meaning unless part of a word. However, Japanese is also written in **kanji** which are quite different to **hiragana** in that they principally have meaning rather than sound. A single **kanji** is a word in its own right, it has a fixed meaning but its pronunciation can change with context. This may seem strange, so think of them as road signs, symbols with fixed meanings but no fixed pronunciation. For example, when you see a curved arrow you know what the sign means but you could call it "curve" or "bend" or "turn" depending on the situation. The sign itself does not have a single pronunciation but it has a definite meaning.

The following **kanji** is a very old one. It comes from a picture of a crescent moon. Its basic meaning is "moon" but it is also used to mean "month," a word that originally comes from "moon" in English too. We have seen this word as **gatsu** がつ in **ichigatsu** (January). This **kanji** is written with four strokes as follows:

HOMEWORK **5** しゅくだい 宿題

1. Say the following numbers aloud in Japanese.

8   4   1   5   2   9   3   10   7   6   0

2. Fill in the blanks to complete the following sentences.

1) Q: にほん の なつ は （　　　　　　　　　） です か。
   na tsu　　　　　　　　　　　　　　　　de su ka.

　A: ろく月 （　　　　　　　） はち月 （　　　　　　　） です。
   ro　gatsu　　　　　　　chigatsu　　　　　　　de su.

2) オーストラリア の えいご （ ） アメリカ の えいご
 Oo su to ra ri a   *go*   *a me ri ka*   *go*
（ ） ちがいます。
          chi ga   ma su

3) A: お でんわ ばんごう は （ ） ですか。
     de   wa ba   *de su ka.*
 B: わたし の うち （ ） です か。
     Wa ta   u chi   *de su ka.*
 A: はい、そう です。
          soo   de su.
 B: うちの （ ） 462 （ ） 3378 です。
     u chi   *de su.*

3. Complete the following sentences using one of the words listed below.

1) （ ） は あついです。 ふゆ は （ ） です。
          a tsu   de su. *fu yu*   *de su.*

2) にほん の 五月 は （ ） です。
          gogatsu   *de su.*

3) にほん の 十月は （ ） です。
          juugatsu   *de su.*

4) "Season" は にほんご で （ ） です。
                         de   *de su.*

きせつ　　つゆ　　　はる　　なつ　　　あき　　さむい
ki se tsu   *tsu yu*   *ru*   *na tsu*   *a ki*   *sa mu*

4. Translate the following sentences into nihongo にほんご.

1) 'Tsuyu" is "wet season" in English. _____

2) Japanese winter is from December to February. _____

_____

3) What is the telephone number of the Japanese embassy? _____

_____

5. ✍ **Let's write in Japanese! Write a HIRAGANA ひらがな or KANJI かんじ in each ___.**

The question word "when" in Japanese is: _____ _____ , and "what number" is: ____ ____ ____ ____

"Summer" in Japanese is: _____ _____. "February" in Japanese is: ____ ____ ____

Let's write some words using the HIRAGANA that you've learned. Write one HIRAGANA in each box.

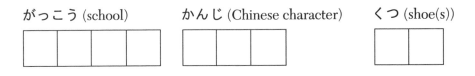

がっこう (school)

かんじ (Chinese character)

くつ (shoe(s))

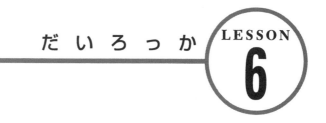

第六課

Note: In this lesson the **roomaji** ローマ字 for the following **hiragana** ひらがな has been removed: くぐにははばおんほぼしじのいえてですずう.

6.1 Going Places   いきます　行きます

When you want to express movement from one place to another, the word you want is い きます (ikimasu). This is like "go" or "going" in えいご (eigo). いきます (ikimasu) is often used with the name of a place and also with the particle に which indicates movement and is rather like "to" in えいご (eigo).

The sentence "I am going to Japan" or "I go to Japan" is:

わたし は にほん に いきます。　　Person は (place) に (go).
wa ta　　　　　*ki ma*

Just as in えいご (eigo) the question word which most often goes with いきます (ikimasu) is どこ (doko where). So, the question "Where are you going?" or "Where do you go?" in にほんご (nihongo) is:

どこ に いきます か。　　　　Where に go か.
do ko　　*ki ma*　*ka.*

■Conversation 6.1 かいわ　会話

A Tokyo morning とうきょう の あさ 東京の朝

This **kaiwa** かいわ takes place at the entrance to a subway station in Tokyo とうきょう one morning. Suzuki すずき and Yasuda やすだ are acquaintances who have just met by chance. It turns out that they are both going to Kanda かんだ, an inner suburb of とうき ょう (tookyoo) known for its offices and shops.

すずき: おはよう ございます。
     ki   *yo*   *go za* *ma*

やすだ: おはよう ございます。
ya *da*   *yo*   *go za* *ma*

すずき: おげんき ですか。
     ki   *ge ki*   *ka*

やすだ: ええ、げんき です。<u>すずき</u>さん は。
ya *da*   *ge ki*   *ki sa*

すずき: げんき です。どこ に いきます か。
     ki ge ki   *do ko*   *ki ma* *ka*

やすだ: <u>かんだ</u> に いきます。
ya *da* *ka* *da*   *ki ma*

すずき: そう です か。わたし も <u>かんだ</u> に いきます。
     ki so   *ka* *wa ta* *mo ka* *da*   *ki ma.*

やすだ: <u>しごと</u> に いきます か。
ya *da* *go to*   *ki ma* *ka.*

すずき: いいえ、<u>かいもの</u> に いきます。
     ki   *ka* *mo*   *ki ma*

やすだ: ああ、そう です か。
ya *da* *a* *a* *so*   *ka*

■Language pattern 6.1　ぶんけい　文型

Q: どこ に いきます か。　　　　　Q: Where (are you) going?
  do ko   *ki ma* *ka*

A: (place) に いきます。　　　　　A: (I'm) going to (place).
         ki ma

6.2 The particle も (mo) (too, also)

The particle も (mo) is used rather like "also" or "too" in えいご (eigo) or like "either" in a negative sentence. When it refers to the subject of the sentence it comes in the same position as は and replaces it as follows:

すずきさん は かんだ に いきます。　Mr./Ms. Suzuki is going to Kanda.
ki sa   ka   da   ki ma.

やすださん も かんだ に いきます。　Mr./Ms. Yasuda is also going to Kanda.
ya da sa   mo ka   da   ki ma

■Practice 6.2　れんしゅう　練習

First, look up your dictionary じしょ (jisho) or the vocabulary list at the end of this text and write the えいご (eigo) in the blanks. Then practice **kaiwa** 6.1 by substituting the destination and the following places, and activities.

しごと　仕事	＿＿＿＿＿	かいもの　　買物	＿＿＿＿＿
go to		*ka mo*	
かいしゃ 会社	＿＿＿＿＿	パーティー	＿＿＿＿＿
ka sha		*pa a tii*	
がっこう 学校	＿＿＿＿＿	しゅっちょう 出張	＿＿＿＿＿
ga kkoo		*shu cchoo*	
だいがく 大学	＿＿＿＿＿	さんぽ　　散歩	＿＿＿＿＿
da ga		*sa po*	

6.3 Here and there　ここ, そこ, あそこ

Just as there were three words for "this" and "that," the words for "here" and "there" vary with the proximity of place to speaker or listener.

ここ *ko ko*	here	(a position nearer the speaker than the listener)
そこ *so ko*	there	(a position nearer the listener than the speaker)
あそこ *a so ko*	there	(a position not nearer either of them)

6.4 Japanese Cities　にほん の まち　日本の町

Here is a list of the major cities of にほん. The word for "city" or "town" is まち (machi). The names of the まち (machi) are written in ひらがな (hiragana) and in かんじ (kanji). Half of them are located on this map, ちず A (chizu) and the other half on ちず B at the end of the lesson. Work with your partner にほんご で (nihongo de) using the following かいわ (kaiwa) to fill in the names of the missing まち (machi) in the blanks. Since you are pointing to the まち (machi) on a ちず (chizu) they are near you and so you will always say ここ (koko).

A:ここ は どこ です か。(pointing to chizu) 　　*ko ko*　　*do ko*　　*ka*	A:Where is this? (pointing to map)
B:(name of city) です。	B:It's (name of city)

ちず (chizu) A　地図A

おおさか　大阪
sa ka

ふくおか　福岡
fu　　ka

とうきょう　東京
too　kyoo

かごしま　鹿児島
ka go　ma

きょうと　京都
kyoo　to

なごや　名古屋
na go ya

さっぽろ　札幌
sa p po ro

ひろしま　広島
hi ro　ma

こうべ　神戸
koo be

なは　那覇
na

ながさき　長崎
na ga sa ki

かなざわ　金沢
ka na za wa

せんだい　仙台
se　da

にいがた　新潟
ga ta

にいがた
ga ta

ひろしま
hi ro　ma

こうべ
koo be

ふくおか
fu　ka

とうきょう
too　kyoo

なごや
na go ya

かごしま
ka go　ma

LESSON **6** 第六課

78

6.5 The negative of ikimasu

To make "go" into "don't go" we just change the ます (masu) part of いきます (ikimasu) to ません (masen).

Q: だいがく に いきますか。
<small>da ga ki ma ka</small>

A1: はい、いきます。
<small>ki ma</small>

A2: いいえ、いきません。
<small>ki ma se</small>

Q: Are (you) going to university?

A1: Yes, (I'm) going.

A2: No, (I'm) not going.

 ■Conversation 6.5　かいわ　会話

A trip to Japan

John ジョン is going to にほん this year. Yamada やまだ asks him about his proposed trip. Listen to the tape and fill in the blanks in hiragana ひらがな.

やまだ: ジョンさん、いつ ＿＿＿＿＿ へ いきますか。
<small>ya ma da Jo n sa tsu e ki ma ka</small>

ジョン: 十月 に いきます。
<small>jo n juugatsu ki ma</small>

やまだ: ＿＿＿＿＿ です ね。あき です ね。
<small>ya ma da ne. a ki ne</small>

ジョン: ええ、そう です ね。
<small>jo n e e soo ne</small>

やまだ: にほん の どこ へ いきます か。
<small>ya ma da do ko e ki ma ka</small>

ジョン: とうきょう と おおさか へ いきます。
<small>jo n too kyoo to sa ka e ki ma</small>

やまだ: きょうと へ も いきます か。
<small>ya ma da kyoo to e mo ki ma ka</small>

ジョン: ＿＿＿＿＿、いきません。
<small>jo n ki ma se</small>

Practice the above (kaiwa) かいわ by substituting the months, seasons, and cities.

Notes:

1. The particle へ (e) has the same usage as に. Which you use is largely a matter of preference. The point to remember about へ (e) is that it is written with the hiragana へ (he) and not with the hiragana え (e).

2. いい です ね (ii desu ne) is the reply you use when someone tells you about something good that is going to happen. The word いい is "good" or "nice" as we saw previously in いいてんき (ii tenki). In えいご (eigo) this expression would be like "That sounds good, doesn't it;" "That's good, I envy you;" or "That'll be nice for you, won't it" depending on circumstance.

3. にほん の どこ (nihon no doko). Although えいご で (eigo de) we say "where in Japan," にほんご で (nihongo de) this becomes "Japan's where," i.e. にほん の どこ (nihon no doko).

4. と (to) is one version of "and." It joins nouns together, e.g. やまださん と わたし (yamada san to watashi) (Yamada and I). We have also seen it joining nouns in a somewhat different way in the language pattern **A wa B to chigaimasu**.

5. へ も (e mo). The particle も can also follow a place. In such cases it combines with the particles に or へ (e) in the following fashion:

LESSON 6 第六課

わたし は きょうと に も いきます。 I am going to Kyoto too.
wa ta   kyoo to   mo   ki ma

おおさか へ も いきますか。 (Are you) also going to Osaka?
sa ka e   mo   ki ma ka

The use of も in にほんご (nihongo) avoids the type of ambiguity which can occur in English sentences such as "I'm going to Osaka too." which could mean either of the following:

わたし は おおさか へ も いきます。
wa ta   sa ka   e mo   ki ma

わたし も おおさか へ いきます。
wa ta   mo   sa ka   e   ki ma

6.6 Time expressions   ときのひょうげん 時の表現

In the last lesson we had one type of time expression—the months of the year. When a month is used to express the time when something happens, it is followed by the particle に. This is rather like the use of "in" in えいご (eigo).

Q: いつ いきます か。 Q: When (are you) going?
tsu   ki ma   ka

A: 九月 に いきます。 A: (I'm) going in September.
kugatsu   ki ma

In general the particle に is used to express direction or time. We have seen it used to indicate movement to a place e.g. おおさか に いきます (oosaka ni ikimasu). In this case it is like "to" えいご で (eigo de). In the above example it expresses the time at which an event occurs. This に is like the えいご (eigo) "in," "on," or "at."

Although に can be replaced by へ (e) when it follows a place to which movement occurs, this is not possible for に when it follows a time. Therefore the sentence **kugatsu e ikimasu** is incorrect; it has to be 九月 に いきます (kugatsu ni ikimasu).

In the case of the following time expressions no particle is required. These words refer to relative time e.g. "tomorrow" rather than to absolute time e.g. "Friday." The general rule for both えいご (eigo) and にほんご (nihongo) is that relative time expressions do not take prepositions while absolute time expressions do. For example, we say "on Saturday," "in June," "at 3 p.m.," "on the 25th" but we don't say "on tomorrow," "in last month," etc. In にほんご (nihongo) all the above absolute time expressions would be followed by に while the relative time expressions would take no particle.

わたし は 一月 に にほん へ いきます。　　I am going to Japan in January.
wa ta　　ichigatsu　　　e　ki ma

わたし は あした にほん へ いきます。　　I am going to Japan tomorrow.
wa ta　　a　ta　　　　e　ki ma

6.7 Greetings used at home いえ で の あいさつ 家での挨拶

1. When leaving the house to go out it is customary for にほんじん (nihonjin) to say "ittekimasu" as they leave. Whoever is staying at home replies "itterasshai." These set phrases sound somewhat strange when translated into えいご (eigo) as there is no equivalent custom.
いってきます (ittekimasu) means "go and come back," as a short way of saying "I'm going out for a bit and will be back in a while."
いってらっしゃい (itterasshai) means "go and please return."

2. When a person returns to the house they say "tadaima" as they enter. Whoever is in the house will reply "okaerinasai."
ただいま (tadaima) means "just now" which is short for "I'm just back now."
おかえりなさい (okaerinasai) means "please come home" or "welcome home."
さようなら (sayoonara) and こんにちは (konnichi wa) are not appropriate when leaving and returning home.

■Conversation 6.7　かいわ　会話

Going out and coming home

Linda リンダ (rinda) is an アメリカ じん (amerikajin) staying with a host family in とうきょう (tookyoo). She is going out sight seeing for the day to あさくさ (asakusa) and うえの こうえん (ueno kooen). Yoshiko, the にほんじん (nihonjin) she is staying with, asks her where she is going just as she is about to go out.

リンダ: きょう は いい てんき です ね。
ri n da　kyoo　　　　ki　　　ne

よしこ: ええ。リンダ さん、きょう どこ へ いきます か。
yo　ko　　　ri n da　sa　　kyoo　do ko　e　ki ma　ka

リンダ: あさくさ と うえの こうえん へ いきます。
ri n da　a sa　sa to　　koo　　　　ki ma

よしこ: いいです ね。じゃ、いってらっしゃい。
yo　ko　　　　ne　ja　　　ra　　ssha

リンダ: いってきます。
ri n da　　　tte ki ma

When she returns later that day Linda says:

リンダ: ただいま。
ri n da　ta da　ma

よしこ: あ、リンダ さん。おかえりなさい。
yo　ko　a　ri n da　sa　　　ka　ri na sa

Notes:

あさくさ Asakusa (浅草) is a suburb of Tokyo near the Sumida River which is known for its rather traditional feel. There is a large temple complex not far from the station called せんそうじ Sensooji (浅草寺). The gateway to this complex has a well known gate called かみなりもん kaminari mon (雷門) which translates as "Thunder Gate" and houses statues of the gods of thunder and wind. In the narrow streets around Sensooji there are numerous shops and restaurants.

うえの Ueno (上野) is another older suburb not far from Asakusa. It has a large station, but is best known for its large park こうえん (kooen) which contains a zoo, and a number of art galleries and museums.

These two suburbs of Tokyo are the best known suburbs of the older area of Tokyo referred to as したまち shitamachi (下町) which means "lower town," so named as it

LESSON **6** 第六課

occupies the low lying area along the Sumida River (すみだがわ). This area was the commercial district of Edo (江戸), the old name of Tokyo とうきょう.

The large red lantern which hangs in かみなりもん.

6.8 Verbs　どうし　動詞

Verbs are words which indicate action, a typical example of a verb is "go." In にほんご (nihongo) "go" is いく. However, at this stage we will encounter this verb in its polite form, which is いきます (ikimasu) in the present tense. In Japanese, verbs comprise two parts: a stem which conveys the meaning, e.g. いき (iki); and an ending which shows the tense and whether the verb is positive or negative, e.g. ます (masu) when the verb is positive and refers to the present or future.

In えいご (eigo) there are three basic verb tenses—future, present, and past, but in にほんご (nihongo) there are two basic tenses—future/present and past. We have already seen the first of these in the previous かいわ (kaiwa). When we refer to an event which is going to happen (or not happen), the verb which comes at the end of the sentence will end in ます (masu) if the sentence is positive and ません (masen) if the sentence is negative.

When referring to an event in the past, the verb ends in ました (mashita) if it is positive and in ません でした (masen deshita) if it is negative.

いく to go 行く		
Tense	**positive**	**negative**
Future/present	いきます ki ma	いきません ki ma se
Past	いきました ki ma ta	いきません でした ki ma se ta

Unlike えいご (eigo), there is no change in the verb for present and future tense in にほんご (nihongo).

6.9 Future and present time expressions

Using the dictionary (じしょ jisho) at the back of this text, write the えいご (eigo) for the following relative time expressions.

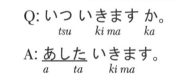

あした (あす) *a ta a*	_____	明日
あした の あさ *a ta a*	_____	明日の朝
あした の ばん *a ta*	_____	明日の晩
あさって *a sa tte*	_____	明後日
きょう *kyoo*	_____	今日
けさ *ke sa*	_____	今朝
こんばん *ko*	_____	今晩

■Conversation 6.9　かいわ　会話

Where are you going?

Practice the above time expressions with your partner (aite) あいて using the following short かいわ (kaiwa).

Q: いつ いきます か。
　　tsu   ki ma   ka
A: <u>あした</u> いきます。
　　a   ta   ki ma

6.10 Past time expressions

The following time expressions will all take the past tense.

きのう *ki*	_____	昨日

きのう の あさ ki　　　　a sa	_____	昨日の朝
さくばん sa	_____	昨晩
おととい to to	_____	一昨日

 ■Practice 6.10　れんしゅう　　練習

With a partner, use the following two short かいわ (kaiwa) to practice the relative time expressions above using the past tense.

1. Q: いつ いきました か。
　　　　tsu　　ki ma　　ta ka

　　A: きのう いきました。
　　　　ki　　　　ki ma　　ta

2. Q: きのう なごや に いきました か。
　　　　ki　　　na go ya　　　　ki ma　　ta ka

　　A: はい、 いきました。
　　　　　　　　ki ma　　ta

　　Or

　　A: いいえ、 いきませんでした。
　　　　　　　　ki ma se　　　　ta

6.11 Past tense of です　「です」の かこけい　「です」の過去形

We can make the past tense of です by changing the ending from す to した (shita) just as we did for いきます (ikimasu).

	です **to be**	
Tense	**positive**	**negative**
Future/present	です	ではありません a ri ma se
Past	でした ta	では ありません でした a ri ma se　　　　ta

■Practice 6.11　れんしゅう　練習

1. Practice the following short exchange using the past time expressions in 6.10 and the vocabulary from 3.3.

A:きのう の ばんごはん は なん でしたか。
　 ki　　　　　　　　　　　　na　　　 ta ka

B:さかな でした。
　 sa ka na　　　 ta

A:そう で すか。
　 so　　　 ka

Note how A still says そうですか (soo desu ka). This is because the people are talking now and A is just acknowledging being told something; it's like "Oh," "Uh huh," and "Right." If you say そうでしたか (soo deshita ka), you are indicating you have just worked something out, or had a sudden realization about something. It means something like "Oh, was that what it was!" or "Ah, now I've got it!"

6.4 ちず B

Answers こたえ 答え
Conversation 6.5　にほん; いい; いいえ.

86

Writing Japanese script 6.12

You have learned the verb "go" **ikmasu** いきます, but need the **hiragana ki** き to be able to write it. **ki** き is written with four strokes in the handwriting style given below. In the printed form the last stroke is often joined. When てんてん is added き becomes **gi** ぎ.

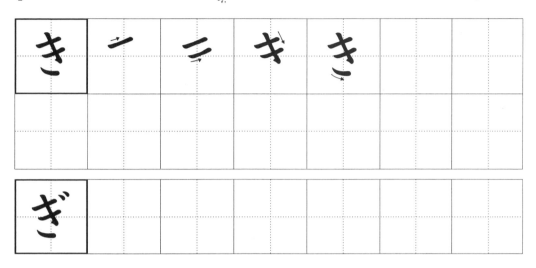

This next hiragana is **ma** ま. It is written with three strokes. Make sure the curl finishes downwards.

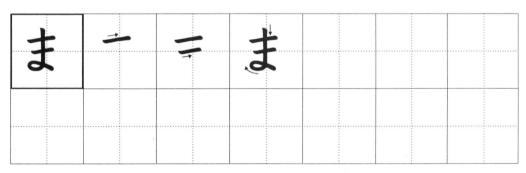

You have often met **se** せ in the negative verb endings: **masen** ません and **de wa arimasen** ではありません. It is written with three strokes. When てんてん is added せ becomes **ze** ぜ.

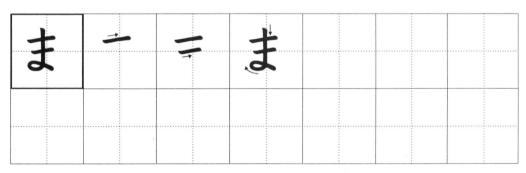

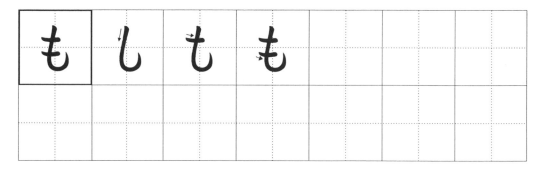

ぜ

You have learned the particles は, の, and に so far. The next is **mo** which is written with three strokes thus: も. This particle is similar to "also" or "too" in English.

も し も も

The **hiragana** へ is usually pronounced "**he**" when spelling a word, but when used as a particle it is pronounced "**e**." (However, it is always typed into the word processor as "he.") Be careful to distingish it from **e** え which is never used to write the particle. When てんてん is added to **he** へ it becomes **be** べ.

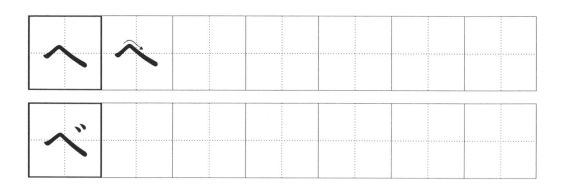

へ へ

べ

The hiragana of the "h" line of the hiragana chart, i.e. ha は hi ひ fu ふ he へ ho ほ can be further transformed by the addition of a small circle which is referred to as "maru" まる. This transforms は to pa ぱ, へ to pe ぺ, and ほ to po ぽ.

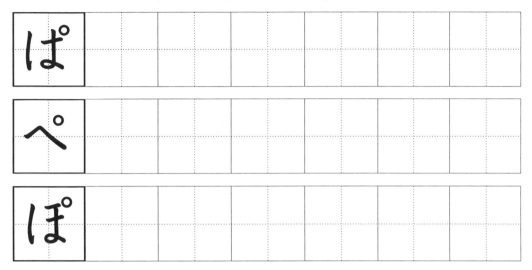

1. **Fill in the blanks with one or two HIRAGANA ひらがな to complete the following sentences.**

    1) Q: どこ （　　　　　） いきます か。
          do ko　　　　　　　　*ki ma*　*ka.*

       A: きょうと （　　　　　） いきます。
          kyoo to　　　　　　　*ki ma.*

       Q: おおさか （　　　　　） いきますか。
          saka　　　　　　　　*ki ma*　*ka.*

       A: いいえ、おおさか （　　　　　） いきません。
               sa ka　　　　　　*ki ma se n.*

    2) あした わたし は パーティー （　　　　） いきます。 すずきさん （　　　　）
       a   ta wa ta　　*paa   tii*　　　　　　*ki ma*　　　*ki sa*

       パーティー （　　　　） いきます。
       paa   tii.　　　　　　*ki ma*

    3) Q: （　　　　） いきますか。
             ki ma　*ka.*

       A: 九月 （　　　　） いきます。
         kugatsu　　　　　　*ki ma*

    4) Q: にほん （　　　　） どこ （　　　　） いきます か。
                do ko　　　　　　*ki ma*　*ka.*

       A: ながさき （　　　　） いきます 。
         na ga sa ki　　　　　　*ki ma.*

2. **Fill in the blanks with the appropriate form of いきます to complete sentences.**

    1) Q: あした とうきょう へ （　　　　　　　　） か。
          a   ta too kyoo   e　　　　　　　　*ka.*

       A: いいえ、（　　　　　　　　）。

    2) Q: きのう だいがく へ （　　　　　　　　） か。
          ki   da ga   e　　　　　　　　*ka.*

       A: いいえ、（　　　　　　　　）。

3. Answer the following questions.

1) What is the reply to "いってきます (ittekimasu)?"

_____

2) What is the reply to "ただいま (tadaima)?"

_____

3) What is the word for "here" in Japanese?

_____

4.Translate the following sentences into にほんご.

1) A: I'm going to Nagasaki tomorrow morning.

_____

   B: That's good!

_____

2) Mr. Tanaka went to Osaka and Kyoto in March.

_____

5. ✍ Let's write in Japanese! Write a HIRAGANA in each ___.

When you leave home you say: ___ ___ ___ ___ ___ ___

"Season" in Japanese is: ___ ___ ___. "Lawyer" in Japanese is: . ___ ___ ___ _

Write the following words using HIRAGANA ひらがな and put the English meanings in the ( ).

かいもの (   )   さんぽ (   )   かべ (   )

第七課

Note: In this lesson the roomaji (ローマじ) for the following has been removed: くぐに はばおしじいえんのすずてでほぼううとどこごなよしょ.

7.1 Time　　じかん　時間

じかん (jikan) is the general word for "time." The じ part of the word means "hour" and, just as we added がつ (gatsu) to the numbers to get the months of the year, we can add じ to get the hours of the day. The only difference between the numbers used with the months and those with the hours is the number four. Instead of し a shortened form of よん (yon) is used, i.e. よじ (yoji) (4 o'clock).

いちじ *chi*	一時	しちじ *chi*	七時
にじ	二時	はちじ *chi*	八時
さんじ *sa*	三時	くじ	九時
よじ	四時	じゅうじ *juu*	十時
ごじ	五時	じゅういちじ *juu*　　*chi*	十一時
ろくじ *ro*	六時	じゅうにじ *juu*	十二時

Note: the above refer only to the hours by the clock とけい (tokei). They cannot be used to mean amounts of time, e.g. "one hour."

To make the question word **"what time?"** we just add じ to the question word for "what?" なん to get なんじ.

To make the **half hour intervals** you add はん "half" to the hour as follows:

にじ はん	half past two	二時半
じゅういちじ はん <small>juu chi</small>	half past eleven	十一時半

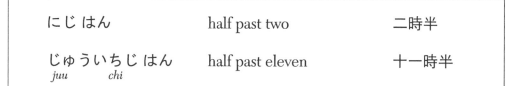

■Language pattern 7.1　ぶんけい　文型

Q:なんじ です か。	Q: What time is it?
A:いちじ です。 <small>chi</small>	A: It's one o'clock.

■Conversation 7.1　かいわ　会話

Asking the time

Person A is in the street and has forgotten his **tokei** とけい. He needs to know the time so he goes up to someone (B) and asks her the time.

A:　すみません、いま なんじ です か。
<small>　　　mi ma se　　　　　ma　　　　　　ka</small>

B:　いちじ はん です。
<small>　　chi</small>

A:　どうも すみません。
<small>　　　mo　　mi ma se</small>

B:　いいえ。

Note: It is not always necessary to use the word いま (ima) "now," but in this situation it is usual.

7.2 Fractions of an hour

In telling the time we generally round up or down to the nearest five minute interval.
Since there are sixty minutes in an hour we need the following numbers:

5	五	ご	35	三十五	さんじゅうご <small>juu</small>
10	十	じゅう <small>juu</small>	40	四十	よんじゅう <small>juu</small>

15	十五	じゅうご *juu*	45	四十五	よんじゅうご *juu*
20	二十	にじゅう *juu*	50	五十	ごじゅう *juu*
25	二十五	にじゅうご *juu*	55	五十五	ごじゅうご *juu*
30	三十	さんじゅう *sa juu*			

To make these numbers into minutes the suffix ふん (fun) is added to the five minute intervals and ぷん (pun) is added to the ten minute intervals. Therefore, 5:05 is ごじご ふん (goji gofun) and 5:10 is ごじじゅっぷん (goji juppun).

Note that one syllable is skipped in the ten minutes. This is indicated in **hiragana** by a small つ (tsu) which is not pronounced, and in ローマじ (roomaji) by a doubling of the letter. This difference is only in pronunciation and not in meaning, both ふん (fun) and ぷん (pun) refer to minutes. In fact, when written in かんじ (kanji) there is no difference, 五分 (ごふん), 十分 (じゅっぷん).

2:05	二時五分	にじごふん *fu*	2:10	二時十分	にじじゅっぷん *ju ppu*
2:15	二時十五分	にじじゅうごふん *juu fu*	2:20	二時二十分	にじにじゅっぷん *ju ppu*
2:25	二時二十五分	にじにじゅうごふん *juu fu*	2:30	二時三十分	にじさんじゅっぷん *sa ju ppu*
2:35	二時三十五分	にじさんじゅうごふん *sa juu fu*	2:40	二時四十分	にじよんじゅっぷん *ju ppu*
2:45	二時四十五分	さんじよんじゅうごふん *juu fu*	2:50	二時五十分	にじごじゅっぷん *ju ppu*
2:55	二時五十五分	にじごじゅうごふん *juu fu*	3:00	三時	さんじ *sa*

Whereas in えいご we say "five past five" for the time 5:05, in にほんご this is expressed as "five o'clock five minutes." There is no special term in にほんご for "a quarter past" or "a quarter to." Although it is possible to express times in terms of before the hour, i.e. "ten to two" in にほんご, for the present we will concentrate on the method that gives this time as "one fifty."

■Conversation 7.2　かいわ　　会話

At a bus stop バス ていで　バス停で

You (A) are waiting at a bus stop バスてい (basu tei) for a バス (basu). You don't know when the バス (basu) will come so you ask another person what time なんじ the next bus つぎ の バス (tsugi no basu) is. Fortunately they know and tell you, but if they didn't know, what would they say?

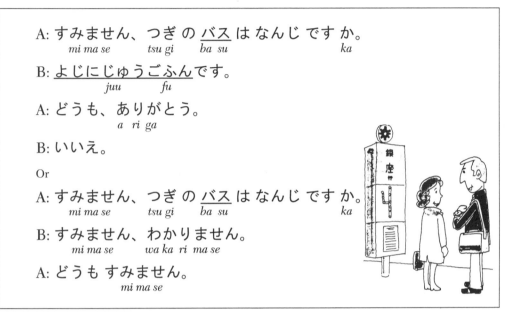

A: すみません、つぎ の バス は なんじ です か。
　　mi ma se　　　*tsu gi*　*ba su*　　　　　*ka*

B: よじにじゅうごふんです。
　　　　juu　　*fu*

A: どうも、ありがとう。
　　　　　a ri ga

B: いいえ。

Or

A: すみません、つぎ の バス は なんじ です か。
　　mi ma se　　　*tsu gi*　*ba su*　　　　　*ka*

B: すみません、わかりません。
　　mi ma se　　　*wa ka ri ma se*

A: どうも すみません。
　　　　　　mi ma se

■Practice 7.2　れんしゅう　　練習

The following are a number of means of transportation. Look up the じしょ to find out the えいご. With your partner, practice asking the times using the above kaiwa かいわ and substituting the means and times.

Sheet A　　　　　　　　　　　　　　　　　　えいご

バス	6:45	バス	_____
ba su			
でんしゃ	___:___	電車	_____
sha			
しんかんせん	11:05	新幹線	_____
ka se			
フェリー	___:___	フェリー	_____
fe rii			

| ひこうき
hi ki | 8:15 | 飛行機 | _____ |
| れっしゃ
re ssha | ___ : ___ | 列車 | _____ |

7.3 Arrival and departure times

It is very useful to be able to ask the time a form of transportation arrives or leaves. To make the appropriate questions we need two new verbs, つく (tsuku) and でる (deru).

つく　to arrive, get to (a destination)　着く

Tense	positive	negative
Future/present	つきます *tsu ki ma*	つきません *tsu ki ma se*
Past	つきました *tsu ki ma ta*	つきません でした *tsu ki ma se ta*

でる　to depart, leave, get out of　出る

Tense	positive	negative
Future/present	でます *ma*	でません *ma se*
Past	でました *ma ta*	でません でした *ma se ta*

📖 ■Language pattern 7.3　ぶんけい　文型

The question "What time (does it) arrive?" is made by adding なんじ as follows:

1. Q: なんじ に つきますか。
　　　　　tsu ki ma ka　　　　　　Q: What time (does it) arrive (at)?

　A: いちじ に つきます。
　　　chi　　　*tsu ki ma*　　　　　A: It arrives at one o'clock.

2. Q: なんじ に でますか。
　　　　　　　ma ka　　　　　　　Q: What time (does it) leave?

　A: くじ に でます。
　　　　　ma　　　　　　　　　A: It leaves at nine o'clock.

Note: the particle に is needed after なんじ in the question and after the time in the answer. に follows absolute times rather like "at" in えいご. Whereas the "at" can be left out in the question in えいご, the に must be included in にほんご.

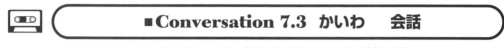

■Conversation 7.3　かいわ　会話

Passenger and conductor じょうきゃく と しゃしょう 乗客と車掌

A passenger じょうきゃく (jookyaku) (A) is on a でんしゃ (densha) on her way to Sendai. She thinks her station えき(eki) must be coming up so she asks the conductor しゃしょう (shashoo) (B).

A: つぎ の えき は どこ です か。
　　　tsu gi　　　ki　　　　　ka

B: せんだい です。
　　se　da

A: なんじ に つきます か。
　　　　　tsu ki ma　　ka

B: よじ に じゅっぷん に つきます。
　　　　ju　　ppu　　　tsu ki ma

　あと じゅうごふん です ね。
　a　　juu　　fu　　　　　ne

A: ありがとう ございます。
　　a ri ga　　　za　　ma

B: いいえ。

Note: あと (ato) means "after" or "later" but in this sentence it would normally be translated as "in fifteen minutes." The ね (ne) at the end can't really be translated as "isn't it" (as we have seen earlier) because it would sound unnatural. In にほんご, ね (ne) is used more often and in more situations than "isn't it" in えいご. The ね (ne) indicates that the information being given is shared. In this case, the しゃしょう (shashoo) 車掌 has made the calculation but is assuming that the passenger could also have done so.

7.4 Arriving at and departing places

We have learned how to express leaving and arriving at certain times so now we can try adding the points of departure and destinations. To make these longer sentences you need to know that the verb つく (tsuku) works just like the verb いく but the verb でる (deru) is different.

1. しんかんせん は いちじはん に おおさか に つきます。
　　ka　se　　　chi　　　　　sa ka　　tu ki ma

　The shinkansen arrives in Osaka at half past one.

2. しんかんせん は にじはん に とうきょう を でます。
   ka se   *kyoo*   *wo*   *ma*

    The shinkansen leaves Tokyo at half past two.

In the second sentence a new particle を (**wo** which is pronounced "o") is needed. We will look at this particle in more detail in Lesson 13. For the moment, just learn the pattern below.

■Language pattern 7.4　ぶんけい　文型

> 1. topic は time に place に つきます。   arrive at a place or time
> 2. topic は time に place を でます。   leave a place or time

7.4 Reading comprehension　　どっかい　読解

あした、うえのさん は なごや に いきます。あさ はちじはん に うち を
a ta   *sa*   *ya*   *ki ma*   *a sa*   *chi*   *chi wo*

でます。しんかんせん は じゅうじ に とうきょうえき を でます。
ma   *ka se*   *ju*   *kyoo*   *ki wo*   *ma*

じゅういちじ ごじゅっぷん に なごや に つきます。
ju   *chi*   *ju*   *ppu*   *ya*   *tsu ki ma*

Questions　しつもん　質問 ─────────

1. うえのさん は いつ なごや に いきますか。
        sa   *tsu*   *ya*   *ki ma*   *ka*

2. うえのさん は なんじ に うち を でますか。
        sa   *chi wo*   *ma*   *ka*

3. しんかんせん は じゅうじ に どこ を でますか。
       ka se   *juu*   *wo*   *ma*   *ka*

4. しんかんせん は なんじ に なごや に つきますか。
       ka se   *ya*   *tsu ki ma*

7.5 Finding the right train

1. To find the right でんしゃ (densha), you need to identify which one it is and find out which platform it leaves from. In にほん it is the tracks or lines rather than the platforms which are numbered. The numbering system uses a number, a word for "number" ばん and then a word meaning "line" せん (sen) as follows:

📼	いちばんせん *chi* *se*	一番線	Number one line (or first line)
	にばんせん *se*	二番線	Number two line (or second line)
	さんばんせん *sa* *se*	三番線	Number three line (or third line)
	よんばんせん *se*	四番線	Number four line (or fourth line)

The question "What line" is just as you would expect if you recall the telephone numbers.

📼 なんばんせん です か。   何番線ですか。
     se   *ka*

2. You can identify trains by their destinations. To do this you say the name of the destination e.g. Osaka, then ゆき (yuki), which means "going to," to get おおさか ゆき (oosaka yuki) which means "going to Osaka." Since this phrase describes the word でんしゃ (densha), it precedes it and is joined to でんしゃ (densha) by the particle の. The resultant question is:

Q: おおさか ゆき の でんしゃ は なんばん せん です か。
        sa ka yu ki   *sha*   *se*   *ka*

A: さんばん せん です。
    sa   *se*

📼 ■Conversation 7.5 かいわ　会話

Looking for the train to Nagoya

A じょうきゃく (jookyaku) is at an えき (eki) looking for the でんしゃ (densha) which goes to Nagoya なごや. She asks a station attendant (ekiin) えきいん which track the train is on.

じょうきゃく: すみません。 *joo* *kya* *mi ma se*	
なごや ゆき の でんしゃ は なんばん せん です か。 *ya yu ki* *sha* *se* *ka*	
えきいん: ななばん せん です。 *ki* *se*	

99

じょうきゃく: なんじ に でます か。
joo *kya* *ka*

えきいん: <u>じゅうじ じゅうごふん</u> に でます。
ki *juu* *juu* *fu*

じょうきゃく: どうも すみません。
joo *kya* *mo* *mi ma se*

えきいん: いいえ。

Practice the above かいわ (kaiwa) with a partner (あいて aite) substituting the destinations, track numbers, and departure times.

7.6 Opening and closing times

We have previously done から (kara) and まで (made) as equivalents to "from" and "till." These terms can also be used with a time to indicate business hours or starting and finishing times.

1. Q:なんじ から です か。 　　　*ka ra*　　*ka*	Q: What time does (it) open / start?
A:九じ から です。 　　*ku*　*ka ra*	A: (It) opens / starts at nine o'clock.
2. Q:なんじ まで です か。 　　　　*ma*　　*ka*	Q: What time does (it) close / finish?
A:五じ まで です。 　　*go*　*ma*	A: (It) closes / finishes at five o'clock.

■Conversation 7.6 かいわ 会話

Asking what time the bank opens

When you are in にほん you may want to know what time shops open and close and what time classes start and finish.

A: ぎんこう は なんじ から です か。
　　gi　　　　　　　　*ka ra*　　　*ka*

B: 八じ はん から です。
　　hachi　　*ka ra*

A: なんじ まで です か。
　　　　　ma　　　*ka*

B: 五じ まで です。
　　go　*ma*

A: ありがとう ございます。
　　a ri ga　　*za*　*ma*

7.7 A.M. and P.M.　　ごぜん と ごご　午前と午後

When we need to indicate that a time is before or after midday in えいご we say "a.m." or "p.m." after the time, e.g. "seven thirty a.m." "four fifty-five p.m."
In にほんご a.m. is ごぜん (gozen) which literally means "noon before," and p.m. is ごご which literally means "noon after." These words come before the time, e.g.

ごぜん しちじ はん. 7:30 a.m.　　　　ごごにじ　2:00 p.m.
　　ze　　*chi*

■Practice 7.7 れんしゅう　練習

When you are in にほん you will probably need to ask what time shops or offices open and close or what time things start and finish. With an aite あいて practice conversation 7.6 including ごぜん (gozen) and ごご as appropriate to fill in the following chart.

Part A

ぎんこう	銀行	8:30 a.m. – 4:00 p.m.
gi		
がっこう	学校	____:____ – ____:____
ga kkoo		

ゆうびんきょく *yu bi kyo*	郵便局	9:00 a.m. – 5:00 p.m.
デパート *de paa to*	デパート	____:____ – ____:____
おみせ *mi se*	お店	8:00 a.m. – 7:00 p.m.
レストラン *re su to ra n*	レストラン	____:____ – ____:____
じゅぎょう *juu gyoo*	授業	7:30 p.m. – 9:00 p.m.
だいがく *da ga*	大学	____:____ – ____:____

7.8 Listening Comprehension　ききとりれんしゅう　聞き取り練習

Tonight's movie こんばん の えいが　今晩の映画

You (B) want to find out what movie えいが (eiga) is on this evening and what time it starts and finishes. You call a movie theatre えいがかん (eigakan) in a part of central Tokyo called Ginza ぎんざ. This えいがかん (eigakan) is called "Ginza Shinema."

The following かいわ (kaiwa) is on the telephone でんわ (denwa). When the woman at the えいがかん (eigakan) answers the でんわ (denwa) she first says "はい" and then gives the name of the えいがかん (eigakan). You start your enquiry with the hesitation "anoo あのう." Write the missing words and times in the blanks in **hiragana**.

A: (ring! ring!) はい、ぎんざ シネマ です。
　　　　　　　　　　　　gi za shi ne ma

B: あのう、こんばん _____ えいが は _____ です か。
　a　　　　　　　　　　　　　　　*ga*　　　　　　　　　*ka*

A: _____ の えいが _____ ゴジラ です。
　　　　　　　　　　　ga　　　　　　　　　　*go ji ra*

B: そう です か。_____ から です か。
　so　　*ka*　　　　　　　　*ka ra*　　　*ka*

A: _____ から です。
　　　　　ka ra

B: なんじ まで _____ か。
　　　　　ma　　　　　　　　*ka*

A: ＿＿＿＿＿＿＿ まで です。
　　　　　 ma

B: どうも ありがとう。
　　 mo a ri ga to

A: ＿＿＿＿＿＿＿、 どういたしまして。
　　　　 do 　　 *ta* 　 *ma*

ゴジラ

絶賛上映中！！

Questions　しつもん　質問 ────────────

1. えいがかん の なまえ は なん です か。　　　＿＿＿＿＿＿＿＿＿＿
　　 ga ka 　　　 *ma* 　　　　　 *ka*

2. こんばん の えいが の なまえ は なん です か。　＿＿＿＿＿＿＿＿＿＿
　　　　　　 ga 　　 *ma* 　　　　 *ka*

3. えいがかん は どこ です か。　　　　　　　　＿＿＿＿＿＿＿＿＿＿
　　 ga ka 　　 *do* 　　 *ka*

4. えいが は なんじまで です か。　　　　　　　＿＿＿＿＿＿＿＿＿＿
　　 ga 　　　 *ma* 　 *ka*

5. ゴジラ は にほん の えいが です か。　　　　＿＿＿＿＿＿＿＿＿＿
　 go ji ra 　　　　　 *ga* 　 *ka*

Notes

1. あのう **anoo** is a hesitation sound which is often used before asking a question. It can also be used when you are thinking of a reply. Hesitating in this fashion gets the listener ready to receive a question so it is a way of showing consideration to the listener. Hesitation strategies are used a lot in にほんご and do not imply that the speaker is confused or shy.

2. ぎんざ (銀座) **Ginza** is a part of central Tokyo famous for its **depaato** デパートand high-class night life.

3. ゴジラ (**Gojira**) You are probably more familiar with the えいご version—"Godzilla." In にほん many えいが have been made about this monster.

4. どう いたしまして **doo itashimashite** is the full form of the reply to ありがとう **arigatoo**. Previously we saw only the shortened form いいえ. It is equivalent to the えいご "not at all, don't mention it."

103

7.9 Combined start and finish times

When you want to ask both the starting and finishing times in one question the following structure is used:

Q:ぎんこう は なんじ から なんじ まで です か。
　 gi　　　　　　　　 ka ra　　　　 ma　　　　 ka

A:八じ はん から 四じ まで です。
　hachi　　　 ka ra yo　 ma

Examples　れい 例 ──────────

きのう の えいが は 七じ から 十じ まで でした。
ki　　　　　 ga　 shichi ka ra juu　 ma　　　 ta

あした、しごと は 八じはん から 五じはん まで です。
a　 ta　　　 to　 hachi　　 ka ra go　　　　 ma

7.10. Transportation in Japan: shinkansen
にほんのこうつう しんかんせん　　日本の交通 新幹線

The transportation system in Japan is highly developed. There are regular train and bus services to almost every part of the country. There are also air services between the major cities and numerous ferries between the islands and up the lower reaches of the larger rivers.

Perhaps the best known form of transportation in Japan is the **shinkansen** しんかんせん system. Although referred to outside Japan as the "bullet train," the word **shinkansen** (新幹線) actually refers to the line rather than to the train. It means "new trunk line" because they are built along side older rail lines. The first しんかんせん (shinkansen) was opened between Tokyo and Osaka in 1964 and since then the system has been greatly extended. The current routes are as follows:

Tokaido Shinkansen	From Tokyo to Nagoya, then to Osaka.
Sanyo Shinkansen	From Osaka to Hiroshima, then to Hakata in Kyushu through an undersea tunnel.
Tohoku Shinkansen	From Tokyo north to Sendai, then to Morioka
Joetsu Shinkansen	From Tokyo to Niigata

The busiest route is the Tokaido with trains leaving Tokyo for Osaka about every five minutes and covering the 515 km between the two cities in about three hours.

Shinkansen Routes

Tokaido Shinkansen
とうかいどう しんかんせん ───────

Sanyo Shinkansen
さんよう しんかんせん ─・─・─・─・─

Tohoku Shinkansen
とうほく しんかんせん ·················

Joetsu Shinkansen
じょうえつ しんかんせん ─ ─ ─ ─ ─

もりおか

にいがた

せんだい

やまがた

ひろしま

はかた

とうきょう

なごや

しんおおさか

older style Shinkansen

new style Shinkansen

7.2 Sheet B				えいご
バス *ba su*	____:____	バス		_____
でんしゃ *sha*	4:20	電車		_____
しんかんせん *ka se*	____:____	新幹線		_____
フェリー *fe rii*	12:55	フェリー		_____

ひこうき *hi ki*	____:____	飛行機	_____
れっしゃ *re ssha*	9:40	列車	_____

7.7 Part B

ぎんこう *gi*	銀行	____:____ – ____:____
がっこう *ga kkoo*	学校	9:00 a.m. – 3:30 p.m.
ゆうびんきょく *yu bi kyo*	郵便局	____:____ – ____:____
デパート *de paa to*	デパート	10:00 a.m. – 8:00 p.m.
おみせ *mi se*	お店	____:____ – ____:____
レストラン *re su to ra n*	レストラン	6:30 p.m. – 11:30 p.m.
じゅぎょう *ju gyoo*	授業	____:____ – ____:____
だいがく *da ga*	大学	9:30 a.m. – 4:30 p.m.

Answers こたえ 答え

7.4 Reading comprehension
1. あした いきます。　2. あさ はちじはんにでます。　3. とうきょうえきをでます。
4. じゅういちじごじゅっぷんにつきます。

7.8 Listening comprehension
の; なん; こんばん; は; なんじ; 7じ10ぷん; です; 9じはん; いいえ.

Questions
1. ぎんざシネマです。　2. ゴジラです。　3. ぎんざです。　4. 9じはんまでです。
5. はい、そうです。

✏️ Writing Japanese script 7.11

The numbers 1 through 4 are written in **kanji** as follows: ichi 一 ; ni 二 ; san 三 ; shi or yon 四.

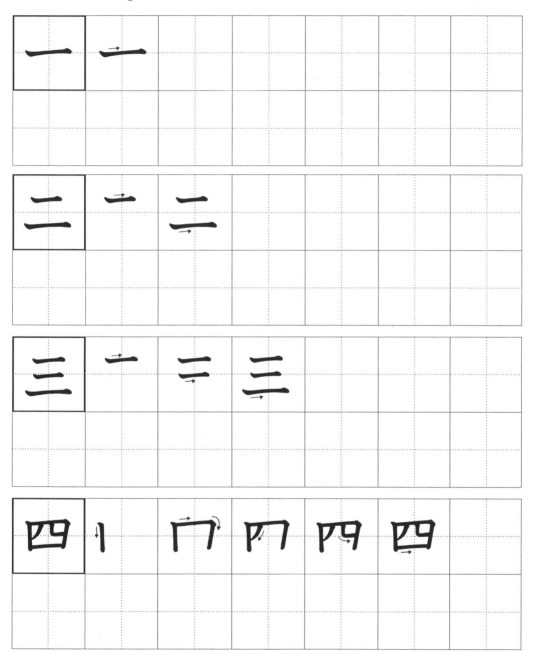

We have often used the respectful title **san** さん which follows a person's family name or given name. To write it you need **sa** さ and ん. The handwritten form is written in three strokes but in the printed character two of these are usually joined. With てんてん it becomes **za** ざ. Be careful not to confuse さ with き **ki**

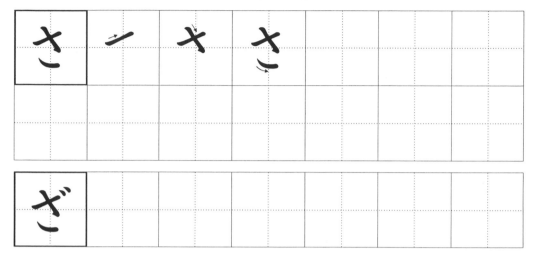

The next **hiragana** we'll learn is ら **ra**, as in なんじ から です か. It is written in two strokes. On some computers it can also be keyed in as "la."

See if you can read these sentences:

かとう さん は にほんご がっこう の せんせい です。

おの さん は いつ かんこく へ いきます か。

しごと は 三月 から です。

1. Say the following times in Japanese.

3:00	8:00	5:30	12:30	4:15	9:05
1:45	7:50	10:00	a.m.	11:25	p.m.

2. Fill in the blanks to complete the following sentences using は, に, の, から, or まで.

1) おおさか ゆき（　　　　　　　）でんしゃ（　　　　　　　）にばんせん です。
   saka yu ki   sha   se

2) ひこうき（　　　　　　　）ごぜん はちじ（　　　　　　　）でます。
  hi   ki   ze   chi   ma

3) こんばん（　　　　　　　）パーティー（　　　　　　　）ろくじ（　　　　　　　　）
                  paa   tii   ro
   くじはん（　　　　　　　）です。

3. Fill in the blanks to complete the following questions.

1) つぎ の えき は（　　　　　　　）ですか。
  tsugi   ki   ka

2) Q: この でんしゃ は（　　　　　　　）に つきますか。
        sha   tsu ki ma   ka.
   A: 三じ はん に つきます。
             tsu ki ma

3) Q: かんだゆき の でんしゃ は（　　　　　　　）ですか。
     ka da yu ki   sha   ka
   A: 3ばんせん です。
      se

4. Translate the following sentences into にほんご.

1) Excuse me. What time is it now? _____

2) The next bus departs at half past five. _____

LESSON **7** 第七課

109

3) The movie is from 4:00 to 6:30. _____

4) A: Thank you very much. _____

   B: You are welcome. _____

5. ✍ Let's write in Japanese! Write a HIRAGANA in each ___ .

1) "Goodbye" は にほんごで ____ ____ ____ ____ ____ です。

2) ____ ____ ____ は えいご で "cherry blossoms" です。

Write the following words in にほんご using かんじ.

January   April   February   March

_____ _____ _____ _____

5. Read the following sentences aloud and then write the meanings in えいご.

1) さとうさん は こんばん おのさん と ぎんざ へ いきます。

_____

2) ぎんこう は くじ から さんじ まで です。

_____

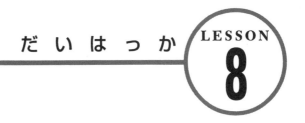

第八課

In this lesson the roomaji ローマじ for the following has been removed: くぐにおはば
しじのんほぼいえてですずとどここごなよしょうかがつづ月.

8.1 Answering the telephone　でんわをうける　電話を受ける

 When the denwa でんわ (phone) rings you pick up the receiver じゆわき (juwaki) and
say はい (or もしもし moshi moshi) followed by (your family name) です.

はい、やまだ です。
　　　ya ma da

If you are working in a company you first say the company name and use the formal
version of です which is degozaimasu でございます.

はい、ソニー でございます。
so nii　　　*za　ma*

■**Practice 8.1　れんしゅう　　練習**

 Imagine you are working at one of the following にほん の かいしゃ (nihon no
kaisha). Practice answering the phone using the sentence above .

さくら ぎんこう *sa　ra　gi*	さくら銀行	Sakura Bank
とうしば でんき 　　　　*ki*	東芝電気	Toshiba Electric
くまがい ぐみ *ma*　　*mi*	熊谷組	Kumagai Constructions
しせいどう *se*	資生堂	Shiseido Cosmetics

111

にほん こうくう	日本航空	Japan Airlines
みつびし じどうしゃ *mi bi sha*	三菱自動車	Mitsubishi Motors
だいまる デパート *da ma ru de paa to*	大丸デパート	Daimaru Department Store
にほん こうつう こうしゃ *sha*	日本交通公社	Japan Travel Bureau

8.2 Making a phone call　でんわをする　電話をする

1. When someone answers the phone on the other end the first thing you usually say is:

もしもし、(なまえ) です が。
mo mo (your family name)

Note: もし もし (moshi moshi) is what you say when you first start to talk on the でんわ (denwa). It literally translates as "I say, I say" but is equivalent to "Hello." It is also used when getting someone's attention, especially when they are dozing. (See later note on が).

2. Then you ask for the person to whom you wish to speak. There are a number of ways of doing this but the following is the simplest:

(なまえ) さん おねがい します。　　　　"Could I have Ms. _____ please."
ma sa ne ma

3. If you've got the person you want they will usually reply with:

わたし です。　　　　"It is I. (It's me)."
wa ta

If the person is a young man or boy and the situation is informal he may use another word for "I," which is ぼく (boku), and reply:

ぼく です。　　　　"It is I. (It's me)."

4. If you get another person they will probably ask you to wait while they get the person you want by saying:

しょう しょう おまち ください。　　　　"Please wait a little."
ma chi da sa

5. If the person is out, you're in trouble because you probably won't understand the explanation. You can get out of the problem with:

すみません、わかりません。また でんわ します。　　　"Sorry, I don't understand.
mi ma se wa ri ma se ma ta wa ma　　　　　I'll call again."

Hang on moment

Person B さとう(Satoo) is calling to speak to **Honda Hiroshi**. His mother (A) answers and asks B to wait while she gets ひろし Hiroshi (C).

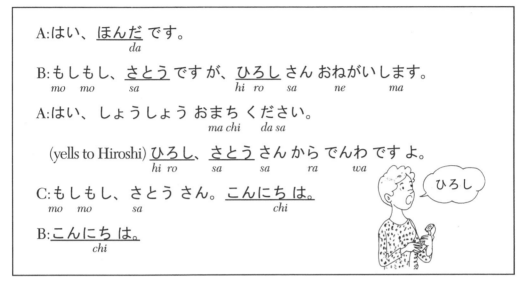

A:はい、 <u>ほんだ</u> です。
　　　　　　da

B:もしもし、 <u>さとう</u> ですが、 <u>ひろし</u> さん おねがいします。
　　mo mo　　*sa*　　　　　　*hi ro sa*　　*ne*　　　　*ma*

A:はい、 しょうしょう おまち ください。
　　　　　　　　　　ma chi　　*da sa*

(yells to Hiroshi) <u>ひろし</u>、 <u>さとう</u> さん から でんわ です よ。
　　　　　　　　　　hi ro　　　*sa*　　*sa*　　*ra*　　　*wa*

C:もしもし、 さとう さん。 <u>こんにち</u> は。
　　mo mo　　*sa*　　　　　　　　*chi*

B:<u>こんにち</u> は。
　　　chi

Practice the above かいわ (kaiwa) with two あいて (aite) substituting the names and the greetings.

Notes:

1. The が on the end of さとう ですが is difficult to translate. Sometimes it is like "but" in えいご. However, in this situation が is used to soften the statement and to indicate that the speaker has more to say, usually in the form of a request.

2. The よ on the end of でんわですよ is also untranslatable. It functions somewhat like an exclamation mark and indicates that the speaker is telling the listener something new to them.

3. Remember, you never use さん (san) after your own name.

8.3 From place to place

We have seen から (kara) and まで (made) used with times but they can also be used for movement from and to places. So far, the only verb of movement we have come across is "go" as in:

かいしゃ に いきます。　　　Or　　かいしゃ へ いきます。
sha　　*ki ma*　　　　　　　　　　　*sha*　*e*　*ki ma*

To say "I went from the post office to the bank" we need to use から as follows:

ゆうびんきょく から ぎんこう へ いきました。
yu　*bi*　*kyo*　　*ra gi*　　　　*e*　*ki ma*　*ta*

If we substituted まで for へ in the above sentence the meaning would be altered:

ゆうびんきょく から ぎんこう まで いきました。
yu　*bi*　*kyo*　　*ra gi*　　　*ma*　*ki ma*　*ta*
This sentence means "I went from the post office **as far as** the bank."

8.4 Verbs of movement

Some other common verbs of movement which work just like いきます (ikimasu) are:

1. きます (kimasu) come　　来ます

The dictionary form of this verb is くる (kuru) (rather than **kiru** as you might have expected) making it one of the two irregular verbs which occur in にほんご. Otherwise its forms are just like いく.

きます	kimasu	come, will come
きません	kimasen	don't come, won't come
きました	kimashita	came, did come
きません でした	kimasen deshita	didn't come

In にほんご, きます (kimasu) is used by the speaker to indicate movement to the place where the speaker is. To indicate movement to another place, the verb いきます (ikimasu) must be used. This is much the same as in えいご. We say "come here" and "go there." However, while we can't use "go" to refer to movement towards us, i.e. we can't say, "go here," it is possible to use "come" to refer to movement away from ourselves. For example, a person can say "I'll come to the party" even though the person speaking isn't at the place where the party will be held. In にほんご this is different, you would have to say "I'll go to the party" in such a case. "Come" can only be used to refer to movement toward where you are (were, or will be). For example, if person A were in Tokyo and person B (メイ) were in London, they could have a phone conversation like this:

A: メイさん、なつ に にほん に きますか。　　A: Are you coming to Japan this summer?
　　　me i　　　　　　　　　　　　　ki ma

B: ええ、八月 に いきます。　　　　　　　　B: Yes, I'm going in August.
　　　hachi　　　　ki ma

Since メイ is not in Japan, he can't say "coming to Japan," he must say "going to Japan."

2. かえります (kaerimasu) return home, come home, go home, get home　帰ります
The dictionary form of this verb is かえる (kaeru). It is quite regular in its forms but its usage can be a little difficult. It indicates movement to the speaker's home, home town, or home country. It doesn't matter whether the person is coming or going home.

A: なんじ に かえりますか。　　A: What time are you coming / going home?
　　　　　　　　ri ma

B: じゅうじ ごろ かえります。　　B: I'm coming / going home about ten o'clock.
　　ju　　　ro　　　ri ma

Note: The use of ごろ 頃
ごろ (goro) is used after a time in place of the particle に to indicate that the time is only approximate. It is like the えいご "around" or "about."

あした、ろくじ に いきます。　　I'll go tomorrow at six.
　a　　ta　ro　　　　　ki ma

あした、ろくじ ごろ いきます。　　I'll go tomorrow around six.
　a　　ta　ro　　　ro　　ki ma

The thing to remember is that ごろ replaces に.

■Conversation 8.4 かいわ　会話

Arranging a visit

Nakatani なかたに (A), who is traveling, calls his old friend Tomoda Michio's (B) place in Tokyo, to tell him when he will arrive. At first, he doesn't recognize Michio's voice on the でんわ (denwa). He thinks it is another member of the Tomoda family.

Listen to the tape and fill in the blanks in **hiragana** ひらがな.

A: もしもし、<u>ともだ</u>さん です か。
　　mo *mo* 　　 *mo da*

B: はい、そう です。
　　　　　so

A: <u>なかたに</u> です が、 みちおさん おねがい します。
　　 ta 　　　　 *mi chi* 　　 *ne*

B: ああ、<u>なかたに</u>さん、＿＿＿＿ です。＿＿＿＿＿＿＿。いま、どこ です か。
　 a a 　 *ta* 　　　　　　　　　　　　　　 *ma*

A: <u>ひろしま</u> の えき です。こんばん <u>ひろしま</u> から ＿＿＿＿＿ まで いきます。
　 hi ro ma 　 *ki* 　　　　 *hi ro ma* 　　　　　　 *ma* *ki*

B: そう です か。 いつ <u>とうきょう</u> に きますか。
　 so 　　　　　　　 *kyo* 　 *ki ma*

A: <u>あさって</u> の ごご <u>とうきょう</u> に つきます。 ＿＿＿＿ ごろ <u>みちお</u>さん の うち
　 a 　　　　 *kyo* 　 *ki ma* 　　　　　 *ro* *mi chi* 　　　　 *chi*

に つきます。いい です か。
　 ki ma

B: ええ、 ＿＿＿＿ です よ。<u>四じ</u> ごろ です ね。 じゃ、また。
　　　　　　　　　　　 yo *ro* 　 *ne* 　　　 *ma ta*

A: ええ、さようなら。
　　　　　　　 ra

Notes:

1. ごご in this context means "afternoon," so ごぜん can be used to mean "morning."

2. うち (uchi) means "home," unless specified otherwise it refers to one's own home.

3. The following simple question is used to ask permission to do something:

　Q: いい です か。　　Q: Is it all right ?

　A: いい です よ。　　A: It's all right. / No problem.

The よ on the end is used to emphasize that it is all right.

Practice the dialogue above with your あいて (aite) substituting names, times, and places.

8.5 Reading comprehension どっかい　読解

A postcard はがき 葉書

Read the following postcard (**hagaki** はがき) written by a にほんじん traveling in にほん and then answer the しつもん **shitsumon** below.

郵便はがき

１０１-□□

東京都千代田区内神田
4-5-6
小野 明子 様

あきこさん、おげんきですか。わたしはとても
げんきです。けさ、こうべからひろしまにつきま
した。とてもいいてんきですよ。ごご、へいわ
きねんこうえんに いきます。あした ひろしま
から はかた まで いきます。あさっての ばん
とうきょうへ かえります。では、また。
　　　　　　　　　　　　　　　うえの たかこ
9月12日

Note: へいわ きねん こうえん (**heiwa kinen kooen**) refers to Peace Memorial Park in Hiroshima.

Questions しつもん　質問 ─────────────

1. Who wrote the はがき？　　　　　＿＿＿＿＿＿＿＿＿＿＿＿
2. Where is she today?　　　　　　＿＿＿＿＿＿＿＿＿＿＿＿
3. What is the weather like there?　＿＿＿＿＿＿＿＿＿＿＿＿
4. Where is she going this afternoon?＿＿＿＿＿＿＿＿＿＿＿＿
5. Where is she going tomorrow?　　＿＿＿＿＿＿＿＿＿＿＿＿
6. When is she returning home to Tokyo?＿＿＿＿＿＿＿＿＿＿＿＿

LESSON **8** 第八課

117

8.6 Introducing people　しょうかい する　紹介する

In Lesson 1 you learned how to introduce yourself, but there are many situations in which you have to introduce other people. The way you do this will change according to the situation. The verb "to introduce" is しょうかい します (shookai shimasu) which literally means "do introduction." When it is preceded by the honorific prefix ご it is used as a set phrase:

📼 ごしょうかいします。　　　　Let me introduce you.
　　　　　ma

This is a fairly formal way to start an introduction which is often used in business. In formal situations you need to be careful to refer to people in the correct way using appropriate titles, e.g. せんせい (sensei) or their positions rather than simply using さん (san) after their family names. Some common titles are:

しゃちょう *sha cho*	for the CEO of a company	社長
ぶちょう *bu cho*	for a departmental head in a company	部長
かちょう *cho*	for a section head in a company	課長

You should use the polite form of "this" which is こちら (kochira) rather than the general form これ (kore), when referring to people with whom you are not closely connected (see note).

When introducing people, introduce the person you know better first. If both people are unfamiliar to you, introduce the younger one to the older person first.

Practice the following three かいわ in groups of three.

📼 **■Conversation 8.6.1 かいわ　　会話**

A formal introduction

Ikeda いけだ is introducing Komatsu こまつ, whom he knows, to Allan アレン whom he has recently met.

> いけだ:　ごしょうかい します。こちら は こまつさん です。
> 　　*ke da*　　　　　　　　　　　　　*chi ra*　　*ma sa*
>
> 　こちら は アレンさん です。
> 　*chi ra*　　*a re n sa*

こまつ: はじめまして、こまつ です。どうぞ よろしく。
ma   *me ma*   *ma*   *zo*   *ro*

アレン: アレン です。こちらこそ、どうぞ よろしく。
a re n   *a re n*   *chi ra*   *so*   *zo*   *ro*

Notes:

1. こちら (kochira) is used for equals or superiors who have no direct connection with you or your organization. これ (kore) "this person / this one" is used for subordinates and members of your own organization or family.

2. こちらこそ (kochirakoso) is a polite phrase which is used in many situations with the meaning of "I am the one who should be…," or in this case "…glad to meet you," but in other cases it could mean "…thanking you" or something similar depending on the situation.

Practice the above substituting your own names.

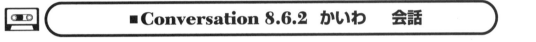

■Conversation 8.6.2 かいわ　会話

Introducing your boss

Mr. Miki みき is introducing his departmental head (ぶちょう), whose family name is Ono おの, to Ms. Ross ロス who is from another company.

みき: ロスさん、ごしょうかい します。ぶちょう の おの です。
mi ki   *ro su sa*   *ma*   *bu choo*

おの: おの です。どうぞ よろしく。
           zo   *ro*

ロス: ロス です。よろしく おねがいします。
ro su   *ro su*   *ro*   *ne*   *ma*

Note:

ぶちょう の おの です: There is no さん after Ono's name. You do not add さん to the names of other people who are members of the same family, company, school, or other organization (i.e. members of your group) when talking to people outside your group. In a business situation, Japanese regard people who work in the same company as if they were members of the same family. This is why you should not use the respectful title さん when referring to them. Using such a title for them is, in this situation, tantamount to using it for yourself.

Practice the above かいわ substituting the names and title.

At the front door げんかん で　玄関で

Matsui まつい has just arrived home with a guest Bill Kelly ビル ケリー whom he introduces to his wife Tamiko たみこ.

LESSON **8** 第八課

まつい: ただいま。
　　　ma　　*ta da*　*ma*

たみこ: おかえりなさい。
ta mi　　　　　*ri*　*sa*

まつい: <u>ケリー</u>さん、<u>かない</u> です。
ma　　*ke rii*　*sa*

ケリー: はじめまして、<u>ビル ケリー</u> です。どうぞ よろしく おねがいします。
ke rii　　*me ma*　　*bi ru ke rii*　　　　　*zo*　*ro*　　*ne*　　*ma*

たみこ: <u>たみこ</u> です。こちらこそ よろしく おねがいします。さあ、どうぞ。
ta mi　　*ta mi*　　　　*chi ra*　*so*　　*ro*　　　*ne*　　*ma*　*sa a*　　*zo*

ケリー: あのう、これ、どうぞ。　(giving a present to Tamiko)
ke rii　*a*　　*re*　　*zo*

たみこ: <u>まあ</u>、どうも ありがとう ございます。
ta mi　*maa*　　*mo a ri*　　　　*za*

ケリー: いいえ、どういたしまして。
ke rii　　　　　　*ta*　*ma*

たみこ: <u>ケリー</u>さん は にほんご が おじょうず ですね。
ta mi　*ke rii*　*sa*　　　　　　　　　*zu*　　*ne*

ケリー: いいえ、まだまだ です。
ke rii　　　　*ma da ma da*

Notes:

1. かない is the word a man uses to refer to his own wife. A woman refers to her husband as しゅじん (shujin).

2. さあ、どうぞ (saa, doozo) さあ is a version of "well" which is used to urge someone to do something. In this case the どうぞ means "please come in."

3. まあ (maa) is an expression of surprise used by women. It is like "oh." In this situation a man would say やあ (yaa).

4. にほんご が おじょうず ですね is often said by Japanese to anyone who can speak some Japanese even if their Japanese is rather basic. It means "Your Japanese is good, isn't it." じょうず means "good at" something.

The most common reply to this compliment is:
いいえ、まだまだ です which means "no, not nearly" or "no, not yet."

5. げんかん (genkan) is the entrance hall to a Japanese house. It is on two levels, you take off your shoes before stepping up into the house.

Practice the above かいわ (kaiwa) substituting the names and roles.

8.7 Cultural Note

Exchanging meishi めいし を こうかん する 名刺を交換する

This is something of a ritual in にほん and its smooth execution makes a good impression, so it is worth getting it right. These are the main points to remember:

1. Have your めいし (meishi) ready so you don't fumble around in your pocket.

2. Hand over the めいし (meishi) as you say your name and just before you bow.

3. You can use one or both hands to hand over your めいし but two hands is better. It is also better to use both hands when receiving another's めいし.

4. When you receive a めいし, always look at it carefully before putting it away carefully. Don't handle the めいし carelessly as it implies a lack of respect for the person who gave it to you.

   If you are going to be meeting a lot of people get a meishi holder (meishi ire めいしいれ).

5. Don't give out worn めいし or write on the めいし that you receive.

Answers こたえ 答え

Conversation 8.4
ぼく; こんばんは; おおさか; よじ (四じ); いい.
8.6 Reading comprehension
1. Takako Ueno. 2. In Hiroshima. 3. Very good. 4. To Heiwa Kinen Koen. 5. To Hakata. 6. On the evening of the day after tomorrow.

The numbers 5 through 10 are written in かんじ as follows:
go 五 ; roku 六 ; shichi or nana 七 ; hachi 八 ; ku or kyuu 九 ; juu 十.

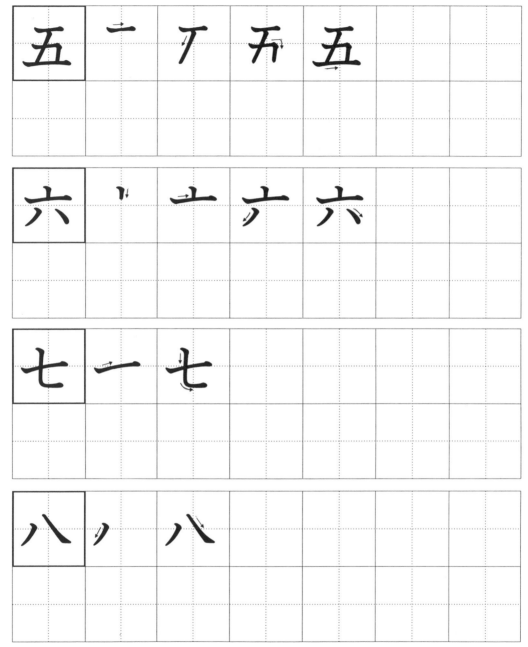

Notice the difference between the printed form of **hachi**, which often has a top i.e.八, and the handwritten form above which doesn't. You should use the handwritten form in your own writing.

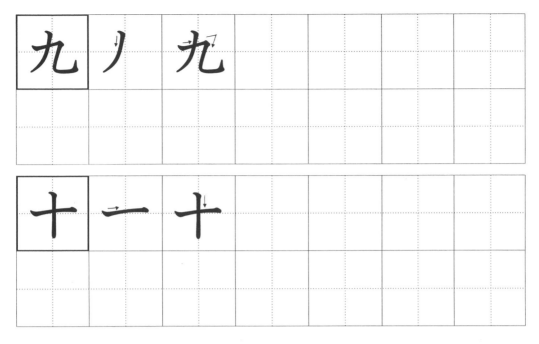

Note: In Japanese, both Arabic (1,2,3…) and かんじ numerals are used. Which one to use is not always clear. In general, Arabic numerals are prefered in horizontal writing and かんじ numbers in vertical writing. In this text we use the かんじ forms more often than usual so that you will get practice in recognizing them.

HOMEWORK 8 しゅくだい 宿題

1. Complete the following conversations by filling in the blanks in ひらがな.

1) Kato called to talk to Ueno Tomoko, but Tomoko's mother answered the phone first.

うえの: ＿＿＿＿＿＿＿、うえの です。
かとう: もしもし、かとう ＿＿＿＿＿＿＿、ともこさん ＿＿＿＿＿＿＿。
うえの: はい、しょうしょう ＿＿＿＿＿＿＿。
ともこ: もしもし、かとうさん。こんばんは。

2) Sato introduces his friend, Mr. Ueno, to Ms. Ono.

さとう: ＿＿＿＿＿＿＿ します。
は うえのさん です。＿＿＿＿＿＿＿ は おのさん です。
うえの: ＿＿＿＿＿＿＿、うえの です。どうぞ よろしく。
                              zo   ro
おの: おの です。＿＿＿＿＿＿＿、どうぞ よろしく。
                         zo   ro

123

2. Choose the correct ones to complete the dialogues.

1) A: いつ わたし の うち に （いきます）/（きます）か。
wa ta   chi   ki ma   ki ma

   B: あさって （いきます）/（きます）。
a sa   ki ma   ki ma

   A: いい ですか。

   B: （いい ですよ）/（いい ですね）。
ne

2) A: にほんご が おじょうず です ね。
ne

   B: （はい、そう です）/（いいえ、まだまだ です）。
so   ma da ma da

3. Translate the following sentences into にほんご.

1) I will arrive in Ginza around 5:00 p.m.

_____

2) Ms. Ueno didn't come to my house yesterday.

_____

3) I will go to Kyoto from Osaka tomorrow afternoon.

_____

4) I will go home around 7:00.

_____

5) I will call (you) again.

_____

4. ✍ Let's write in Japanese! Write the months May to October vertically using かんじ.

 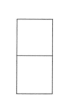

第九課

The **roomaji** ローマじ for the following characters: くぐにおはばぱしじいえほぼぽん のてですずとどこごなよしょうかがつづ月きぎませぜもへべぺ has been removed.

9.1 Large numbers

So far we have seen the multiples of ten which are quite regular as follows:

🎞	10	じゅう *ju*	十	60	ろくじゅう *ro　ju*	六十
	20	にじゅう *ju*	二十	70	しちじゅう *chi ju*	七十
	30	さんじゅう *sa　ju*	三十	or	ななじゅう *ju*	
	40	よんじゅう *ju*	四十	80	はちじゅう *chi ju*	八十
	50	ごじゅう *ju*	五十	90	きゅうじゅう *kyu　ju*	九十

The next set of numbers are the hundreds. There are a couple of irregularities here so for the time being, we will just look at 100, 200, 500, and 700 :

🎞	100 ひゃく *hya*	200 にひゃく *hya*	500 ごひゃく *hya*	700 ななひゃく *hya*
	百	二百	五百	七百

After this come the thousands. Again there are a few irregularities so we will just do 1000, 2000, 5000, and 7000 for the moment. We'll do hundreds and thousands in more detail in Lesson 11.

	1000	せん	2000	にせん	5000	ごせん	7000	ななせん
		千		二千		五千		七千

The next unit is one which is not used in European languages, but which is common in Asian languages. This is the ten thousand unit—まん. Since this one is important in large prices, besides being quite regular, we will look at all the main combinations.

	10000	いちまん *chi*	一万	60000	ろくまん *ro*	六万
	20000	にまん	二万	70000	ななまん	七万
	30000	さんまん *sa*	三万	80000	はちまん *chi*	八万
	40000	よんまん	四万	90000	きゅうまん *kyu*	九万
	50000	ごまん	五万	100000	じゅうまん *ju*	十万

As you can see 100,000 (one hundred thousand) is expressed as 10,0000 (ten **man**). The units in which numbers over 9000 are expressed are quite different and can be rather confusing at first. The key point to working out large numbers is to place the comma after each set of four zeros, e.g. 8,0000, rather than after three zeros as in えいご.

	100	ひゃく *hya*	百	100,0000	ひゃくまん *hya*	百万
	1000	せん	千	1000,0000	いっせんまん	一千万
	1,0000	いちまん *chi*	一万	1,0000,0000	いちおく *chi*	一億
	10,0000	じゅうまん *ju*	十万			

9.2 Japanese money　にほん の おかね　日本のお金

There is only one unit of おかね **(okane)** in にほん and that is the えん (yen). Rather than have two units, e.g. dollars and cents, all calculations are in えん only. Since 1えん is roughly equivalent to one cent, large numbers are needed when talking about prices ねだん **(nedan)**. When writing a price the かんじ which is used is 円, pronounced えん. It is written after the number, i.e. 10円 or 十円.

9.3 Japanese currency　にほん の つうか　日本の通貨

The denominations of Japanese currency are as follows:

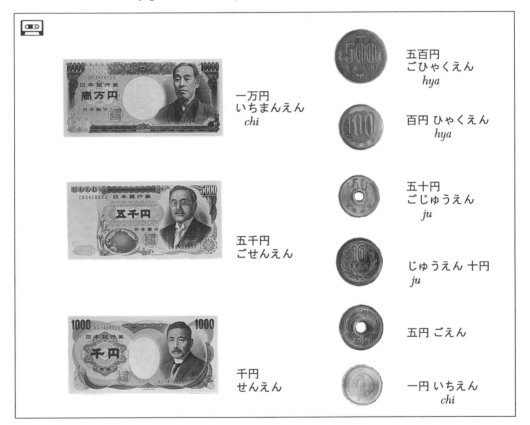

一万円
いちまんえん
chi

五千円
ごせんえん

千円
せんえん

五百円
ごひゃくえん
hya

百円 ひゃくえん
hya

五十円
ごじゅうえん
ju

じゅうえん 十円
ju

五円 ごえん

一円 いちえん
chi

The coins are from 一円 **(ichi en)** to 五百円 **(500en)**, and the notes are 千円 **(1000en)**, 五千円 **(5000en)**, and 一万円 **(10000en)**. When referring to the actual coin or bill, rather than the amount of money, the suffix だま **(dama)** is added for coins and さつ **(satsu)** for bills:

| ひゃくえん だま | 百円玉 | せんえん さつ | 千円札 |
| *hya*　　　*da* | *100 yen* coin | *sa* | *1,000 yen* note (bill) |

9.4 Asking prices　ねだん を きく　値段を聞く

The question word for "How much" when referring to a price is いくら (ikura) in にほん
ご. The easiest way to ask the price of something is to point at it and ask:

Q: いくら です か。 　　　ra	Q: How much is it?
A: にまん えん です。	A: It's 20000 yen.

■Practice 9.4　れんしゅう　　練習

Ask your あいて(aite) the following prices (ねだん nedan),using the question above.

100円	1000円	5000円	1,0000円	1,2250円	9,0100円
250円	1200円	5200円	1,1000円	2,2000円	10,0000円
160円	1500円	5500円	1,2000円	3,5060円	11,0000円
500円	1580円	5550円	1,5000円	7,2500円	20,0000円
570円	2010円	5230円	1,5500円	4,5250円	30,5000円

9.5 Brands of Japanese goods
にほん の メーカー の なまえ　日本のメーカーの名前

にほん produces a great variety of consumer goods, TVs, watches, cameras among other
things. The names of Japanese manufacturers (meekaa メーカー) have become known
throughout the world. Here are some major brand names for cameras (kamera カメラ).
Write the えいご in the blanks.

📼 にほん の メーカー の なまえ		日本のメーカーの名前	
ニコン *ni ko n*	_____	リコー *ri koo*	_____
フジ *fu ji*	_____	ミノルタ *mi no ru ta*	_____

キャノン ＿＿＿＿＿　　　　オリンパス ＿＿＿＿＿
kya no n　　　　　　　　　*o ri n pa su*

サクラ ＿＿＿＿＿
sa ku ra

■Conversation 9.5　かいわ　　会話

At a camera shop カメラや で　カメラ屋で

Before you decide which **kamera** to buy you usually have a look at what the different manufacturers (**meekaa** メーカー) have to offer. When you want to ask the てんいん at the カメラや (**kameraya**) the make of the **kamera**, you can use the following question:

Q: どこ の カメラ です か。
　　　　　ka me ra

A: ニコン の です。
　　ni ko n

In the following かいわ the customer きゃく (**kyaku**) is looking at various カメラ (**kamera**) and asking the brands.

きゃく：　これ は どこ の カメラ です か。
　　　　　　re　　　　　　　*ka me ra*

てんいん：ニコン の です。
　　　　　ni ko n

きゃく：　これ も ニコン の です か。
　　　　　　re　　*ni ko n*

てんいん：はい、それ も ニコン の です。
　　　　　　　　so re　　*ni ko n*

きゃく：　これ も ニコン の です か。
　　　　　　re　　*ni ko n*

てんいん：いいえ、それ は ニコン の
　　　　　　　　　　so re　　*ni ko n*
　　　　　では ありません。
　　　　　　　a ri
　　　　　それ は フジ の カメラ です。
　　　　　so re　　*fu ji*　　*ka me ra*

Practice the above かいわ with an あいて (**aite**) substituting **meekaa no namae**.

LESSON **9** 第九課

Notes:

1. When the word kamera カメラ is understood from the context, it is left out. But the preceding の is retained, i.e. nikon no kamera desu becomes nikon no desu. This is like saying "a Nikon one" rather than "a Nikon camera."

2. The particle は changes to も when the meaning of "also" is added but when the reply is negative the particle reverts to は .

9.6 Shopping　　かいもの　　買物

When you go shopping in にほん it is fairly likely that you will spend quite a bit of おかね . To avoid spending too much おかね it is wise to ask いくら (ikura) before buying something. However, if the ねだん (nedan) is right you will buy it by saying:

これ を ください。 *re wo da sa*	(I'll have) this please.

Then you will hand over the おかね (okane).

Notes:

1. ください (kudasai) is the word for "please." It comes at the end of a request.

2. を is a new particle . It is written in ローマじ as "o" or "wo" and is pronounced 'o'. However, the hiragana is different from the お you have seen so far. This hiragana を is not used in ordinary spelling, it is only used for this particle. The particle を follows the object of a sentence. Since "this (thing)" is what is requested, it is the object of ください (kudasai). You will come across を in contexts which demonstrate its usage more clearly in later lessons.

 ■Conversation 9.6　かいわ　　会話

At an electrical goods store でんきやで　電気屋で

Imagine you are in にほん and you (A) go to an electrical goods store でんきや (denkiya). You are considering buying a video ビデオ (bideo). There are many bideo in the でんきや (denkiya) and they have quite different ねだん (nedan). You want to find out the meekaa so you talk to one of the てんいん working in the でんきや (denkiya). After finding out the,メーカー (meekaa), you ask the prices. You don't want to buy an expensive たかい (takai) one, you want a cheap やすい (yasui) one. The てんいん recommends one by saying:

これ は いかが です か。 *re*	How about this (one)?
	How would this one be?

きゃく： すみません。これ は どこ の ビデオ です か。

てんいん：サンヨー の です。

きゃく： これ も サンヨー の です か。

てんいん：いいえ、それ は ひたち の です。

きゃく： ああ、そう です か。これ は いくら です か。

てんいん：四まん円 です。

きゃく： たかい です ね。

てんいん：じゃ、これ は いかが です か。三まん円 です よ。

きゃく： やすい です ね。どこ の です か。

てんいん：みつびし の です。いい ビデオ です よ。

きゃく： じゃ、それ を ください。

てんいん：ありがとう ございます。

Questions しつもん 質問

1. How much are the videos?　　　2. What brand does he buy?

Notes:

1. いかが is the question word used in offering or suggesting. It is like "How about" or "What do you think of" in えいご.

You will also come across いかが when asking the condition of something or someone,

e.g:　　てんき は いかが です か。　　　　How is the weather?

　　　　やまださん は いかが です か。　　　How's Mr./Ms. Yamada?

2. The "thank you" used by the てんいん in the above かいわ (kaiwa) is in the present tense, i.e. it ends in ます. When the transaction is completed and the きゃく (kyaku) is about to leave the shop the てんいん will use the past tense and say: ありがとう ございました (arigatoo gozaimashita).

3. When a てんいん address a customer the term of address used is おきゃくさん (okyaku san). The honorific お is placed before the word きゃく and さん after it to make it more polite.

9.7 Electrical goods in Japan
にほん の でんき せいひん　　日本の電気製品

If you want to buy a video in にほん you should first check whether you can use it in your own country. The system used in Japan is NTSC which is the same as in the US. However, many countries use PAL, such as Australia, New Zealand, and the UK, or SECAM so you should check that the video is compatible with the system used in your own country. If the system in your country is different you may consider getting a multisystem (maruchishisutemu) so you can watch videos of Japanese television テレビ (terebi) back home. Another thing to consider is the voltage. In Japan it is 110 volts. To find out this kind of information you could ask questions such as the following:

これ は パル・システム です か。   Is this a PAL system?
re   pa ru   shi su te mu

これ は ひゃくじゅう ボルト です か。   Is this 110 volts?
re   hya   ju   bo ru to

■Practice 9.7　れんしゅう　　練習

With your partner practice a かいわ (kaiwa) similar to 9.6 using the pictures below and substituting the goods, prices, and manufacturers. Try to extend the conversation by asking about the system and voltage. The goods you want to buy are:

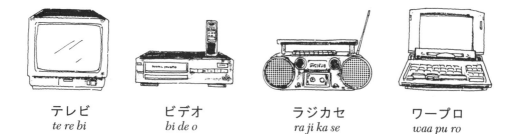

テレビ　　　　ビデオ　　　　　ラジカセ　　　　ワープロ
te re bi　　　　bi de o　　　　ra ji ka se　　　　waa pu ro

Some well known **nihon no meekaa** にほん の メーカー for such goods are the following:

とうしば	東芝	サンヨー *sa n yoo*	三洋
アカイ *a ka i*	アカイ	ひたち *hi ta chi*	日立
ソニー *so nii*	ソニー	みつびし *mi bi*	三菱
シャープ *shaa pu*	シャープ	NEC *enuiishii*	NEC 日本電気 *nihonden ki*

9.8 Exchange rate　　かわせレート　　為替レート

When traveling overseas the current exchange rate is always of interest. In にほんご "dollar" is **doru** ドル, so "American dollar" is **amerika doru** アメリカ ドル. When you are at a ぎんこう you can ask the rate for アメリカ ドル (**amerika doru**) with the following question:

Q: いま、 アメリカ ドル は いくら です か。
　　　　a me ri ka do ru　　　　　*ra*

A: いち ドル は＿＿＿＿＿＿ 円です。
　　chi do ru　　　　　　　*en*

You may also wish to work out price equivalents between アメリカ ドル (**amerika doru**) and Japanese Yen 日本円 (**nihon en**). To do this, you need to use the particle で to make the question:

"How much is 10 dollars in Japanese yen?"

Q: じゅうドル は 日本円 で いくら です か。
　ju　　*do ru*　*nihon en*　　　　*ra*

A: (日本円 で)＿＿＿＿＿＿ 円 です。
　nihon en　　　　　　　*en*

Check the current rate and write it in the blanks.

Foreign exchange がいこく かわせ 外国為替

Here are a number of currencies つうか with some hypothetical exchange rates. The names of the currencies given on the left are how you would refer to them when talking. The next column shows the way they appear in the newspaper (some are abbreviated).
With an あいて (aite) use the A and B sheets with the question and answer below to fill in the blanks.

Q: <u>ドイツ・マルク</u> は 日本円で いくらですか。
   do i tsu   ma ru ku   nihon en   ra

A: 1 <u>マルク</u> は＿＿＿＿＿円です。
   ma ru ku   en

When giving the rates you will need to use decimals. The decimal point is called てん so, seventy two point two five (72.25) is said as: なな じゅう に てん に ご
                                     ju

        point zero four (0.04) is said as: れい てん れい よん
                                     re   re

Sheet A

つうか	通貨	日本円
アメリカ・ドル *a me ri ka do ru*	米ドル	83.15
ニュージーランド・ドル *nyuu jii ra n do do ru*	ニュージーランドドル	＿＿＿
カナダ・ドル *ka na da do ru*	カナダドル	61.67
オーストラリア・ドル *oo su to ra ri a do ru*	豪ドル	＿＿＿
シンガポール・ドル *shi n ga poo ru do ru*	シンガポールドル	58.94
ホンコン・ドル *hon ko n do ru*	香港ドル	＿＿＿
たいわん・ドル *ta wa do ru*	台湾ドル	3.22
イギリス・ポンド *i gi ri su po n do*	英ポンド	＿＿＿
ドイツ・マルク *do i tsu ma ru ku*	独マルク	60.25

フランス・フラン *fu ra n su fu ra n*	仏フラン	———
スイス・フラン *su i su fu ra n*	スイスフラン	73.28
ちゅうごく・げん *chuu ge*	中国元	———
タイ・バーツ *ta i baa tsu*	タイバーツ	3.42
マレーシア・リンギ *ma ree shi a ri n gi*	マレーシアリンギ	———
インド・ルピー *i n do ru pii*	インドルピー	4.37
スペイン・ペセタ *su pe i n pe se ta*	スペインペセタ	———
イタリア・リラ *i ta ri a ri ra*	イタリアリラ	0.153
オランダ・ギルダー *o ra n da gi ru daa*	オランダギルダー	———

Sheet B

つうか	通貨	日本円
アメリカ・ドル *a me ri ka do ru*	米ドル	———
ニュージーランド・ドル *nyuu jii ra n do do ru*	ニュージーランドドル	62.34
カナダ・ドル *ka na da do ru*	カナダドル	———
オーストラリア・ドル *oo su to ra ri a do ru*	豪ドル	71.08
シンガポール・ドル *shi n ga poo ru do ru*	シンガポールドル	———
ホンコン・ドル *ho n ko n do ru*	香港ドル	11.05

たいわん・ドル *ta wa do ru*	台湾ドル	_____
イギリス・ポンド *i gi ri su po n do*	英ポンド	140.35
ドイツ・マルク *do i tsu ma ru ku*	独マルク	_____
フランス・フラン *fu ra n su fu ra n*	仏フラン	17.32
スイス・フラン *su i su fu ra n*	スイスフラン	_____
ちゅうごく・げん *chuu ge*	中国元	10.63
タイ・バーツ *ta i baa tsu*	タイバーツ	_____
マレーシア・リンギ *ma ree shi a ri n gi*	マレーシアリンギ	30.44
インド・ルピー *i n do ru pii*	インドルピー	_____
スペイン・ペセタ *su pe i n pe se ta*	スペインペセタ	0.87
イタリア・リラ *i ta ri a ri ra*	イタリアリラ	_____
オランダ・ギルダー *o ra n da gi ru daa*	オランダギルダー	63.92

The following かんじ is the number 1000. It is pronounced せん and is written with three strokes.

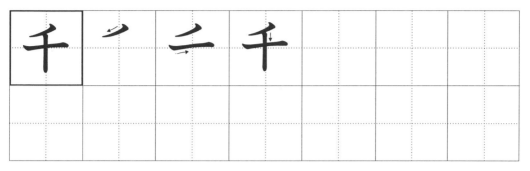

Here is a かんじ which you will often see on Japanese money. Its basic meaning is "circle" but it is most commonly seen as the unit of currency, the yen. In Japanese this is pronounced えん and always written with this かんじ. It is written with four strokes. Be careful not to confuse it with 月.

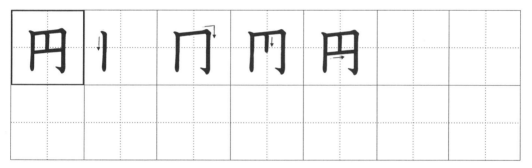

We have done one ひらがな (hiragana) for "o" but here is another ひらがな which is pronounced "o." This is the ひらがな which is used for the particle **wo** を which follows the object of the sentence. This ひらがな is never used as a part of a word, unlike the previous **o** お. It can be written in ローマじ (roomaji) as **o** or **wo**. We have used **wo** to distinguish it from the other **o** お and because that is how it is typed into a word processor. However, the two usually have the same pronunciation. It is written in three strokes.

The first of the fourth line of the ひらがな chart is **ta** た. The first two strokes are as in な and the next two are like こ. When てんてん is added **ta** た changes to **da** だ.

た

だ

The next ひらがな is **ri** り. It is written in two strokes. In some typefaces these are joined, e.g. り. Be careful not to confuse り with い. On some word processors it can also be typed in as "li."

り

Try reading these words: ください, いただきます, 五十円

1. Read the following aloud in Japanese.

180円 670円 4000円 3500円

5005円 29000円 60020円 142000円

2. Match the Japanese words with their English meanings by joining them with a line.

てんいん   electrical goods shop

ねだん   customer
ne da

でんきや   money
ya

おかね   shop assistant
ne

きゃく   price
kya

てんき   shopping

かいもの   weather

3. Fill in the blanks with question words and particles as appropriate.

1) Q: これ は (   ) です か。
   re
   A: 千円 です。
   sen en

2) Q: えき は (   ) です か。
   A: あそこ です。
   a so

3) Q: これ は (   ) テレビ です か。
   re   *te re bi*
   A: とうしば の です。

4. Fill in the blanks with は, か, も, を, の, と, ね (ne), で, or よ.

1) これ は 900円 です。 あれ（　　　）900円 です。 それ（　　　）400 円 です。
re　　en　　a re　　　　　　en　　　so re　　　　　en

2) A: これ は いかが です（　　　）。いい カメラ です（　　　）。 20000 円 です。
re　　　　　　　　　　　　　　me ra

B: やすい です（　　　）。じゃ、それ（　　　）ください。
ya　　　　　　　　ja　so re　　　　da

3) おのさん（　　　）さとうさん は がくせい です。

4) 1ドル は にほん 円（　　　）65 円 です。
do ru　　　　　en　　　　en

5. ✍ Let's write in Japanese! Write a ひらがな in each ___.

The reply to "ただいま" is: __ __ __ __ __ __.

"I'd like some eggs, please" は にほんご で:「たまご __ __ __ __ __」です。

Write the following words using かんじ.

５０えん

７０００えん

８０えん

第十課

In this lesson the ローマじ for the following characters: くぐにおはばぱしじいえほぼぽん のてですずとどこごなようかがつづ月きぎませぜもへべペー二三四らさざ has been removed.

10.1 Days of the week　ようび　曜日

When you look at 日本 の カレンダー (nihon no karendaa) you will see that the days of the week are marked with the following かんじ.

日　　月　　火　　水　　木　　金　　土

These かんじ are the first parts of the names of the days and therefore correspond to the abbreviations used in えいご i.e. Sun., Mon., Tue., etc. The full names of the days of the week are as follows:

にちようび 日曜日 _chi_ _bi_		どようび 土曜日 _bi_
げつようび 月曜日 _ge_ _bi_		
かようび 火曜日 _bi_		五
すいようび 水曜日 _bi_		日 月 火 水 木 金 土
もくようび 木曜日 _bi_		28 29 30 1 2 ③ ④
きんようび 金曜日 _bi_		⑤ ⑥ 7 8 9 10 11

Calendar:

日	月	火	水	木	金	土
28	29	30	1	2	③	④
⑤	⑥	7	8	9	10	11
12	13	14	15	16	17	18
19	20	21	22	23	24	25
26	27	28	29	30	31	1

As you can see, each ends in ようび (yoobi) which means something like "week day." To make the question "What (week) day is it" we just add ようび (yoobi) to the question word なん (what) to get the following question:

Q: なんようび です か。
　　　　bi

Q: なんよう日 です か。

A: もくようび です。
　　　　　bi

A: 木よう日 です。

Practice asking your あいて (aite) the days of the week by pointing to one of the かんじ above and asking, なんようび です か. It is worth learning to recognize the かんじ for the days as you will often come across them in Japan.

■Conversation 10.1　かいわ　会話

Going to a meeting かいぎ に いきますか 会議に行きますか

Owada おわだ and Katoo かとう are talking about a meeting (かいぎ). Listen to the tape and fill in the blanks with ひらがな.

おわだ:　かいぎ は なんよう日 です か。
wa da　　　　　　　　　　bi

かとう:　金よう日 です。
　　　　kin　　bi

おわだ:　＿＿＿＿＿＿ から です か。
wa da

かとう:　六じ はん ＿＿＿＿ です。 おわださん は いきます か。
roku　　　　　　　　　　　　　　wa da

おわだ:　ええ、＿＿＿＿＿＿＿＿。 かとうさん は。
wa da

かとう:　わたし ＿＿＿＿＿＿ いきます。
wa ta

おわだ:　じゃ、また、金よう日 に。
wa da　　　　ta　　kin　　bi

かとう:　ええ、じゃ また。
　　　　　ja　　ta

Practice the かいわ (kaiwa) with an あいて (aite) substituting days and time.

10.2 Holidays　　やすみ　休み

The word for a "break" or "rest" in にほんご is やすみ (yasumi) and the word for "day"is hi 日. So, not surprisingly, the word for a "rest day" or a "day off" is yasumi no hi やすみ の ひ （休みの日）. However, in general conversation やすみ (yasumi) is used for both rests or breaks and holidays. You have already seen the word やすみ in the expression used when going to bed at night おやすみなさい (oyasuminasai). In this case the meaning of "rest" is extended to include "sleep." Unlike the えいご, "holiday" (holy day), やすみ (yasumi) has no religious connotations.

■Conversation 10.2　かいわ　　会話

Holiday やすみ の ひ 休みの日

Before you go to a museum, art gallery, or department store (depaato) in にほん it is wise to check whether it is open or not. Since the やすみ の ひ (yasumi no hi) is fairly regular for certain establishments, you (A) can usually find out by asking a にほんじん (B).

A: <u>せいぶ デパート</u> の やすみ は なんよう日 ですか。
　　　bu de paa to　　　ya mi　　　　　bi

B: <u>火よう日</u> です。
　　ka　　bi

A: そう です か。ありがとう ございました。
　　so　　　　　　a ri　　　　　　　　ta

■Practice 10.2　れんしゅう　　練習

Following is a list of places and their やすみ の ひ (yasumi no hi). Since half the information is missing on each of Part A and Part B, you can work with your あいて (aite) to complete the tables.

To find out the えいご for the にほんご words you don't know, you can fill in the えいご by asking your あいて (aite):

Q: (Japanese word) は えいご で なん です か。

A: (English word) です。

Then find out the やすみ (yasumi) using かいわ 10.2.

Part A

📼 ばしょ	やすみの日 *ya mi hi*	えいご
いせたんデパート *ta de paa to*	水	Isetan department store
はくぶつかん *bu*	____	_____
びじゅつかん *bi ju*	火	art gallery
どうぶつえん *bu*	____	_____
としょかん	水	library
みつこしデパート *mi de paa to*	____	_____
ぎんこう	土 と 日	_____
ゆうびんきょく *yu bi*	____	_____

10.3 Weekly schedule   しゅう の よてい   週の予定

If you are a busy person, it is likely you go somewhere every day of the week and each day of your diary につき is full. To say that you are going somewhere on a certain day in にほんご, you need to follow the name of the day with the particle for time に, e.g. "I'm going to a movie on Saturday." or "I'll go to a movie on Saturday." in にほんご is:

わたし は 土よう日 に えいが に いきます。
wa ta   do   bi

To ask the question "Where are you going on Saturday ?" we just substitute どこ:
土よう日 に どこ に いきますか。
do   bi

■Conversation 10.3　かいわ　会話

At a tour company りょこうがいしゃで　旅行会社で

Two secretaries ひしょ (hisho) at a tour company りょこうがいしゃ (ryokoogaisha) are trying to work out the schedules for next week for two of their tour guides ガイド (gaido) Satoo and Honda.

ひしょ A: さとう さん は <u>日よう日</u> に どこ に いきますか。
hi　　　　　　*nichi bi*

ひしょ B: <u>くうこう</u> に いきます。
hi

ひしょ A: なんじ に でます か。
hi

ひしょ B: <u>ごぜん 七じ はん</u> に でます。
hi　　　*shichi*

ひしょ A: そう です か。
hi　　　*so*

ひしょ B: ほんだ さん は <u>金よう日</u> に どこ に いきますか。
hi　　　*da*　　　*kin bi*

ひしょ A: <u>金よう日</u> は やすみ です。
hi　　　*kin bi ya mi*

ひしょ B: ああ、 そう です か。
hi　　　*a a so*

なんじに
でますか。

■Practice 10.3　れんしゅう　練習

Here are next week's schedules スケジュール (sukejuuru) for the two tour guides ツアー・ガイド (tsuaa gaido) who work with Japanese tourists in the Gold Coast region of Australia. They each take out tours ツアー (tsuaa) five days a week. The tours are:

ゴールド コースト・ツアー　　　　　　　to sights along the Gold Coast
goo ru do koo su to tsu aa

ゴルフ・ツアー　　　　　　　　　　　　to play golf
go ru fu tsu aa

カジノ・ツアー *ka ji no tsu aa*	to the casino
バーベキューパーティー *baa be kyuu paa tii*	to a barbeque party
かいがん・ツアー *tsu aa*	along the coast line (かいがん)

They have one day やすみ (**yasumi**) and one day picking up guests from the airport (くうこう).

With your あいて (**aite**) practice かいわ (**kaiwa**) 10.3 to fill in the following:

Part A

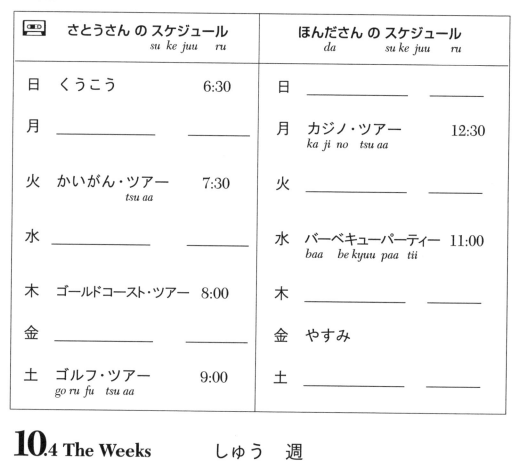

🔲 さとうさん の スケジュール *su ke juu ru*		ほんださん の スケジュール *da su ke juu ru*	
日　くうこう	6:30	日　＿＿＿＿＿	＿＿＿
月　＿＿＿＿＿	＿＿＿	月　カジノ・ツアー *ka ji no tsu aa*	12:30
火　かいがん・ツアー *tsu aa*	7:30	火	
水　＿＿＿＿＿	＿＿＿	水　バーベキューパーティー *baa be kyuu paa tii*	11:00
木　ゴールドコースト・ツアー	8:00	木　＿＿＿＿＿	＿＿＿
金　＿＿＿＿＿	＿＿＿	金　やすみ	
土　ゴルフ・ツアー *go ru fu tsu aa*	9:00	土　＿＿＿＿＿	＿＿＿

10.4 The Weeks　　しゅう　週

We have already learned the names of the days of the week but before we can use these words to refer to "next Sunday" or "last Saturday," we need to learn the words for "next week" and "last week." This brings us to three prefixes which are used quite a lot in にほんご, らい for "future," こん for "present,"and せん for "past."
When combined with しゅう we get:

📼 らいしゅう *ra shu*	next week	来週
こんしゅう *shu*	this week	今週
せんしゅう *shu*	last week	先週

These prefixes can also be combined with げつ (getsu) to make "next month" らいげつ
（来月）etc. Note how 月 is pronounced げつ rather than がつ.

To get "next Sunday" we just use "next week" to describe "Sunday" by joining the two
words with the particle の as follows:

📼 らいしゅう の にちようび *ra shu chi bi*	next Sunday	来週の日曜日
こんしゅう の どようび *shu bi*	this Saturday	今週の土曜日
せんしゅう の きんようび *shu bi*	last Friday	先週の金曜日

There are also some terms that don't occur in えいご.

さらいしゅう *ra shu*	the week after next	再来週
せんせんしゅう *shu*	the week before last	先々週

■**Practice 10.4 れんしゅう　練習**

Practice these expressions by asking your あいて (aite) "When are you going?" or "When
did you go?" Substitute the weeks and days.

📼 Q: いつ いきますか。 A: <u>らいしゅう の 木よう日</u> に いきます。 　　*ra   shu   moku   bi* Or Q: いつ いきましたか。 　　　　　　　*ta* A: <u>せんしゅう の 木よう日</u> に いきました。 　　*shu   moku   bi*

10.5 Somewhere and nowhere　どこか と どこへも

When asking about another person's activities we often avoid the direct question "Where are you going tomorrow?" in favor of the more indirect "Are you going anywhere tomorrow?" In にほんご we make the term for "anywhere" or "somewhere" by adding か to the question word どこ to get どこか.

> Q: あした、どこか へ いきますか。
> 　　*a　　ta*

The reply to this could either be はい, followed by the place you are going:

> A: はい、ゴールド コースト へ いきます。
> 　　*goo　ru do koo　su to.*

or "No, I'm not going anywhere," which in にほんご is:

> A: いいえ、どこ へ も いきません。

■Language pattern 10.5　ぶんけい　文型

To make "not anywhere" or "nowhere" we follow どこ with も, but the も comes after the particle へ or に.

Q: どこか へ いきますか。	Q: Are you going somewhere (anywhere)?
A: いいえ、どこへ も いきません。	A: No, I'm not going anywhere.

■Conversation 10.5　かいわ　会話

A day off

Tomorrow is a やすみ (yasumi). Yamamoto 山本 and Yamada 山田 are talking about their plans.

山本: <u>あした</u> は やすみ です ね。やまださん は どこか へ いきます か。
　　a　ta　　　ya mi　　　ne　ya da

山田: いいえ、どこ へ も いきません。やまもとさん は。
　　　　　　　　　　　　ya

山本: わたし は <u>うきよえ びじゅつかん</u> へ いきます。
　　wa ta　　　　　　bi ju

山田: ああ、そう です か。いい です ね。
　　a　a　so　　　　　　　　*ne*

148

Practice the above かいわ (kaiwa) substituting destinations. Then try converting it to the past tense.

Notes:

1. うきよえ is a style of painting which flourished in にほん in the 17th, 18th, and 19th centuries. Typically these were wood block prints (はんが) of actors and courtesans; themes which gave the name, "floating world pictures" (ukiyoe 浮世絵) to the genre. However, うきよえ extend beyond these topics to landscapes, street scenes, and aspects of everyday life. Well known artists include Hiroshige ひろしげ (広重), Hokusai ほくさい (北斎), Utamaro うたまろ (歌麿), and Sharaku しゃらく (写楽).

2. いい です ね is what you say when someone tells you about something good that they are going to do or is happening to them. It is like the えいご "Oh, that's nice, isn't it," "That sounds good," or "That's great."

When referring to a past event, the いい part changes to よかった (yokatta), so the expression becomes: よかった です ね (yokatta desu ne).

10.6 The use and non-use of に 「に」のつかいかた 「に」の使い方

We have seen that in sentences which contain verbs of action, the particle always follows absolute time expressions such as clock times, months, days of the week, and special days. However, に is not used following relative time expressions such as "now," "tomorrow," and "last week."

きょう かいしゃ に いきます。
　　　　sha

土よう日 に かいしゃ に いきます。
do　*bi*　　　*sha*

せんしゅう ひろしま に かえりました。
　　shu　*hi ro*　　　　*ri*

六月 に ひろしま に かえりました。
roku　　*hi ro*　　　*ri*

In the case of question words the general "when" いつ is not followed by に. Specific questions, however, such as なん月, なんよう日 (nanyoobi), and なんじ require に.

いつ 日本 へ いきますか。
nihon

なん月 に ちゅうごく に いきました か。
chu   *ta*

なんよう日 に きます か。
bi

なんじ に がっこう に いきました か。
ta

Compound time expressions will take に depending upon what kind of expression comes last. For example, せんしゅう (senshuu) doesn't take に but 火よう日 (kayoobi) does, so "last Tuesday" せんしゅう の 火よう日 (senshuu no kayoobi) will be followed by に. Conversely, 水よう日 (suiyoobi) takes に while あさ (asa) doesn't, so "Wednesday morning" 水よう日のあさ is not usually followed by に. However, in this last case に can be used for emphasis.

Examples れい 例

らいしゅう の 日よう日 に いきます。
ra   *shu*   *nichi*   *bi*

木よう日 の ばん いきます。
moku   *bi*

あした の 七じ に いきます。
a   *ta*   *shichi.*

金よう日 の ごご かえりました。
kin   *bi*   *ri*   *ta*

10.2 Part B

ばしょ	やすみの日 *ya mi hi*	えいご
いせたんデパート *ta de paa to*	————	————
はく ぶつかん *bu*	木	museum
びじゅつかん *bi ju*	————	————
どうぶつえん *bu*	火	zoo

としょかん	_____	_____
みつこしデパート *mi de paa to*	月	Mitsukoshi department store
ぎんこう	土 と 日	_____
ゆうびんきょく *yu bi*	_____	_____

10.3 Part B

さとうさん の スケジュール *su ke juu ru*		ほんださん の スケジュール *da su ke juu ru*	
日 _____ _____		日 ゴールド コースト ツアー 8:30 *goo ru do koo su to tsu aa*	
月 バーベキューパーティー 11:00 *baa be kyuu paa tii*		月 _____ _____	
火 _____ _____		火 ゴルフ・ツアー 9:30 *go ru fu tsu aa*	
水 カジノ・ツアー 12:00 *ka ji no tsu aa*		水 _____ _____	
木 _____ _____		木 かいがん・ツアー 7:00 *tsu aa*	
金 やすみ *ya mi*		金 _____ _____	
土 _____ _____		土 くうこう 6:00	

Answers こたえ 答え

Conversation 10.1
なんじ; から; いきます; も.

Writing Japanese Script 10.7

The hiragana hi ひ is written with only one stroke. When it takes てんてん it is pronounced bi び. When "maru" (まる) is added its pronunciation changes from hi ひ to pi ぴ.

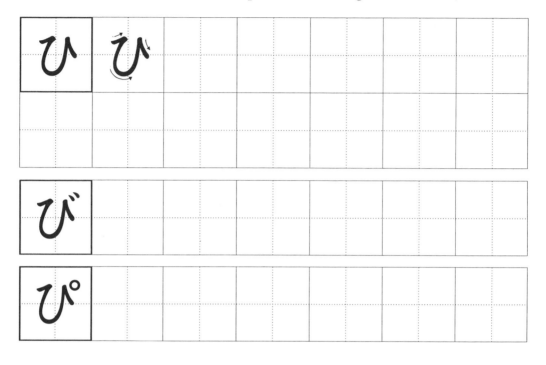

This next かんじ means "day" or "sun." It was originally a circle with a dot in it but was squared off to: 日. It is pronounced hi ひ as in この日 (this day) or bi び as in どよう日 (Saturday), or as nichi にち as in 日よう日 (Sunday), まい日 (every day), こん日 は (Good Day!). It is written with four strokes.

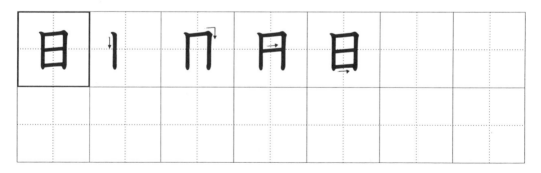

The next ひらがな is so そ. It is written in one or two strokes depending on which form is used. Below we give you the one stroke version. When it takes てんてん it is pronouced zo ぞ. You can now write the third line of the ひらがな chart: さ、し、す、せ、そ。

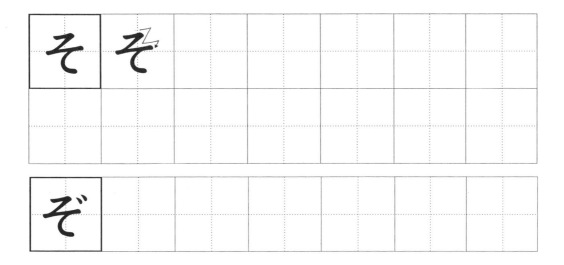

You have come across this next ひらがな at the end of sentences with the meaning "isn't it?" It is ne ね and is written in two strokes.

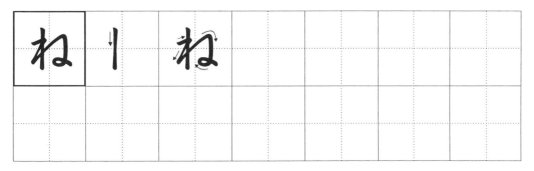

Try reading the following: そうで すね, どうぞ, おねがいします

1. Choose the correct word from the list below and write it in the appropriate blank.

いつ   なん月   なんじ   なんようび

1) Q: いま（   ）ですか。
   A: 四じはん です。

2) Q: かいぎ は（   ）ですか。
   A: すいようび です。
        bi

3) Q:（   ）おおさか に いきましたか。
   A: きのう いきました。

4) Q:（   ）に にほん へ いきますか。
   A: 三月 に いきます。

2. Fill in the blanks with one ひらがな to complete the dialogues.

1) Q: もくようび（   ）どこ（   ）いきました か。
        bi
   A: ぎんざ に いきました。

2) Q: としょかん（   ）やすみ は いつ です か。
                                ya mi
   A: きんようび（   ）すいようび です。
        bi

3) Q: こんばん どこ（   ）へ いきますか。
   A: はい、えいが へ いきます。

3. Translate the following sentences into にほんご.

1) The bank is open from Monday to Friday. _____

2) Ms. Sato didn't go anywhere yesterday. _____

3) The holiday is next Wednesday. _____

4. ✍ Let's write in Japanese! Write a ひらがな in each ___.

1) When you offer something to someone you say: _____ _____ _____.

2) "Money"は にほんごで: _____ _____ _____

3) _____ _____ _____ _____ は えいご で "plane" です。

4) Write the following words in ひらがな and かんじ; also write the meaning of the first word in parentheses.

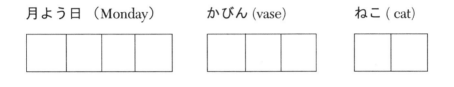

月よう日 （Monday）　　　かびん (vase)　　　ねこ (cat)

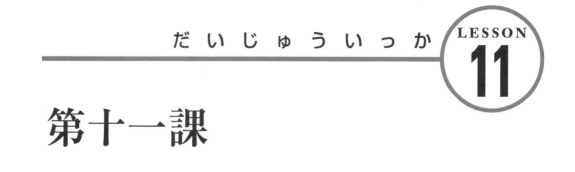

第十一課

The ローマじ for the following characters has been removed: くぐにおはばぱしじいえほぼぽんのてですずとどここごなよしょうかがつづ月きぎませぜもへべペー二三四らさざ五六七八九十.

11.1 Counting hundreds

You have already learned that "one hundred" is ひゃく (hyaku) in にほんご. As you would expect "two hundred" is therefore にひゃく (nihyaku). However, it isn't all so easy; there are some pronunciation changes which affect those numbers marked with an asterisk below. These changes are not just capricious variations designed to annoy the novice, rather they are examples of more general rules which you will encounter in later lessons. These can be summarized as follows:

1. When words are compounded of two words such as "three" and "hundred," the first syllable of the second word may undergo a pronunciation change if it is possible for it to take two dots てんてん. In the case of 300, instead of being read さん plus ひゃく (hyaku) the ひ of ひゃく takes てんてん to become び (bi) so the word becomes さんびゃく (sanbyaku). This kind of change often occurs after the sound "an."

2. In compounds which are difficult to pronounce the first part may be contracted. In such cases the first syllable of the following part will take まる (maru) if it can. For example, hachi hyaku is considered difficult to say so the ち (chi) of はち is deleted and replaced by the unvoiced chiisai つ to make ha' はっ. Consequently, the ひ of ひゃく (hyaku) takes まる to become ぴ (pi). The result is ha' pyaku はっぴゃく which is conventionally typed as happyaku. Remember to skip your voice over the chiisai つ.
   These contractions only affect pronunciation, so they don't change the way the numbers are written in かんじ only in ひらがな. This is analogous to pronouncing "eight hundred" in えいご as "ei'dundred," as many people in fact do, but still writing it as "eight hundred."

	100	ひゃく *hya*	百
	200	にひゃく *hya*	二百
	300*	さんびゃく *bya*	三百
	400	よんひゃく *hya*	四百
	500	ごひゃく *hya*	五百
	600*	ろっぴゃく *ro* *ppya*	六百
	700	ななひゃく *hya*	七百
	800*	はっぴゃく *ha* *ppya*	八百
	900	きゅうひゃく *kyu* *hya*	九百
	1000	せん	千

As for units of tens, they are counted as you would expect.
Just remember よん, なな, and きゅう (kyuu).

	110	ひゃくじゅう *hya* *ju*	百十
	220	にひゃくにじゅう *hya* *ju*	二百二十
	340	さんびゃくよんじゅう *bya* *ju*	三百四十
	670	ろっぴゃくななじゅう *ro* *ppya* *ju*	六百七十
	790	ななひゃくきゅうじゅう *hya* *kyu* *ju*	七百九十

Counting thousands

These numbers are fairly regular. Just remember there is no "one" on "one thousand," and that 3000 and 8000 require a pronunciation change.

1000	せん	千	6000	ろくせん *ro*	六千
2000	にせん	二千	7000	ななせん	七千
3000*	さんぜん	三千	8000*	はっせん	八千
4000	よんせん	四千	9000	きゅうせん *kyu*	九千
5000	ごせん	五千	10000	いちまん *chi*	一万

Notes: For numbers over 10, よん and なな tend to be used rather than し and しち. However, in the unit position these are interchangeable. For example, 24 can be にじゅうよん or にじゅうし, and 57 can be ごじゅうなな or ごじゅうしち.

 ■**Practice 11.1 れんしゅう　練習**

With an あいて partner test your reading of the following prices in えん (円). Point to one and ask いくら ですか。

480円、850円、690円、930円、560円、1500円、7770円、9040円、
13000円、110円、2300円、1005円、325円、198円、8700円、
234円、677円、74200円、548円、399円.

11.2 Coffee Shops　　きっさてん　喫茶店

In にほん there are many きっさてん. These きっさてん are not simply purveyors of coffee (koohii コーヒー) but also function as places to sit and talk with friends, do some reading, or just as a refuge from the crowded streets. For this reason the コーヒー (koohii) is rather takai たかい; you are really paying for the atmosphere and not just the コーヒー. Also, the price of coffee varies greatly from きっさてん to きっさてん. Some きっさてん sell a wide range of コーヒー from all over the world. These are named according to country of origin or by type as in the case of the famous "Blue Mountain." However, all きっさてん will sell a rather strong house blend called burendo ブレンド and a mild blend called amerikan アメリカン. Burendo ブレンド seems to be the more popular of the two and is often ordered simply as "hotto" ホット (hot). In なつ cold black coffee with ice and a sweet syrup on the side is also popular. This is referred to as "aisu" アイス (ice) when ordering.

きっさてん not only sell コーヒー, they also have English-style tea which is known as koocha こうちゃ, not to be confused with ocha おちゃ (Japanese tea), as well as cakes and light meals. こうちゃ comes either with miruku ミルク or with lemon レモン. When you sit down in a きっさてん you are usually given a glass of ice water and a small moist towel called oshibori おしぼり with which you wipe your hands (and face if you like) and freshen up.

In the mornings (asa あさ) many きっさてん offer a reasonably priced set breakfast called mooningu setto モーニングセット which can be either Japanese or European style and comes with コーヒー or こうちゃ. When more than one setto is offered they are often labeled A setto (A セット) and B setto (B セット). These setto are usually displayed in the window or next to the door.

■**Conversation 11.2　かいわ　会話**

At a coffee shop　きっさてん で喫茶店で

The following かいわ takes place in a きっさてん one なつ. It is between a customer (きゃく kyaku) and a woman working in the coffee shop (てんいん). The きゃく (kyaku) is a foreign visitor who has trouble reading the menyu (メニュー). She has heard that コーヒー can be rather たかい (takai) so she checks the price before ordering.
Listen to the tape and fill in the blanks.

てんいん: いらっしゃいませ。 ごちゅうもん は…。
　　　　　　　　　　　　　　 sha　　　　　　chuu
きゃく:　あのう、 コーヒー は ＿＿＿＿ ですか。
　　　　　　a　　　 koo　hii
てんいん: アイス ですか、 ホット ＿＿＿＿ か。
　　　　　 a　i　su　　　　　　ho　tto
きゃく:　ホット は いくら ですか。
　　　　　ho　tto
てんいん: ＿＿＿＿ 円 です。
　　　　　　　　　　 en
きゃく:　じゃ、 ホット を ＿＿＿＿。
　　　　　　　　　 ho　tto
てんいん: はい、 かしこまりました。
　　　　　　　　　　　　　　 ri　　　 ta

Notes:

1. いらっしゃいませ **irasshaimase** means "welcome to our shop." It is the greeting used by store clerks when a customer comes in.

2. ちゅうもん **chuumon** is a restaurant order. When ご is attached the word becomes more polite and therefore refers to "your order." This ご is an honorific prefix like the お we encountered earlier.

3. ごちゅうもん は is an unfinished question meaning "Your order…?"

4. かしこまりました **kashikomarimashita** means "certainly." It is used in the service industry. It is a polite form of わかりました **wakarimashita**.

メニュー　menyuu

****

コーヒー		koohii
ブレンド	450円	burendo
アメリカン	450円	amerikan
アイスコーヒー	480円	aisukoohii

紅茶 こうちゃ		koocha
ミルクティー	450円	mirukutii
レモンティー	450円	remontii
アイスティー	480円	aisutii

モーニングセット　　　mooningu setto

A セット	450円	A setto
トースト、ゆでたまご、 コーヒー／こうちゃ		toosuto, yudetamago, koohii/koocha
B セット	500円	B setto
おにぎり、みそしる、サラダ、 たまご、コーヒー／こうちゃ		onigiri, misoshiru, sarada, tamago, koohii/koocha

Notes:

1. ティー **tii** is English-style tea (i.e. from Sri Lanka or India). It is not used alone but appended to words such as アイスティー **aisutii**.
2. トースト **toosuto** is toast.
3. ゆでたまご **yudetamago** is boiled egg.
4. サラダ **sarada** is salad (a very small bowl is usual).
5. おにぎり **onigiri** is a triangular shaped lump of compressed rice often with something inside.

■Practice 11.2　れんしゅう　練習

Practice かいわ 11.2 substituting various pairs of words below and varying the prices.

アイス ／ ホット
a i su　*ho tto*

レモンティー ／ ミルクティー
remo n tii　　*mi ru ku tii*

ブレンド ／ アメリカン
bu re n do　　*a me ri ka n*

A セット ／ B セット
　se tto　　*se tto*

■Language pattern 11.2　ぶんけい　文型

Just by doubling the question you can convey the meaning "Would you like A or B?" This is a convenient type of question which is often used.

A です か、B です か。	Would you like A or B?
アイス です か、ホット です か。 *a i su*　　　*ho tto*	Would you like ice coffee or hot coffee?

11.3 This thing and that thing これ、それ、あれ／この、その、あの

We have seen words for "this" これ (**kore**) and "that" それ (**sore**), あれ (**are**). With these we can make questions such as "Is this tofu?" これはとうふですか or statements like "That is my magazine" それはわたしのざっしです. In such sentences the topic is "this" or "that." This is fine so long as we are referring to something obvious or can indicate by pointing to the object. However, in many cases we need to make the topic more specific and refer to "that magazine" rather than to simply "that" in order to make statements such as "That magazine is mine." In such cases we cannot just place これ (that) in front of ざっし (magazine) as is the case with えいご. Instead, we must use different forms of "this" and "that" as follows:

この ざっし	this magazine
その ざっし *so*	that magazine
あの ざっし *a*	that magazine (over there)

その ざっし は わたし の です。 That magazine is mine.
so　　　　*wa ta*

It is wrong to say "**kore zasshi**," this sounds like a pidjin form of "これはざっしです" (this is a magazine) and will not be understood by にほんじん as "this magazine."

The rule is that これ, それ, and あれ are pronouns. They stand alone and replace the name of the thing. In contrast, この (**kono**), その (**sono**), and あの (**ano**) are adjectives that can only precede the name of the thing and cannot stand alone.

■Conversation 11.3　かいわ　会話

Lost things　わすれもの　忘れ物

The class is leaving the きょうしつ. The teacher sees a pair of spectacles (**megane** めがね) which have been left on a つくえ and wants to find out who they belong to. The question word for "who" is だれ (**dare**). In にほんご we don't need a special word for "whose," we simply add の to get だれの.

せんせい:	この めがね は だれの です か。 　　*me ne*　　*da re*
がくせい:	わたしの じゃ ありません。それ は すずきくんの です。 *wa ta*　　　*a ri*　　　*so re*
せんせい:	そう です か。すずきくん！ わすれもの です よ。 *so*　　　　　　　　　　*wa re*
すずき:	はい。
せんせい:	この めがね は きみ の です か。 　　*me ne*　*mi*
すずき:	はい、ぼくの です。どうも すみません。 　　*mi*

Notes:

くん is a title placed after a person's name in the same way as さん. However it is only used when referring to subordinates or friends. It is often used after the names of boys and young men.

きみ (kimi) is one of the words for "you." It is a familiar, informal form often used among friends or by superiors to subordinates with whom they are familiar.

ぼく means "I" but it is more informal than わたし **watashi**. It is only used by boys and men. In the above situation a woman would use わたし.

じゃ ありません (ja arimasen) is the negative of です. The では part of ではありません can be contracted to **ja** じゃ to give the alternative form: じゃありません.

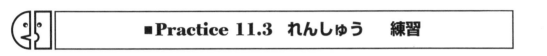

■Practice 11.3　れんしゅう　練習

Practice this かいわ (kaiwa) with two あいて (aite) substituting the なまえ and the わすれもの (wasuremono). Here are some things which are often forgotten:

じしょ	辞書	dictionary
けしゴム *ke go mu*	消ゴム	eraser
かさ	傘	umbrella
ノート *noo to*		notebook
じょうぎ	定規	ruler
きょうかしょ	教科書	textbook

Q: だれ の ですか。　　　　Q: Whose is it?
  da re

A: わたしの です。　　　　A: It's mine
  wa ta

"I" is transformed to "my" by adding の.　　わたし → わたしの　　watashi → watashino
"Who" becomes "whose" by adding の.　　　だれ → だれの　　　dare → dareno

11.4 The station kiosk えき の ばいてん　駅 の 売店

Most Japanese railway stations (えき) have a small kiosk (ばいてん) at which you can buy a range of items. Most people buy their newspapers (shinbun しんぶん) at such ばいてん or have them delivered. In addition to しんぶん (shinbun) and ざっし, ばいてん usually sell まんが (comics), various drinks, snacks, and miscellaneous small items.

🎧　■**Conversation 11.4　かいわ　　会話**

At the station kiosk えき の ばいてん で　駅 の 売店 で

This conversation is between a customer きゃく (客) and the person working in the kiosk ばいてん の てんいん (店員). Fill in the blanks in ひらがな (hiragana).

客:　すみません、＿＿＿＿ ざっし は ＿＿＿＿ ですか。
          mi

店員:＿＿＿＿円 です。
      en

客:　＿＿＿＿ ざっし は。

店員: その ざっし ＿＿＿＿ 300円 です。
     so　　　　　　　　*en*

客:　じゃ、これ を ください。
       re wo　*da*

　　その ジュース ＿＿＿＿ いくら ＿＿＿＿ か。
    so　*juu su*

店員: これ は ＿＿＿＿ 円 です。
         en

客:　じゃ、それ も ください。
      so re　*da*

店員: ぜんぶ で ＿＿＿＿＿ 円 です。
      bu   *en*

客: はい。(hands over the money)

店員: ありがとう ＿＿＿＿＿ た。
      a ri

Note: ぜんぶ で (zenbu de) means "altogether." ぜんぶ means "the lot."
When you pay for something, you say はい as you hand over the money.

■Practice 11.4　れんしゅう　練習

The following is a list of items commonly sold at a ばいてん with their prices. First work out what the items are and then practice the かいわ (kaiwa) above with your あいて (aite), with one of you taking the role of the てんいん (Sheet A) and the other that of the きゃく (kyaku) (Sheet B at the end of this lesson). Write the ねだん (nedan) in the blanks on Sheet B. Swap roles after you have completed eight items.

Sheet A　ばいてんのていいん　売店の店員

しなもの 品物	ねだん 値段	しなもの 品物	ねだん 値段
たばこ 煙草	300円	ジュース	100円
ペン	75円	サンドイッチ	150円
ライター	100円	パン	90円
ハンカチ	450円	コーヒー	150円
ティッシュ	50円	おにぎり	100円
フイルム	320円	まんが　漫画	250円
しんぶん　新聞	90円		
ざっし　雑誌	350円		
べんとう　弁当	500円		
ぎゅうにゅう　牛乳	60円		

Notes: 1. You should be able to guess the following **katakana** words:

ティッシュ	tisshu	ペン	pen
サンドイッチ	sandoicchi	ジュース	juusu
フイルム	fuirumu	ライター	raitaa
コーヒー	koohii	ハンカチ	hankachi

2. If you know some **furansugo**, パン **pan** will also be obvious.

3. べんとう is a small portable prepared meal, usually cold and comprising rice, fish or meat, and vegetables. Some えき are famous for their particular variety of **ekiben** えきべん (short for えきのべんとう). べんとう is also used for any cooked food which you pack in a container to take somewhere (e.g. to work or school) to eat. The box you use is called a べんとうばこ.

4. おにぎり (onigiri) are small triangular cakes of compressed rice which make a convenient snack. There are many kinds, but most have something inside such as dried salmon (**sake** さけ), preserved plum (**umeboshi** うめぼし), or pickled cucumber (おしんこう), and many are wrapped in **nori** のり. They are also referred to as **omusubi** おむすび.

5. ぎゅうにゅう (gyuunyuu) is cows' milk. たばこ (tabako) is cigarettes.

6. まんが are cartoons or comics. In にほん comics are not only for children but for people of all ages. They are very popular and there are まんが about everything from romantic fiction to economics and Chinese classics.

11.5. Which?   どれ と どの

Just as there are two forms of "this" これ, (kore) and この, there are also two forms of the question word "which." These are **dore** どれ, which stands alone, and どの, which must precede a noun.

どれ ですか。 *re*	Which is it?
どの ほん ですか。	Which book is it?

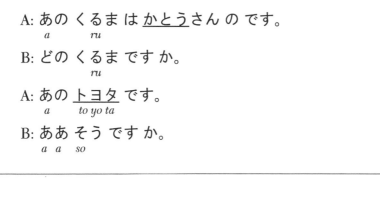

■Conversation 11.5 かいわ 会話

Pointing at someone's car

Person A is pointing out Kato's car (kuruma くるま). Since there are many くるま
(kuruma) to be seen, person B can't tell which one A is referring to.

A: あの くるま は かとう さん の です。
    a   *ru*

B: どの くるま です か。
    ru

A: あの トヨタ です。
    a   *to yo ta*

B: ああ そう です か。
  a a *so*

■Practice 11.5 れんしゅう 練習

Here is a list of common kuruma no meekaa no namae くるまのメーカーのなまえ.
Many of them are from にほん but others are from various くに. First practice the above
かいわ (kaiwa) substituting the make of the くるま. Then ask each other where the
various makes come from using the following:

A: ボルボ は どこ の くるま です か。
  bo ru bo   *ru*

B: スウェーデン の です。
  su *ee* *de n*

A: ああ そう です か。
  a a *so*

📟 くるまの メーカー

toyota	トヨタ	hooruden	ホールデン
suzuki	スズキ	bentsu	ベンツ
foodo	フォード	nissan	ニッサン
subaru	スバル	borubo	ボルボ
mitsubishi	みつびし	biiemu	ビーエム
matsuda	マツダ	runoo	ルノー
daihatsu	ダイハツ	honda	ホンダ
fiatto	フィアット	hyundai	ヒュンダイ
saabu	サーブ	jagaa	ジャガー

11.4 Sheet B.

しなもの 品物	ねだん 値段	しなもの 品物	ねだん 値段
たばこ 煙草	_____ 円	べんとう 弁当	_____ 円
ペン	_____ 円	ぎゅうにゅう 牛乳	_____ 円
ライター	_____ 円	ジュース	_____ 円
ハンカチ	_____ 円	サンドイッチ	_____ 円
ティッシュ	_____ 円	パン	_____ 円
フイルム	_____ 円	コーヒー	_____ 円
しんぶん 新聞	_____ 円	おにぎり	_____ 円
ざっし 雑誌	_____ 円	まんが 漫画	_____ 円

Answers こたえ 答え
Conversation 11.2 / いくら; です; 350; ください.
Conversation 11.4 / この; いくら; 350; この; も; は; です; 100; 450; ございまし.

Writing Japanese script 11.6

The first ひらがな in the ひらがな chart and the first ひらがな in the じしよ is a あ. It is written in three strokes. Now you can write the first line of the chart, あ、い、う、え、お.

The last line of the ひらがな chart starts with **wa** わ. This is not the particle **wa** which is written は. This is the **wa** used in spelling words such as **watashi** わたし. It is written in two strokes. There is some difference in the handwritten and printed forms. Use the handwritten version below in your writing.

The next ひらがな is **re** れ: as in これ, and それ. It is written with two strokes. On some word processors it can be input as "le."

LESSON **11** 第十一課

This next かんじ means "fire" 火. You have come across it in the name of the weekday Tuesday, pronounced **kayoobi** and written with this かんじ and another you have already learned: 火よう日. In this word the かんじ 火 is pronounced "**ka.**" It is written in four strokes.

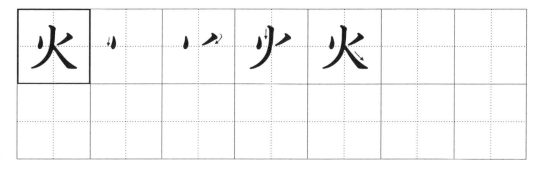

Another day of the week is Wednesday which is called すいようび and written with the かんじ 水 as follows: 水よう日. This かんじ has the meaning of "water" and is pronounced "**sui**" in compounds. However, when this かんじ is used to refer to water itself it is written as a single character, 水, and pronounced **mizu**. Most かんじ have different pronunciations depending on whether they are part of a word which comprises two or more かんじ or whether they are used independently.

1. Complete the following conversation by filling in the blanks.

Situation: At a coffee shop. The waiter/waitress welcomes the customer and requests the order. The customer orders a "morning set B" which comes with coffee or tea. The waiter/waitress asks whether s/he wants coffee or tea. S/he decides on tea.

てんいん：　いらっしゃいませ。＿＿＿＿＿＿＿＿＿＿は。
　　　　　　　　　　　sha

　きゃく：　あのう、モーニングセット の B ＿＿＿＿＿＿＿＿＿。
　　kya　　　*a*　　　*moo ni n gu se tto*

てんいん：　はい 。コーヒー ＿＿＿＿＿＿＿＿、こうちゃ ＿＿＿＿＿＿＿。

　きゃく：　こうちゃ ＿＿＿＿＿＿＿＿＿。
　　kya　　　*cha*

てんいん：　はい、＿＿＿＿＿＿＿＿＿。

2. Fill in the blanks with これ, この, どれ, どの, or どこ.

1) Q: スズキ は （　　　　　） の くるま です か。
　　　su zu ki　　　　　　　　*ru*
　 A: にほん の です。

2) （　　　　　　） は にほんご の じしょ です。

3) Q: うえの さん の かさ は （　　　　） です か。
　 A: あれ です。
　　　a re

4) （　　　　　） ほん は わたし の です。

3. Fill in the blanks with a ひらがな.

1) この ざっし は かとうさん （　　　　　） です か。

2) ぜんぶ （　　　　） 千円 です。
　　　bu　　　　*sen en*

3) Q: べんとう（　　　　　　）いくら です か。

　A: この べんとう は 500円 です。その べんとう（　　　　　　）500円 です。

　　　　　　en　　　*so*　　　　　　　　　　　　　　　　　　　　　*en*

4. Translate the following sentences into にほんご.

1) A: This umbrella is 1500 yen. That umbrella (near person B) is 1300 yen.

_____

　B: Well, I'll take (buy) this (near B).

_____

2) Whose textbook is this?

_____

3) That one (near you) is not mine.

_____

5. Read the following aloud and then translate it into えいご.

1) わたし は 火よう日 と 水よう日 に としょかん へ いきます。

_____

2) すみません、わかりません。また、でんわ します。

_____

3) これ は たなか くん の わすれもの です。

_____

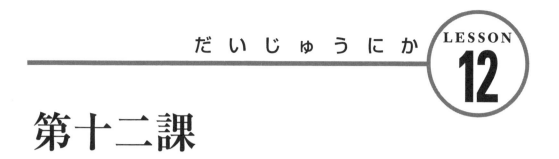

第十二課

The ローマじ for くぐにおはばぱしじんいえほぼぽのてですずうとどこごよなかがつづ月きぎませぜもへべぺらさざをただりー二三四五六七八九十千円 is omitted in this lesson.

12.1 Making sentences ぶんをつくる 文を作る

Japanese sentences are constructed differently from English sentences. In にほんご the order of information in the sentence goes from general to specific. The sentence starts with the topic and the time and then moves on to the action. This is rather like the script for a play or a film scenario. Before anything specific can happen the scene must be set, i.e. we first need the time, the actors, and the topic. Then the action can take place. In a Japanese sentence the verb comes at the end and the time and topic start the sentence. This means that any further details will come in the middle. In a simple sentence such as: この人 は たなかさん です (kono hito wa tanaka san desu), there is no action, only information about the topic, "this person." The time isn't stated either since we assume it to be "now." This kind of sentence can be summarized conceptually as:

(time(に))	topic は	information です。

In sentences in which action does occur, such as movement to a place, the general pattern of the Japanese sentence is more clearly evident. For example:

土よう日 に たなかさん は きょうと に いきました comprises the following components:
do   *bi*

time (に)	topic / actor は	place に	move(tense).
		scene	action

In this sentence there are four components; the first two set the scene and the last two give the action. Each of the first three components is followed by a particle which indicates its function in the sentence and the last component, the verb, ends in a suffix (i.e. ます) which indicates its tense and whether it is positive or negative. The time component always comes early in the sentence, either before or immediately after the topic depending on which you want to emphasize. When more details are added to a sentence they are usually placed after the topic and before the action. The resultant pattern is as follows:

| topic / actor は | time (に) | further details place *scene* | に | move(tense). *action* |

12.2 A visit to the Kamakura Daibutsu
かまくら の だいぶつ　　鎌倉の大仏

In the following story we build upon a basic sentence by adding details in the following way.

a) Tanaka is a かいしゃいん (kaishain) from **Kyushu** きゅうしゅう who is visiting a company in **Yokohama** よこはま. One of the people from the company in よこはま is going to take him to **Kamakura** かまくら to see the famous big Buddha statue. かまくら is not far from よこはま. It was once capital of Japan and has many old buildings and temples, but its most famous monument is the big bronze statue of the Amida Buddha which is referred to as the だいぶつ (daibutsu). It was cast in the 13th century and was originally housed inside a temple. Since the temple was destroyed in the 15th century it has stood outside. Watch how we can build up sentences about Tanaka's proposed visit to かまくら on Sunday. The word for "person" in にほんご is ひと (hito), which is written in かんじ as 人. We can introduce Tanaka たなか as follows:

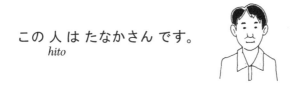

この 人 は たなかさん です。
　　hito

日よう日 に たなかさん は かまくら に いきます。
nichi　　*bi*

b) Now we intoduce another person, **Yoshida** (よしだ), who will go with Tanaka.

この 人 は よしださん です。
hito

日よう日 に たなかさん は よしださん と かまくら に いきます。
nichi   bi

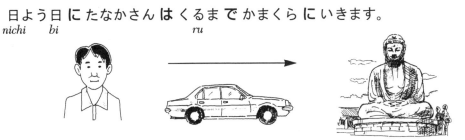

In this sentence we have introduced a person who is not the topic but who is added to the topic using the particle と.

c) Next we say by what means Tanaka is going to かまくら.

日よう日 に たなかさん は くるま で かまくら に いきます。
nichi   bi   *ru*

The particle で is used after the means of transportation.

d) Finally, we can combine all the information into one sentence.

日よう日 に たなかさん は よしださん と くるま で かまくら に いきます。
nichi   bi   *ru*

The structure of the previous sentences can be represented as follows.

> time に topic person は additional person と method で place に/へ verb ます/ました
> *time*　　 *topic*　　　　　*details*　　　　　　　　 *action*

However, the positions of the "time" element and the "topic" could also be switched:

topic person は　time に　additional person と　method で　place に　(or へ)　verb(tense).

12.3 Making questions　しつもんぶん を つくる　　質問文を作る

If someone wanted to ask a set of questions to find out all the information about Tanaka's proposed outing contained in the above sentence, they would have to ask about: the time, the destination, the person Tanaka is going with, and the means of getting there.
We already know how to ask some of these questions:

a) Asking about destination (place)　いきさきをく　行き先を聞く

The question word refering to place is どこ. This is combined with the particle に or へ.
たなかさん は どこ に いきますか。

b) Asking about time　じかん を きく　時間を聞く

We could do this two ways:

1. Ask the day of the week.
(たなかさん は) なんよう日 に かまくら に いきますか。
　　　　　　　　　 bi

2. Ask the more general question "when."
(たなかさん は) いつ かまくら に いきますか。

Usually the topic would be omitted since it was established in the first question, but when it is needed it is usually placed before the question about time.

c) Asking about the companion　だれ と いくか きく　だれと行くか聞く

The question word who is だれ (dare). This is combined with the particle と.
(たなかさん は 日よう日 に) だれ と (かまくら に) いきますか。
　　　　　 nichi　 *bi*　　　 *re*

Again, those parts of the question which are already known could be left out.

d) Asking about transport なん で いくか きく 何で行くか聞く

A くるま (kuruma) is a thing and the question word referring to things is なん. When combined with the particle で, the meaning becomes "what means" or "by what." In えいご "how" is often used with this meaning.

(たなかさん は 日よう日 に) なんで (かまくら に) いきますか。
nichi bi

12.4 Companions　　　どうこうしゃ　　　同行者

Here are some general ways you can refer to with whom you went. Look up the dictionary (じしょ) at the end of this text to find out the えいご.

ともだち chi	友達	_____
がっこう の ともだち chi	学校の友達	_____
かぞく zo	家族	_____
かいしゃ の ひと sha　　hi	会社の人	_____
おきゃくさん kya	お客さん	_____
かない	家内	_____
しゅじん shu	主人	_____
せんせい	先生	_____

If you went alone you say ひとり で hitori de (一人 で) which means "by myself."

■Practice 12.4　れんしゅう　　練習

Practice the words above with an あいて (aite) using the following かいわ (kaiwa).

A: だれ と いきましたか。
　　re
B: ともだち と いきました。
　　chi
A: ああ そう ですか。
　a　a　so

12.5 Transportation   こうつうきかん   交通機関

The following are the main forms of transport you will come across in にほん. Look up
the dictionary (じしょ) at the end of this text to find out the えいご.

くるま *ru*	車	_____
でんしゃ *sha*	電車	_____
ちかてつ *chi*	地下鉄	_____
しんかんせん	新幹線	_____
ひこうき *hi*	飛行機	_____
ふね *fu ne*	船	_____
フェリー *fe rii*	フェリー	_____
じてんしゃ *sha*	自転車	_____
タクシー *ta ku shii*	タクシー	_____
バス *ba su*	バス	_____

■Practice 12.5 れんしゅう   練習

With an あいて (aite) practice the above vocabulary using the following short かいわ.

A: なん で いきました か。

B: でんしゃ で いきました。
  sha

A: ああ そう です か。
  a a so

■**Conversation 12.5 かいわ　会話**

A trip to Kamakura

Person A is asking Tanaka about his trip to かまくら.

A: たなかさん、かまくら に いきましたか。

B: はい、<u>日よう日</u> に いきました。
　　　　 nichi　 *bi*

A: <u>一人</u> で いきましたか。
　 hitori

B: いいえ、<u>かいしゃ の 人</u> と いきました。
　　　　　　　 sha　　 *hito*

A: ああ そう ですか。だれ と いきましたか。
　 a a so　　　　　 *re*

B: <u>よしださん</u> と いきました。

A: <u>かいしゃ の くるま</u>で いきましたか。
　 sha　　　　 *ru*

B: はい、そう です。
　　　　 so

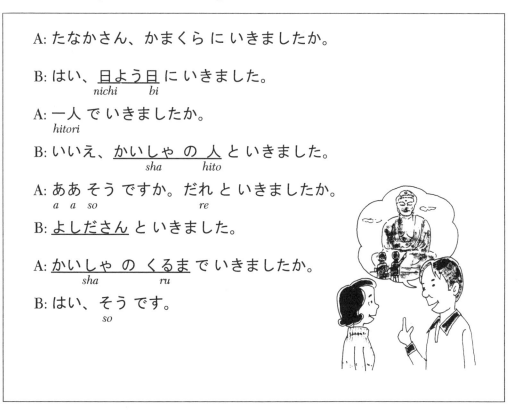

Practice by substituting the days, companions, and transport underlined.

12.6 Flower viewing　　はなみ　　花見

In はる haru (spring) in にほん it is almost mandatory to go and have a party beneath the cherry blossoms (さくら). Viewing the blossoms this way is called はなみ hanami. People usually go to parks in groups and sit together eating and drinking too much and often singing and dancing as well.

 ■**Conversation 12.6 かいわ　会話**

Flower viewing in Hakone

In the following かいわ Suzuki has already (もう) been to はなみ (hanami) and Tanaka is interested in finding out when, where, and with whom. Suzuki shows her some photos しゃしん (shashin). Listen to the tape and fill in the blanks.

たなか: いい _____ ですね。
　　　　　　　　　　ne

　　　　すずきさん は もう おはなみ に いきましたか。
　　　　　　　　　　　　　　　　　　mi

すずき: ええ、_____。

たなか: そう ですか。　_____ いきましたか。
　　　　so

すずき: せんしゅう の 土よう日 に いきました。
　　　　　　　shu　　　do　　bi

たなか: _____ に いきましたか。

すずき: はこね に いきました。
　　　　　　ne

たなか: _____ いきましたか。

すずき: ともだち の もりさん の くるま _____ いきました。
　　　　　　　　chi　　　　　　　　　　　ru

たなか: そうですか。
　　　　so

すずき: これは はなみ の しゃしん です。　(show photo)
　　　　　re　　　mi　　sha

たなか: もりさん は _____ 人 ですか。
　　　　　　　　　　　　　　　hito

すずき: ちがいます。もりさん は この おとこ の 人 です。
　　　　chi　　　　　　　　　　　　　　　　　　hito

たなか: ああ そう ですか。この 人たち は だれ ですか。
　　　　a　a　so　　　　　　　hito chi　　re

すずき: もりさん _____ かいしゃ _____ 人たち です。
　　　　　　　　　　　　　　　sha　　　　　　hito chi

Notes:

1. はこね Hakone 箱根 is the name of a mountainous region near the base of Mt. Fuji (ふじさん), a couple of hours from Tokyo. It is a popular area to visit and is renowned for its hot springs (おんせん), pleasant scenery, and lake.

2. もう is used like "already" or "yet" in えいご. For example:

(a) たなかさん は もう はこね に いきました。 Tanaka has already gone to Hakone.

(b) たなかさん は もう はこね に いきましたか。 Has Tanaka gone to Hakone yet?

In えいご "yet" is used in the question while "already" is used in the statement. In にほんご, もう is used in both cases.

3. ともだち の もりさん is the way you say "my friend Mori." ともだち describes who Mori is so it comes before the name and is joined to it by の.

4. おとこ means man. Its more polite from is おとこの人. The word for "woman" is おんな but you should use おんなの人 when referring to a woman.

5. ひとたち hitotachi 人達 is the plural form of 人 (hito). You should only use it when you need to be especially clear.

12.7 Notes on particles　　じょし　　助詞

1. と

(i) This particle attaches one noun to another so that both go together. It is a similar to "and" or "with" in えいご. For example:

A は B と にほん に いきました。	A went to Japan with B.
A と B は にほん に いきました。	A and B went to Japan.
たなかさん と よしださん は にほん人 です。 　　　　　　　　　　　　　　*jin*	Tanaka and Yoshida are Japanese.

(ii) It can also join two nouns in a contrast situation.

たなかさん の かいしゃ は よしださん の (かいしゃ) と ちがいます。
　　　　　　sha　　　　　　　　　　　*sha*　*chi*

Tanaka's company is different from Yoshida's (company).

2. で

This particle follows a means or method by which an action occurs. After transportation it is like the えいご "by" or "in." For example: くるま で いきます "go by car / go in a car." Otherwise it is like "on." For example, "went on a bicycle" じてんしゃ で いきました (jitensha de ikimashita).

In other cases it is like "with," as in "write with a pen" ペン で かきます (pen de kakimasu). As you can see, the English prepositions are not consistent in their meaning; "by," "in," "on," and "with" can all be used to denote method. In Japanese these words would all be replaced by で when a method is being indicated. Here are some illustrative (rei) れい.

Examples れい 例 ───────────────

1. くるま で ひろしま へ いきました。
   ru   *hi ro*

2. "train" は にほんご で なん ですか。

3. はなこさん は 一人 で いきました。
   hitori

12.8 Reading comprehension　　　どっかい　　読解

Aloha Tours アロハ ツアー

A tour guide, called Lisa (リサ), is telling a tour group about their schedule for the next few days in Hawaii.

みなさん、おはようございます。アロハ ツアー の ガイド の リサ です。
a ro ha tsu aa　　*ga i do*　*ri sa*

みなさん は きょう の ごご バス で ダイヤモンド・ヘッド と ハナウマ・ベイ
ba su　　*da i ya mo n do*　*he ddo*　*ha na u ma be i*

に いきます。よる の 7じ ごろ ホテル に かえります。あした ごぜん 8じに
ru　　　　*ro ho te ru*　　　　　　*a*

ホテル を でます。バス で ホノルル くうこう へ いきます。くうこう から ひこ
ho te ru　　　*ba su*　*ho no ru ru*　　　　　　　　　　　*hi*

うき で マウイとう へ いきます。9じはん ごろ つきます。バス でいろいろな
ma u i　　　　　　　　　　　　　　　　　　*ba su*　　*ro*　*ro*

かんこうち に いきます。あさって 5じ に マウイとう から ホノルル に かえり
chi　　　　　　　*a*　　　　*ma u i*　　　*ho no ru ru*

ます。6じはん ごろ この ホテル に つきます。よろしい ですか。
ro　　*ho te ru*　　　　　*ro*

では、2じ にこの ロビー に きてください。
ro bii

どうぞ よろしく おねがいします。
zo　*ro*　　　*ne*

1 いつ ダイヤモンド・ヘッド に いきます か。
  da i ya mondo   he ddo

2. こんばん なんじ に ホテル に かえります か。
  ho te ru

3. あした なんじ に ホテル を でます か。
  a   *ho te ru*

4. マウイとう に なんで いきます か。
  ma u i

5. あした バス で どこに いきますか。
  ba su

6. あさって なんじ に ホテル に つきますか。
  a   *ho te ru*

Notes:

1. アロハ ツアー (aroha tsuaa) is the name of the tour company "Aloha Tours."

2. みなさん "everybody." This is how you talk to a group of people. みな (皆) means "everyone."

3. よる の 7じ means 7 o'clock at night. よる (夜) means "night."

4. いろいろな (iroirona) means "various."

5. かんこうち (kankoochi) means "sight seeing spot." We came across かんこう in Lesson 5 in the word, かんこう あんない for "tourist information."

6. よろしい ですか。 is the polite form of いいですか。 "Is (that) OK?" Here it also has the implied meaning of "Any questions?"

7. ロビー (robii) refers to a hotel lobby.

8. どうぞ よろしく おねがいします。 This introduction phrase is said by guides after they have finished introducing the company, themselves, and the tour.

9. If you have been to Hawaii you should be able to guess the following place names:

ダイヤモンド・ヘッド	daiyamondo heddo
ハナウマ・ベイ	hanauma bei
ホノルル	honoruru
マウイとう	maui too (とう means "island")

■Practice 12.8　れんしゅう　練習

Think up a tour schedule and write your own introduction to the tour, as if you were a tour guide talking to a busload of にほんじん.

Answers　こたえ 答え
Conversation 12.6
てんき; いきました; いつ; どこ; なんで; で; この; の; の.

✏ Writing Japanese script 12.9

The next かんじ: 木 means "tree" or "wood." When written alone it is pronounced き but you have come across it in "Thursday" where it is pronounced もく, i.e. 木よう日.

木	一	十	才	木			

This fairly complex かんじ: 金 means "metal," "gold," or "money." Alone it is pronounced かね as in お金 (money). You have also seen it in "Friday" 金よう日 where it is pronounced きん. It is written with eight strokes.

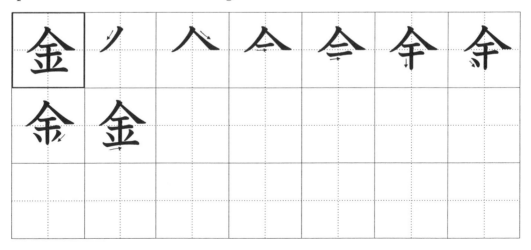

The next かんじ: 人 means "person" or "people." When written alone it is pronounced ひ
と, but in compounds it is pronounced じん. It also has some irregular pronunciations
such as 一人 (hitori). It is written with two strokes and in the handwritten form the left
stroke is longer.

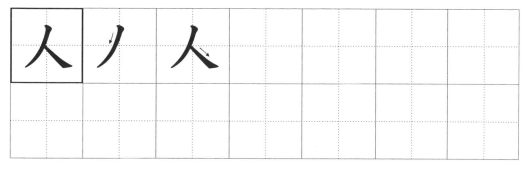

The next ひらがな is ya や. It is written in three strokes.

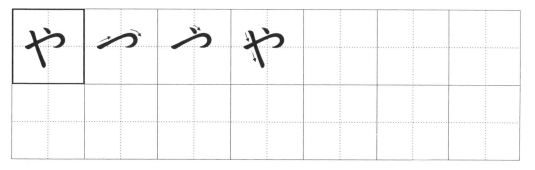

や can be combined with other **hiragana** to form combined syllables.
When combined with し it becomes **sha** しゃ, and with じ it becomes **ja** じゃ.

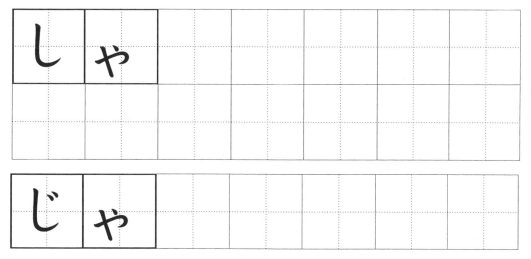

Try reading these combined syllables: きゃ, きょ, きょう, ひゃ, ひょ, ひょう, にゃ, にょ, にょ
う, and these words: びょういん, きょう, おきゃくさん, かいしゃ, とうきょう, てんじょう,
きょうしつ, きょうと, でんしゃ, ひしょ

1. Fill in the blanks with は, も, に, へ, の, と, or で. **If no particle is needed, put an X.**

1) きのう（　　）わたし は くるま（　　）デパート（　　）いきました。

　　　wa　　　　　　　ru　　　　　de paa to

2) この でんしゃ は 九じ（　　）とうきょうえき（　　）つきます。

3) もりさん は わたし（　　）がっこう（　　）ともだち です。

4) わたし（　　）じしょ は かとうさん の（　　）おなじ です。

2. Fill in the blanks with the appropriate question words and particles where needed.

1) A: あした は やすみ です ね。（　　　　　　　）へ いきます か。

　　　a　　　　　　mi　　　ne
　　B: はい、せんだい へ いきます。
　　A:（　　　　　　　）いきます か。
　　B: しんかんせん で いきます。

2) Q:（　　　　　　　）えいが へ いきました か。
　　A: もりさん と いきました。

3) Q: あの 人 は（　　　　　　　）です か。

　　A: はなこさん の えいご の せんせい です。

4) Q:（　　　　　　　）おおさか へ いきます か。
　　A: 六月 に いきます。

3. Translate the following sentences into にほんご.

1) Q: Has Ms. Katoo already gone to Kamakura?

_____

A: Yes, She went (to Kamakura) last Sunday.

2) I went to the airport by car alone.

_____

3) I am going to my friend's house with my wife tomorrow.

_____

4) This is a picture of my company.

_____

4. ✍ Let's write in Japanese!

1) Write the following words. Use かんじ for underlined part.

<u>もく</u>ようび (Thursday)

<u>きん</u>ようび (Friday)

2) How do you say the following words in Japanese? Write them in ひらがな.

a) company employee   b) train   c) telephone number

_____   _____   _____

d) tomorrow   e) cheap   f) expensive

_____   _____   _____

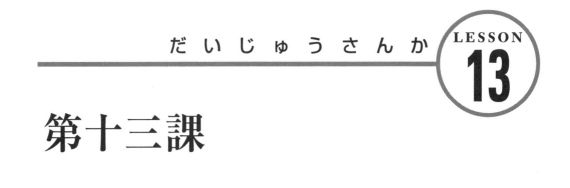

だ い じゅ う さ ん か

LESSON
13

第十三課

The ローマじ for くぐにおははばぱしじんいえほぼぽのてですずうとどこごよなかがつづきぎませぜもへべぺらさざをただりひびぴそぞね月一二三四五六七八九十千円日 is omitted.

13.1 Everyday actions

Here are a number of verbs that apply to everyday life.

たべます　　　のみます　　　かいます　　　つくります
　　　　　　　mi

みます　　　よみます　　　ききます　　　かきます
mi　　　　*mi*

These verbs are all verbs of action. They all refer to situations in which something does an action to another thing, e.g. "John ate a fish."

The thing which has the action done to it is, in grammatical terms, the "object" of the verb, while the thing that does the action is the "subject" of the verb. Therefore, "John" is the subject because he does the eating, and "fish" is the object because it is eaten. In えいご the subject and object are easily distinguished because the subject comes before the verb and the object comes after the verb.

John	ate a	fish.	Mary	writes	letters.	Bill	made	breakfast.
subject	*verb*	*object*	*subject*	*verb*	*object*	*subject*	*verb*	*object*

188

In にほんご the verb always comes at the end so the subject and object both precede the verb, e.g. John fish ate. Also, the subject is often omitted when understood, so the sentence becomes "fish ate." In such a sentence it is not clear whether the fish does the eating or whether it is what is eaten. Therefore, it is necessary in にほんご to use a particle after the object to distinguish it from the subject. This particle is を.

The にほんご pattern is:

John	は	fish	を	ate.	ジョンさん は さかな を たべました。
subject	は	*object*	を	*verb*	

The above pictures can all be described using this pattern:

ばんごはん を たべます。   ビール を のみます。
                                  bii ru   *mi*

ざっし を かいます。   りょうり を つくります。

テレビ を みます。   しんぶん を よみます。
te re bi *mi*   *bu*   *mi*

おんがく を ききます。   てがみ を かきます。
                                         mi

13.2 Transitive verbs   たどうし   他動詞

Only verbs of action can take an object. Such verbs are called transitive verbs. The subject/object relationship is not always as clear as in the above examples. The verb "do" (します) is a transitive verb which is used very frequently in にほんご in cases where another verb would be used in えいご. For example:

スポーツ を します。   play sport(s)   しごと を します。   work, do a job
su poo tsu

でんわ を します。   make a phone call   べんきょう を します。 (do) study
   wa

かいもの を します。   do shopping   カラオケ を します。   do (sing) karaoke
                                                     ka ra o ke

Note: カラオケ karaoke is singing to recorded music. It literally means "without orchestra."

13.3 Intransitive Verbs 　　じどうし　　自動詞

Verbs that cannot take an object are called intranstive verbs. Verbs of movement fall into this category. In going to a place nothing actually is done to the place and so the place can't be the object of the verb "go." The pattern in this case is:

place に move	日本 に いきます。
Or	*hon*
place へ move	日本 へ いきます。
	hon

Another common verb of movement is かえります which indicates movement to one's home, home town, or home country like the えいご go/come home, e.g.

たなかさん は 日本 に かえりました。　　　　　Tanaka went home to Japan.
　　　　　　hon

The verb "arrive" also falls in to this category:

でんしゃは 三じに おおさか に つきます。　　　The train arrives in Osaka at three.
　　sha

Two other common intransitive verbs are:

おきます　　　　　　　　　　　　　ねます

Although these actually refer to the actions of getting up out of bed and lying down in bed rather than to waking or going to sleep, these meanings are included in everyday usage.

Note: There are some intransitive verbs of movement which take the particle を after the place from which the movement begins. One of these is でる (deru), the verb "to go out" or "to exit." It takes the pattern: place を でます。

九じ に うち を でます。　　　　　I'll leave home at 9 o'clock.
　　　　chi

13.4 A usual day　　ふつう の 日　　普通 の 日

🔊 Yoshida is describing an ordinary (futsuu ふつう) day in her life (せいかつ).

これ は わたし の ふつう の 日 のせいかつ です。わたし は ふつう 七じ に おきます。
re　*wa*　　*fu*　　　　　　　　　　　　　　　*wa*　　　*fu*

そして あさごはん を たべます。八じ に うち を で ます。八じ四十ぷん に かいしゃ に
a　　　　　　　　　　*chi*　　　　　　　　　*pu*　　　*sha*

つきます。しごと は 九じ からです。十じはん にコーヒー を のみます。十二じはん に
　　　　　　　　　　　　　　　　　　　　　koo hii　　　*mi*

ひるごはん を たべます。五じ に かいしゃ を でます。六じごろ うち に つきます。
ru　　　　　　　　　　　　*sha*　　　　　　　　*ro*　*chi*

それから ばんごはん を つくります。七じごろ ばんごはん を たべます。七じはん から
　　　re

九じ まで テレビ をみます。それから 本 を よみます。または おんがく を ききます。
　　　　te re bi　*mi*　　　*re*　*hon*　*mi*

十一じはん ごろ ねます。
　　　　ro

Notes: Conjunctions　　せつぞくし　　接続詞
In the above monologue words which join sentences (conjunctions) have been used to improve the flow of speech and link the sentences. There are many conjunctions in にほんご but the following are the most common in conversation.

1. そして is used to join two sentences which are related to the same topic. It is rather like the えいご "and," "as well," or "and then," except that it is often used to start a sentence which follows on from the previous sentence.

きのう ぎんざ に いきました。そして えいが を みました。かとうさん は コーヒー
　　　　　　　　　　　　　　　　　　　mi　　　　　　　　　　*koo hii*
を のみました。そして もりさん は こうちゃ を のみました。
　mi　　　　　　　　　　　　*cha*　　*mi*

たなかさん は だいがく の きょうし です。そして すずきさん の えいご の せ
んせい です。

2. それから (sorekara) is used to join two sentences which occur sequentially in time or as part of a list. It is like the えいご "after that," "and then," "and also."

テニス を しました。それから ビール を のみました。
te ni su　　　　　　　　*re*　*bii ru*　*mi*

しんぶん を ください。それから この ざっし も ください。
　bu　　　　　　　　*re*

191

3. または is used to join two alternatives rather like the えいご "or." As well as starting a sentence, it can also join two nouns.

でんしゃ で いきます。 または バス で いきます。
　　　　sha　　　　　　　　　　*ba su*

でんしゃ、または バス で いきます。
　　　　sha　　　　*ba su*

五月、または 六月 に 日本 へ いきます。
　　　　　　　　　　　　　hon

 ■Practice 13.4　れんしゅう　　練習

Read the above passage aloud a few times. Then try writing a similar passage about your ふつう の 日 or the ふつう の 日 of another person. Instead of going to a かいしゃ you might go to a がっこう or a みせ (mise).

13.5 Doing things at a place

So far we have only come across places as destinations. We can say: "go to China" ちゅうごく に いきます (chuugoku ni ikimasu) or "go back (home) to England" イギリス に かえります (igirisu ni kaerimasu.)

However, places are also the settings for actions, in such cases we are not moving "to" a place but doing something "at," "in," or "on" a place. We therefore need to express this difference with a different particle after the place. This particle is で. For example, "eat lunch at a cafe" is:

きっさてん で ひるごはん を たべます。
　　　　　　　　ru

■Language pattern 13.5　ぶんけい　　文型

person	は	place	で	thing	を	do.

たなかさんは きっさてん で　ひるごはん を たべました。
　　　　　　　　　　　　　　　ru

わたし　　は ばいてん で　ざっし　　　を かいました。
wa

In this case, the particle で is like the えいご prepositions "at," "in," or "on."

Examples れい 例 ────────────────────

1. でんしゃ で しんぶん を よみます。
   　　sha　　　　*bu*　　*mi*
   (I) read the newspaper in the train.

2. あした ぎんざ で えいが を みます。
   　a　　　　　　　　　　*mi*
   (I'm) going to watch a movie in Ginza tomorrow.

3. やまださん は ビーチ で ねました。
   ya　　　　*bii chi*
   Yamada lay on the beach.

We can make two types of questions from this sentence pattern: What? and Where?

1. What: In this case, the question word "what" is not なん but なに. This form is used with various verbs. The なん version is used with です and in compounds such as なんじ, なんよう日, なん月.

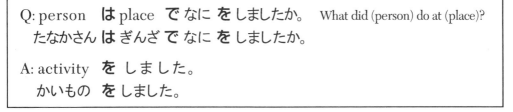

> Q: person **は** place **で** なに **を** しましたか。　What did (person) do at (place)?
> 　たなかさん **は ぎんざ で** なに **を** しましたか。
>
> A: activity **を** しました。
> 　かいもの **を** しました。

2. Where: This is どこ as we have previously seen.

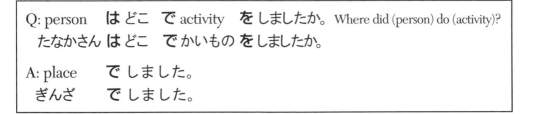

> Q: person 　**は どこ で** activity 　**を** しましたか。Where did (person) do (activity)?
> 　たなかさん **は どこ　で** かいもの **を** しましたか。
>
> A: place 　　　**で** しました。
> 　ぎんざ 　　　**で** しました。

Note: Time can be added to the above patterns quite simply as follows:
person は time (に) activity place (で) を しました。
たなかさん は 日よう日 に うちでべんきょう を しました。

■Conversation 13.5　かいわ　　会話

Shopping in Ginza

It is 月よう日 and Takako (T) is at the office telling a colleague (C) about her shopping trip to Ginza (ぎんざ).

> T: きのう きょうこさん と <u>ぎんざ</u> に いきました。
>
> C: ああ そう です か。<u>ぎんざ</u> で なに を しましたか。
> 　*a*　*a*　*so*

T: もちろん かいもの を しました。きょうこさん は <u>たかい ドレス</u> を かいましたよ。
   chiro   *do re su*

C: そう ですか。たかこさん は なに を かいましたか。

T: わたし は <u>くつ</u> を かいました。それから <u>ハンドバッグ</u> を かいました。
   wa   *re*   *ha n do baggu*

C: どこ で かいましたか。

T: <u>みつこし デパート</u> で かいました。
   mi   *de paa*   *to*

Practice this かいわ substituting the place, the companion, and what you bought.

Notes:

1. ドレス　dress　　　ハンドバッグ　handbag　　　くつ　靴　shoes
  do re su   *ha n do baggu*

2. もちろん (mochiron): means "of course" and is used to indicate that something should be obvious. Don't use it when the conclusion is not obvious as it can sound rude.

3. Ginza 銀座 used to be the section of the city where the silversmiths lived, and the place where coins were minted. This is the origin of the name that translates as "silver guild." In the late 19th century the area was rebuilt and soon become a fashionable shopping district.

■Practice 13.5　れんしゅう　　練習

Let's play a game! ゲームを しましょう！

This is a sentence making game that you can play in class, called 「いつ・だれが・だれ と・どこで・なに を しました」.

You know how to make the following components of sentences:

1	2	3	4	5
person は	time (に)	companion と	place で	activity を しました。

1. You each need a blank sheet of paper which you can cut into five equal strips.

2. On each strip you write a number from 1 to 5. On the back of each strip you write one of the components of a sentence as follows:

On strip no. 1, write **someone's name** は on the back. (Use famous people's names or names of people you know.) E.g. Elvis は, (classmate's name)は etc.

On strip no. 2, write a **time** (に) on the back. (Remember, some times take に and some don't.) E.g. 日よう日に, きのう, なつやすみに etc.

On strip no. 3, write a **companion**と on the back, e.g. せんせい と, (name)と etc.

On strip no. 4, write a **place**で on the back, e.g. がっこう で, えき で, (place name)で etc.

On strip no. 5, write an activity i.e. **activity** を **verb**ました。 There are many possibilities for this part, e.g. えいが を みました, ビール を のみました, かいもの を しました etc.

3. When each person has finished writing all the components of one sentence on five strips of paper, put all the strips into five envelopes according to the numbers. All the **person's name** は strips are in envelope 1, the **time** (に) are in envelope 2, etc.

4. Next, a student selects one paper from each envelope and puts them together to make a sentence. Read out the sentence to the rest of the class.

13.6 Frequency　　　　ひんど　　頻度

1. In your ふつう の 日 の せいかつ there are some things which you do more or less often and some things you seldom or never do. To express the frequency of an action we can use specific words such as "every day" or "every week."

まいにち chi	毎日	every day
まいあさ a	毎朝	_____
まいばん	毎晩	_____
まいしゅう shu	毎週	every week
まいしゅう 金よう日 shu kin	毎週金曜日	every Friday

Such expressions do not require the particle に unless combined with a day of the week.

わたし は まいあさ ジョギング を します。
wa　a　jo gi n gu

すずきさん は まいしゅう 土よう日 に テニス を します。
shu　do　te ni su

195

2. We can also use more relative terms such as "often" or "sometimes."

いつも			always
よく			often
ときどき	時々		sometimes
あまり *a*	余り	(plus negative)	not often, not much
ぜんぜん	全然	(plus negative)	never

The last two frequency adverbs require the verb to be in the negative, e.g.

やまだ さん は あまり おさけ を のみません。
ya   *a*   *ke*   *mi*

"Yamada doesn't often drink alcohol." or, "Yamada doesn't drink alcohol much."

■Practice 13.6　れんしゅう　練習

Questionnaire アンケート

You can find out how often a person does something by asking the question:

    Q:　name さん は よく activity を do か。

For example, たなか is asking さとう if she does much sport:

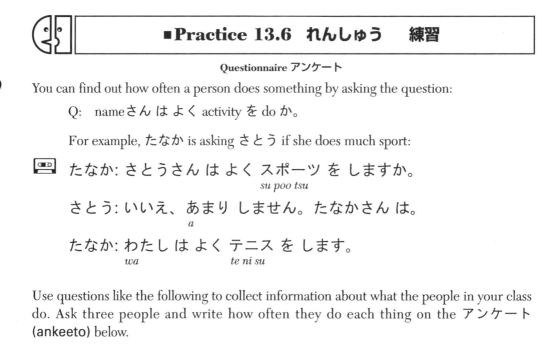

たなか: さとうさん は よく スポーツ を しますか。
                    su poo tsu

さとう: いいえ、あまり しません。たなかさん は。
               a

たなか: わたし は よく テニス を します。
      wa   *te ni su*

Use questions like the following to collect information about what the people in your class do. Ask three people and write how often they do each thing on the アンケート **(ankeeto)** below.

> Q:　name さん は よく テレビ を みますか。
>   *te re bi*   *mi*
> A:　はい、ときどき みます。
>   *mi*
> Or
> Q:　name さん は よく おさけ を のみますか。
>   *ke*   *mi*
> A:　いいえ、ぜんぜん のみません。
>   *mi*

なまえ	さん	さん	さん

personさん は frequency thing を do。

Q: たなかさん は よく りょうり を つくりますか。

A: はい、ときどき つくります。

Or

A: いいえ、あまり つくりません。

Note: These frequency adverbs can be placed in three places in a sentence:

1. もりさん は ときどき えいが を みます。

2. ときどき もりさん は えいが を みます。

3. もりさん は えいが を ときどき みます。

■Conversation 13.6　かいわ　　会話

Seeing movies えいが を みる 映画を見る

The kind of question you asked in the アンケート (ankeeto) is often used in conversation when you want to find out what kind of things the other person does so you can then have a topic for further conversation. Listen to the tape and fill in the blanks.

やまだ: もりさん は ＿＿＿＿ おんがく を ききますか。
ya

もり:　 おんがく ですか。あまり＿＿＿＿＿＿＿ね。でも、よく えいが を みます。
　　　　　　　　　　　　　a　　　　　　　　　　　　　　　　　　*mi*

やまだ: そう ですか。わたし も よく みます。ゴジラ を みましたか。
ya　　　　　　　　　　　　*wa*　　　　*mi*　　*go ji ra*　*mi*

もり:　 ＿＿＿＿ です。やまだ さん は。
　　　　　　　　　　　　ya

やまだ: ええ、＿＿＿＿ に みました。いい えいが ですよ。
ya　　　　　　　　　　*mi*

もり:　 そう ですか。＿＿＿＿ で みましたか。
　　　　　　　　　　　　　　mi

やまだ: ぎんざ シネマ です。
ya　　　*shi ne ma*

Notes:

でも means "but." There are a number of versions of "but" in にほんご. This one is used to start sentences.

いい is "good," so いい えいが means "good movie."

Practice this かいわ with an あいて substituting your names and the movie name.

13.7 もう and まだ

まだ means "not yet" and is actually the opposite of もう (already, yet). まだ is often used in negative replies with, or instead of いいえ, since it has less of a final feeling. It suggests that there is still a possibility that you might do it in the future.

> Q: もう ひるごはん を たべましたか。　Q: Have you eaten lunch yet?
> 　　　　　　　　 ru
> A: いいえ、まだ です。　　　　　　　A: No, not yet.

13.8 Verbs　　どうし　動詞

So far we have come across a number of verbs of movement such as いく, くる, かえる. We have seen these in the sentence pattern: PLACE に いきます。
In this lesson we also learned a number of transitive and intransitive verbs. Here are the verbs you have done so far in both their ます and dictionary forms, and in かんじ. Write the えいご in the blanks.

たべます	たべる	食べる	_____
ねます	ねる	寝る	_____
でます	でる	出る	_____
みます	みる	見る	_____
おきます	おきる	起きる	_____
いきます	いく	行く	_____
つきます	つく	着く	_____
ききます	きく	聞く	_____
かきます	かく	書く	_____

かえります	かえる	帰る	_____
つくります	つくる	作る	_____
のみます	のむ	飲む	_____
よみます	よむ	読む	_____
かいます	かう	買う	_____
きます	くる	来る	_____
します	する		_____

Answers こたえ 答え

Conversation 13.6
よく; ききません; まだ; 日よう日; どこ.

Writing Japanese script 13.9

We finish the days of the week with "Saturday" 土よう日, written with the かんじ for "earth" 土. In this case it is pronounced ど.

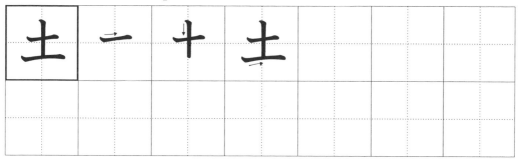

You have seen this かんじ in the name of the country 日本. In this name it has the root meaning of "origin" but we just think of it as a name. The same かんじ also means "book," again it is pronounced ほん and written 本. It is written in five strokes. Be careful not to confuse it with 木.

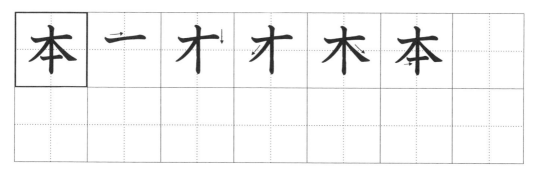

The next ひらがな is mi み. It is written in two strokes.

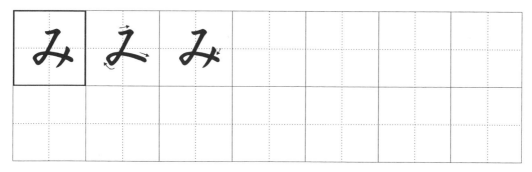

In their dictionary form many verbs end in **ru** る. It is written in one stroke. When typing it into some word processors "lu" can also be used.

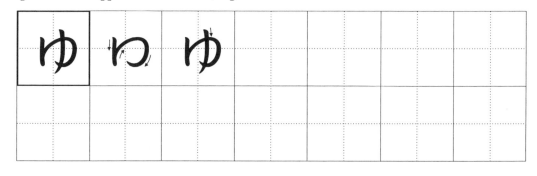

The next ひらがな **yu** ゆ is the last of the three which are used in combined syllables. These are や, ゆ, and よ. This character is written in two strokes in handwriting but in print it often appears as one stroke, e.g. ゆ.

Try reading the following combined syllables: きゅ, きゅう, にゅ, にゅう, みゅ, み ゅう, ぎゅ, ぎゅう, ひゅ, ひゅう, りゅ, りゅう, しゅ, しゅう, びゅ, びゅう, じゅ, じゅう, ぴゅ, ぴゅう,

1. Much up the words with suitable endings by joinining them with a line.

えいが		ききます
ビール *bii　ru*		たべます
おんがく		よみます
ごはん	を	みます
しんぶん *bu*		のみます
かいもの		かいます
くつ		します

2. Fill in the blanks with the appropriate particles. If no particle is needed, put an X.

1) さとうさん は いつも（　）7じ（　）おきます。

2) きのう すずきさん は ともださん（　）としょかん（　）べんきょう
　（　）しました。

3) いつも 8じ（　）うち（　）でます。そして でんしゃ（　）がっこう
　（　）いきます。

4) どこ（　）その ほん（　）かいましたか。

5) よく（　）きっさてん（　）あさごはん（　）たべますか。
　　　　　　　　　　　a

3. Look at the example and make sentences using the given words. Use negative or affirmative, past or present endings on the verbs as appropriate.

Ex.さとうさん きのう すし たべます → さとうさん は きのう すし **を** たべました。

1) もりさん　ときどき　きっさてん　てがみ　かきます →
         mi

_____

2) かない　あまり　りょうり　つくります →
   a

_____

3) たなかさん　せんしゅう　の 日よう日　ぎんざ　かいもの　します →

_____

4) わたし　まいにち　五じごろ　ともだち　テニス　します →
   wa   chi   ro   chi   te ni su

_____

4. Translate the following sentences into にほんご.

1) I never drink tea.

_____

2) I read a book. After that, I went to bed around 11 p.m.

_____

3) On Saturdays Mr. Ueno often plays tennis. Otherwise (or) (he) plays golf.

_____

4) This morning I didn't eat breakfast.

_____

5) Q: Did Ms. Tanaka go home already?

_____

   A: No, not yet.

_____

5. Answer the following questions about yourself in Japanese.

1) よく えいが を みますか。

   _____

2) きのう べんきょう を しましたか。

   _____

3) こんばん なんじごろ ねますか。

   _____

6. ✍ Let's write in Japanese!

Write the following words using かんじ.Write underlined part in ひらがな.

にほんじん (Japanese people)　_____

にほんえん (Japanese yen)　_____

ど<u>よう</u>び (Saturday)　_____

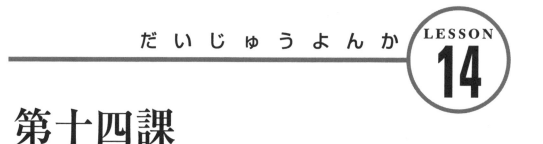

だ い じ ゅ う よ ん か

LESSON
14

第十四課

In this lesson the ローマじ has been removed for the following characters: くぐにおはばぱ しじんいえほぼぽのてですずうとどこごよなかがつづっきぎませぜもへべぺらさざをただりひ びぴそぞねあわれ月一二三四五六七八九十千円日火水.

14.1 Counting people　ひとをかぞえる　人を数える

In 日本ご (にほんご) we count people by adding the suffix にん (人) to the number, e.g. 六にん. This is like saying "six people" since にん has the meaning of "person" or "people." However, the first two numbers in this system don't conform to this pattern in their pronunciation even though the かんじ are written as you would expect.

ひとり	一人	しちにん *chi*	七人
ふたり *fu*	二人	はちにん *chi*	八人
さんにん	三人	きゅうにん *kyu*	九人
よにん	四人	じゅうにん *ju*	十人
ごにん	五人	じゅういちにん *ju* *chi*	十一人
ろくにん *ro*	六人		

To ask "how many people" just add にん (人) to the question word なん to get:

なんにん　　　なん人　　　　　How many people?

206

14.2 Counting large numbers

We have already learned that large numbers are counted in units of ten thousand まん but this can be a little difficult to get used to.

	10,000	いちまん *chi*	一万
	10,0000	じゅうまん *ju*	十万
	100,0000	ひゃくまん *hya*	百万
	1000,0000	いっせんまん	一千万
	1,0000,0000	いちおく *chi*	一億
	10,0000,0000	じゅうおく *ju*	十億
	100,0000,0000	ひゃくおく *hya*	百億

■Practice 14.2　れんしゅう　　練習

Try reading the following numbers.

1,2000	745,0000	1,5000,0000
25,0000	1200,0000	2,6500,0000
98,0000	8000,0000	12,2000,0000
600,0000	5250,0000	3,0500,0000

14.3 Population 　　じんこう　人口

We need large numbers like this when talking about population じんこう (人口) (the か
んじ literally mean "human mouths").

The じんこう of 日本 (にほん) is concentrated on the Pacific coast (たいへいようがわ)
with 40% in the cities of Tokyo, Yokohama, Osaka, and Nagoya. Tokyo is the largest city
with about 8.2 million in the city proper, and about 12 million including the surrounding
urban areas.

To ask the 人口 of 日本 we say:

Q: 日本 の 人口 は なん人 ですか。　　Q: What is Japan's population?
　　hon　 jin koo　　　　nin

A: やく いちおく 二千まん人 です。　　A: It is approximately 12 million
　 ya　　　chi　　　　　　nin　　　　　　 people.

Note: やく yaku 約: means "approximately." It precedes a number but can"t be used
with a time.

■**Practice 14.3　れんしゅう　　練習**

Here are some places and じんこう (人口). Practice the above question with your あい
て to complete the following tables. (Sheet B is at the end of this lesson)

Sheet A

オーストラリア oo　 su to ra ri a	1800,0000	日本	＿＿＿＿＿
ニュージーランド nyuu　jii　ra n do	＿＿＿＿＿	アメリカ a me ri ka	2,4880,0000
カナダ ka na da	2660,0000	イギリス i gi ri su	＿＿＿＿＿
ロンドン ro n do n	＿＿＿＿＿	とうきょう（東京）　820,0000	
ニューヨーク nyuu　yo o ku	730,0000	シドニー shi do nii	＿＿＿＿＿
バンクーバー ba n kuu　baa	＿＿＿＿＿	オークランド oo　ku ra n do	15,0000
きょうと（京都）	142,0000	おおさか（大阪）	＿＿＿＿＿

LESSON 14 第十四課

208

14.4 Family　　かぞく　　家族

People will often ask how many people are in your family. When counting them you include yourself. **Katoo** (かとう) is talking to Smith (スミス).

かとう: スミスさん の かぞく は なん人 です か。
　　　　su mi su　　　　　　　　　　　　*nin*

スミス: 五人 です。
　　　su mi su　　*nin*

Practice asking the others in your class how many people are in their family.

14.5 One's own family and another's family

In 日本ご different words are used when referring to one's own family, to those used when referring to another's family. For example, I refer to "my mother" as はは but to another person's mother as おかあさん. Also, there are different words for brothers and sisters who are older or younger than oneself.

One's own family　じぶん の かぞく　自分の家族

はは	母	one's own mother
ちち *chi chi*	父	one's own father
あね	姉	one's own big sister
あに	兄	one's own big brother
いもうと	妹	one's own little sister
おとうと	弟	one's own little brother

Another's family　ほかのひと の かぞく　他の人の家族

おかあさん゜	お母さん	another's mother
おとうさん゜	お父さん	another's father
おねえさん゜	お姉さん	another's elder sister

おにいさん°	お兄さん	another's elder brother
いもうとさん	妹さん	another's younger sister
おとうとさん	弟さん	another's younger brother

° these words are also used as forms of address when talking to one's own mother, etc. For example, when you talk to your mother you call her おかあさん, (or some contraction of this, e.g. かあさん). This is like "Mom" in えいご. When you talk about your mother to non-family members you use はは. This is like "My mother" in えいご.

14.6 Brothers and sisters　きょうだい　兄弟

In 日本ご one word covers both brothers and sisters, this is きょうだい. This is how you ask if someone has any brothers and sisters.

---

1. Q: たなかさん は きょうだい が いますか。
   A: はい、あに が います。

2. Q: すずきさん は きょうだい が いますか。
   A: いいえ、いません。

■Conversation 14.6　かいわ　　会話

Asking about brothers and sisters

You (A) are asking Mori (B) about her brothers and sisters. In giving the number of きょうだい she doesn't count herself.

A: もりさん は きょうだい が いますか。

B: はい、二人 います。あに が 一人 と いもうと が 一人 います。
　　　fu ta ri　　　　　*hi to ri*　　　　　*hi to ri*

Practice this かいわ by substituting the numbers and きょうだい. If you are an only child you would simply answer、いいえ、いません.

Topic person は family member が います。

わたし　　　は あに　　　　　が います。　　I have a big brother.

すずきさん は きょうだい　　が いません。　Suzuki doesn't have any brothers or sisters.

When a number is added it goes directly before います.

Topic person は family member が number います。

わたし は あに が 二人 います。

1. This pattern is used to refer to the existence of people (or animals). The verb います (いる in its dictionary form) is rather difficult to translate. It means "exist," but in conversation is used rather like "have" or "there is." For example, if I looked through the classroom window and could see Suzuki, I could say to my friend すずきさん が います。to inform them "Suzuki's there." or "There's Suzuki."

2. The particle が is used after the subject of the verb いる, i.e. after the person or people who are there. Its function is to mark the subject of the subsequent verb. The usage of が is somewhat complex so for the moment just learn the above pattern.

3. When referring to family members the verb ある (aru) is often used instead of いる. (see Lesson 16) However, popular usage seems to favour いる.

14.7 Asking how many people are there

There are many situations in which we want to ask how many people are at a particular place. We may wish, for example, to ask how many people were at a party, in a class, or in meeting. The question to use is:

Q: クラス に なん人 いましたか。　　Q: How many people were in class?
　　ku ra su　　　　*nin*

A: 十五人 いました。　　　　　　　　A: There were fifteen.
　　nin

After the place the particle に is used. This is like "in" or "at."

We can divide people according to gender into:

おんな の ひと　　女の人　　woman / women / female(s)
おとこ の ひと　　男の人　　man / men / male(s)

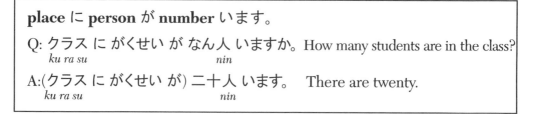

■Language pattern 14.7　ぶんけい　　文型

place　に　person　が います。

あそこ に おんなの人 が います。　　There is woman over there.

When a number is added it is placed just before います. The same goes for the question word which refers to numbers of people, i.e. なん人.

place に person が number います。

Q: クラス に がくせい が なん人 いますか。How many students are in the class?
　　ku ra su　　　　　　　　　　　*nin*

A:(クラス に がくせい が) 二十人 います。　There are twenty.
　　ku ra su　　　　　　　　　　　*nin*

■Conversation 14.7　かいわ　　会話

Asking about clients

A tsuaa koodineetaa ツアー コーディネーター (コ) is talking to a tsuaa gaido ツアー ガイド (ガ) about how many clients (okyakusan おきゃくさん) they have.

コ: あしたの<u>ツアー</u> に <u>おきゃくさん</u> が なん人 いますか。
　　　　　tsu aa　　　　　　　　　　　　*nin*

ガ: <u>二十六人</u> います。 おんな の 人 が <u>十七人</u> と おとこ の 人 が <u>九人</u> います。
　　　nin　　　　　　　　　　*hito*　　*nin*　　　　　*hito*　　*nin*

コ: ああ そう ですか。

Note: We can include the number of women and the number of men in two sentences or in the same sentence in the following ways:

We could write two separate sentences and join them with そして:
おんなの人 が 十七人 います。そして、おとこの人 が 九人 います。

Alternatively, we could make a single sentence using と:
おんなの人 が 十七人 と おとこの人 が 九人 います。

■Practice 14.7　れんしゅう　　練習

Practice the above かいわ by substituting the following word pairs for the underlined parts and also by varying the number of people.

LESSON 14 第十四課

212

📼 かいしゃ/しゃいん 　　　　*sha　sha*	会社／社員
びょういん / いしゃ 　　　　　*sha*	病院／医者
おみせ / てんいん	お店／店員
がっこう/きょうし	学校／教師
ホテル / じゅうぎょういん *ho te ru　ju　　gyo*	ホテル／従業員

Notes:

1. しゃいん is a staff member of a company.
2. びょういん is a hospital.
3. じゅうぎょういん is a general term for employees of companies, shops, agencies, and many other organizations. This term is not used for schools or government offices.

14.8 おみやげ　　お土産

When you go to visit someone in 日本 it is proper to bring a present. Such presents are called **omiyage** おみやげ. 日本人 often give おみやげ (omiyage) when visiting someone and when returning from a trip. People spend considerable time selecting appropriate presents which both please the receiver and characterize the place from where they were bought. In 日本 each region has a variety of characteristic gift items みやげもの (miyagemono) which visitors feel obliged to buy and take home as おみやげ. Typical items are foods, handcrafts, pottery, cloth, and liquor. If you don't know the people well, the best approach is to stick to local products which are consumable or usable, and not easily obtained in 日本. Alternatively, you can find out your host's interests or hobbies (しゅみ shumi) as a guide to what kind of おみやげ to look for. When you give someone おみやげ they will seldom open it immediately, they may thank you for it and then put it somewhere without unwrapping it. In 日本 it is not customary to open a present in front of the person who gave it to you. This is because the receiver doesn't want to upset the giver by being less than thrilled in the event that the present is nothing like they had expected. This type of consideration is quite common in interpersonal relations in 日本, especially in formal situations. The more familiar the relationship, the less such niceties are observed.

14.9 Hobbies   しゅみ   趣味

To ask another person's しゅみ (shumi) you could use the following question in either its complete or incomplete form.

> 🔲 Q: ごしゅみ は (なん ですか)。　Q: What is your hobby?
>   *shu mi*
>
>   A: きってあつめ です。　　　　A: It's stamp collecting.
>   *me*

Note: When referring to another's しゅみ the honorific prefix ご can be attached to make ごしゅみ. This prefix is just like the prefix お which you have already encountered.

In 日本ご the word しゅみ includes not only hobbies but sports (スポーツ **supootsu**) and other interests. The most popular sports are baseball, golf, soccer, and tennis. However, many people learn one of the traditional martial arts and traditional wrestling (すもう) is a popular spectator sport.

Here is a list of typical しゅみ. Find the えいご by looking up the じしょ in the back of this textbook.

🔲 ゴルフ
　 go ru fu　　　　　　　　　　　　_____

　 テニス
　 te ni su　　　　　　　　　　　　_____

　 サッカー
　 sa k kaa　　　　　　　　　　　　_____

　 ラグビー
　 ra gu bii　　　　　　　　　　　　_____

　 ハイキング
　 ha i ki n gu　　　　　　　　　　_____

　 サーフィン
　 saa fi n　　　　　　　　　　　　_____

　 やきゅう　　　　　野球
　 ya kyu　　　　　　　　　　　　　_____

　 すいえい　　　　　水泳　　　　　　_____

　 からて　　　　　　空手　　　　　　_____

じゅうどう	柔道	_____
あいきどう	合気道	_____
すもう	相撲	_____
ダンス *da n su*		_____
カラオケ *ka ra o ke*	空オケ	_____
りょうり	料理	_____
りょこう	旅行	_____
しゃしん *sha*	写真	_____
どくしょ	読書	_____
つり	釣	_____
おんがく	音楽	_____
えいがかんしょう	映画観賞	_____
きってあつめ *me*	切手集め	_____

 ■Conversation 14.9　かいわ　会話

You (A) have been invited to visit Yamaguchi's place to stay for a few days so you are considering what to do about おみやげ.

A: <u>やまぐち</u>さん は きょうだい が いますか。
　　ya　　*chi*

Y: はい、<u>あね</u> と <u>おとうと</u> が います。

A: おねえさん の しゅみ は なん ですか。
            shu mi

Y: しゃしん です。
   sha

A: おとうとさん の しゅみ は。
             shu mi

Y: どくしょ です。

Practice the かいわ substituting family members and しゅみ.

14.10 Spouse and children

Different terms are used to refer to one's own and to another's spouse and children.

かない	家内	one's own wife
しゅじん *shu*	主人	one's own husband
こども	子供	one's own children
むすめ *mu me*	娘	one's own daughter
むすこ *mu*	息子	one's own son
おくさん	奥さん	another's wife
ごしゅじん *shu*	ご主人	another's husband
おこさん	お子さん	another's child(ren)
むすめさん *mu me*	娘さん	another's daughter
むすこさん *mu*	息子さん	another's son

LESSON
14
第十四課

It is not usual to ask someone you have just met whether they are married or not. However, it is not overly rude to ask a person whom you know whether they are single どくしん (独身) or not. Since this is a personal question, it is best to begin with the phrase:

しつれい です が   It's rude (of me) but…

This phrase is often used to introduce a personal question. しつれい means "rude" or "impolite" while the が is a conjunction rather like "but" in えいご.

■Conversation 14.10　かいわ　会話

Do you have any children? おこさん が いますか

You (A) have met Yamada a few times in a business setting but this time you'd like to find out some more personal information.

> A: しつれい です が、やまださん は どくしん ですか。
>   　　　　　　　　　　 _ya_
>
> Y: いいえ、ちがいます。
>   　　　　 _chi_
>
> A: おこさん が いますか。
>
> Y: はい、むすめ が ふたり います。
>   　　　_mu me_　　_fu_

Practice this かいわ with an あいて substituting the underlined parts.

14.11 Asking a person's address　じゅうしょ を きく　住所を聞く

The pattern for asking this common question is just like one we met in Lesson 4.

> Q: じゅうしょ は どこ ですか。　　Q: What is your address?
> A: かながわけん の よこはま です。　A: It's in Yokohama in Kanagawa prefecture.

Remember to use "where" どこ when asking someone's address.

■Conversation 14.11　かいわ　会話

My friend's address

Linda (R) has a penfriend ペンフレンド (penfurendo) called Yoshida who lives in 日本 and Ishida (I) is asking where Yoshida lives. (Note the use of the hesitation: ええと.)

I: リンダさん、日本 に ともだち が いますか。
ri n da　　*hon*　　*chi*

R: はい、<u>かながわ けん</u> に ペンフレンド が います。
ke　　*pe n fu re n do*

I: <u>かながわ けん</u> の どこ ですか。
ke

R: ええと、(looks in address book) <u>よしだ</u>さん の じゅうしょ は これ です。
ju

I: ああ、<u>よこはま</u> ですか。わたし の あね も <u>よこはま</u> に いますよ。

R: ああ そう ですか。

14.12 Japanese addresses　にほん の じゅうしょ　日本住所

When you look at a Japanese address じゅうしょ (juusho) you will notice that the number of the house comes last. When writing a じゅうしょ you first write the largest region and then the smaller divisions, until you narrow it down to the house number. This is probably just the opposite to the type of address you are used to. Another difference is the absence of street names in 日本 の じゅうしょ. Each house has a lot number in an area, rather than a street number. This is similar to the way agricultural land is classified. To understand the way 日本 の じゅうしょ work we need to look at how the country is divided up.

1. The whole country is divided into forty-seven administative districts. There is the capital, とうきょうと (東京都); the two big city regions of おおさかふ (大阪府) and きょうとふ (京都府); all of the northern island ほっかいどう (北海道); and forty-three けん (prefectures) 四十三県.

2. Each of these is again divided into city and town regions called し (市) or into suburban regions called く (区), each of which has a name, e.g. みなとく (港区), かわさきし (川崎市).

3. The next subdivision is the local area name or suburb name.

4. In the city, each suburb is divided into large divisions called ちょうめ (choome) 丁目 which have numbers, e.g. にちょうめ (二丁目). The ちょうめ are further divided into ばんち (banchi) (番地) which are also numbered. The ばんち are again divided into ごう (号) which are the individual blocks of land.

5. There is also a zip code ゆうびん ばんごう (yuubin bangoo) (郵便番号).

The address of a person who lives in the Tokyo suburb of あかさか (赤坂) might be:

107
東京都 港区 赤坂 8-5-3
大木 ようこ様

First is the ゆうびん ばんごう (zip code). Next comes the address: とうきょうと みな とく あかさか 8–5–3, which shows they live on block 3 of ばんち number 5, of number 8 ちょうめ (choome), of the suburb of あかさか, which is in みなとく (minatoku) division of Tokyo city (とうきょうと). Last comes the person's name おおき ようこ which is followed by the polite version of さん, the title さま (様).

The address can also be written vertically as on the following postcard (はがき):

あかさかのちず

The Administrative Districts of the Main Islands
The following are a few of the 47 districts.

ほっかいどう

いわてけん

きょうとふ

ひろしまけん

とうきょうと

かながわけん

おおさかふ

かごしまけん

14.3 Sheet B

オーストラリア *oo su to ra ri a*	_____	日本	1,2360,0000
ニュージーランド *nyuu jii ra n do*	331,0000	アメリカ *a me ri ka*	_____
カナダ *ka na da*	_____	イギリス *i gi ri su*	5720,0000
ロンドン *ro n do n*	677,0000	とうきょう（東京）	_____
ニューヨーク *nyuu yo o ku*	_____	シドニー *shi do nii*	339,0000
バンクーバー *ba n kuu baa*	137,0000	オークランド *o o ku ra n do*	_____
きょうと（京都）	_____	おおさか（大阪）	255,0000

Writing Japanese script 14.13

This next かんじ: 口 means "mouth" or "entrance." When written alone it is pronounced くち. In compounds it is こう as in 人口 (じんこう) "population."

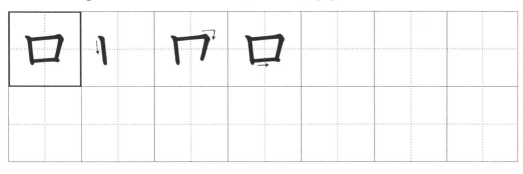

The next ひらがな is chi ち. With てんてん it becomes "ji" but this ぢ is seldom used, usually じ is used for "ji." Be careful not to confuse ち with さ. This completes the fourth line of the ひらがな chart: た、ち、つ、て、と. When using a word processor you can also type this in as "ti."

The next ひらがな is pronounced ke け. You can now write the second line of the ひらがな chart: か、き、く、け、こ. With てんてん, its pronunciation changes to ge げ.

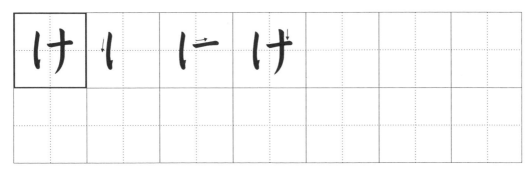

げ

With this next ひらがな, written ふ in three strokes and pronounced hu or fu, you are able to write the sixth line of the ひらがな chart thus: は、ひ、ふ、へ、ほ. When てんてん is added, it becomes bu ぶ and with まる it is pu ぷ.

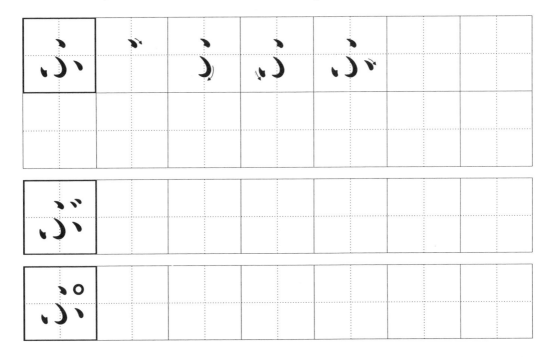

Try reading these words:

ふつう	げんき	ちがいます	まち	ともだち	かいぎ
ちかてつ	ふゆ	けいさつ	つけもの	けさ	ふたつ

HOMEWORK 14 しゅくだい　宿題

1. Read the following aloud in Japanese.

15000　　　　370000　　　　4800000

50000000　　700000000　　82000000000

2. Fill in the blanks with の, は, が, と, に, も **or** で**. If no particle is needed, put an X.**

1) すずき: さとうさん（　　）きょうだい（　　）いますか。
　 さとう: はい。あに（　　）一人（　　）いもうと（　　）二人います。

2) あそこ（　　）がくせい（　　）十人（　　）います。

3) わたし は よこはま（　　）すんでいます。あね（　　）よこはま（　　）
　 すんでいます。

3. Answer the following questions about yourself in 日本ご**.**

1) どこ に すんでいますか。

_____

2) くに の 人口 は なん人 ですか。

_____

3) かぞく は なん人 ですか。

_____

4) しゅみ は なん ですか。

_____

4. Translate the following sentences into 日本ご**.**

1) There are seven clients on this tour.

_____

2) Japan's population is approximately 12 million people.

_____

3) Excuse me, but are you single?

_____

223

4) My father is a company employee.

_____

5) Ms Suzuki's father lives in Osaka.

_____

5. Complete the chart.

わたし の	はは		しゅじん	こども	
おのさん の	おかあさん	おくさん			おねえさん

6. Let's write in Japanese!

How do you say the following words in 日本ご. Write 1) to 5) in ひらがな and 6) in かんじ.

1) family

2) friend

3) gift (when visiting or returning from a trip)

4) address

5) hobby

6) population

だ い じゅ う ご か **LESSON 15**

第十五課

In this lesson the ローマ じ has been removed for the following characters: くぐにおはばぱしじん いえほぼぽのてですずうとどこごよなかがつづきぎませせぜもへべぺらさざをただりひびぴそぞね あわれや月一二三四五六七八九十千円日火水木金人.

15.1 Counting objects もの を かぞえる 物を数える

日本ご uses more than just numbers for counting things. The method depends on what you happen to be counting. We have already learned how to count people. Now we will learn the most general counting system for objects. This system uses ancient Japanese numbers (rather than adopted Chinese numbers) to which the suffix つ is added.

ひとつ	一つ	むっつ *mu*	六つ
ふたつ *fu*	二つ	ななつ	七つ
みっつ *mi*	三つ	やっつ	八つ
よっつ	四つ	ここのつ	九つ
いつつ	五つ	とお	十

This method is used for many objects especially for prepared food and for objects of ill-defined shape. It is only used for the numbers 1 through 10. The question word (how many) relating to this system is いくつ.

225

■Practice 15.1　れんしゅう　練習

With your あいて practice the numbers by pointing at the かんじ on the chart and asking:

> Q: いくつ ですか。
> A: ふたつ です。
>   *fu*

15.2 Fruit　くだもの　果物

Here are some types of fruit which are commonly available in fruit shops（くだものや）in 日本.

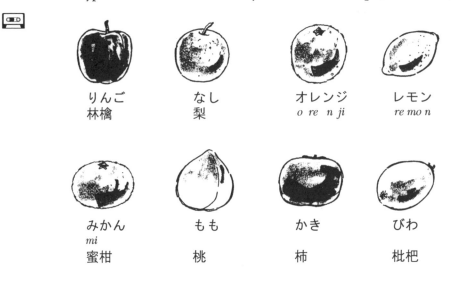

りんご	なし	オレンジ	レモン
林檎	梨	*o re n ji*	*re mo n*
みかん	もも	かき	びわ
mi			
蜜柑	桃	柿	枇杷

■Conversation 15.2　かいわ　　会話

At the fruit shop　くだものやで　果物屋で

There are many small くだものや where you can buy just how many pieces of fruit you want. Note how the てんいん confirms your order in かいわ A and how she clarifies it in かいわ B.

> **かいわ A**
> てんいん:　　いらっしゃいませ。
> きゃく:　　　りんご を 五つ ください。
> てんいん:　　はい、りんご を 五つ ですね。
> きゃく:　　　ええ。

226

```
かいわ B
てんいん：    いらっしゃいませ。
きゃく：      かき を 七つ と なし を 六つ ください。
てんいん：    すみません、かき を いくつ ですか。
きゃく：      七つ です。
てんいん：    かき を 七つ と なし を 六つ ですね。
きゃく：      はい、そうです。
```

Practice the above かいわ by substituting the names of くだもの and the numbers.

📖 ■**Language pattern 15.2 ぶんけい 文型**

thing を number ください。
りんご を 二つ ください。　　　　Two apples please.

15.3 Counting objects of various shapes

In えいご we often count objects by the containers in which they come. For example, we say two bottles of beer and four packets of chips. We also count things by their shape, e.g. two sheets of paper, three sticks of celery, a bunch of flowers. Some types of animals are are counted by their groupings such as, flocks of sheep, schools of fish, and herds of cattle. Animals can also be counted individually by the head, e.g. twenty head of cattle. In 日本ご objects are counted in a similar way, i.e. by shape, container, or type. There are a number of words used in counting in 日本ご, but for the moment we will just learn two common ones:

15.3.1 まい (枚)

This is used for flat things such as postage stamps, sheets of paper, photos, records, CDs, shirts, handkerchieves, biscuits, plates, shirts, but not for books.

📼	いちまい *chi*	一枚	ななまい	七枚
	にまい	二枚	はちまい *chi*	八枚

さんまい	三枚	きゅうまい *kyu*	九枚
よんまい	四枚	じゅうまい *ju*	十枚
ごまい	五枚	じゅういちまい *ju* *chi*	十一枚
ろくまい *ro*	六枚	じゅうにまい *ju*	十二枚

The counter まい is simply attached to the number.
The question word is:　なんまい　　(how many?)　何枚

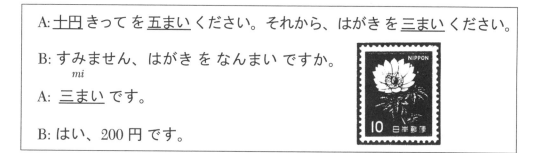

■Conversation 15.3.1　かいわ　会話

At a post office　ゆうびんきょくで　郵便局で

In a ゆうびんきょく (yuubinkyoku) you (A) are buying stamps (きって) and postcards (はがき).

A: 十円 きって を 五まい ください。それから、はがき を 三まい ください。

B: すみません、はがき を なんまい ですか。
mi

A: 三まい です。

B: はい、200 円 です。

Practice with your あいて substituting the value of the stamps, the numbers, and the final price.

15.3.2 ほん (本)

This is used for longish stick-like or string-like things such as bottles, carrots, bananas, sticks, trees, rolls of string, recording tape, film, belts, pens.

📼	いっぽん	一本	ななほん	七本
	にほん	二本	はっぽん	八本
	さんぼん	三本	きゅうほん *kyu*	九本
	よんほん	四本	じゅっぽん *ju*	十本

ごほん	五本	じゅういっぽん *ju*	十一本
ろっぽん *ro*	六本	じゅうにほん *ju*	十二本

This method may seem somewhat irregular but a general rule is being followed. When a word is contracted, the omitted syllable is replaced by chiisai つ and the following ほ changes to ぽ. This happens with 1, 6, 8, and 10. After an "an" sound e.g. さん, the following ほ changes to ぼ. This also occurs with the question word なんぼん (なん本 how many?). You will find that this rule can be applied to other counters as well.

15.4 Alcoholic beverages　さけ　酒

ビール *bii ru*		にほんしゅ *shu*	日本酒
ウイスキー *u i su kii*	(whiskey)	しょうちゅう *chu*	焼酎
ブランデー *bu ra n dee*	(brandy)	うめしゅ *me shu*	梅酒
ワイン *wa i n*	(wine)	みずわり *mi*	水割り

Most of these are kinds of alcoholic drinks (さけ) with which you are familiar. However, you may not know the four on the right. The first is Japanese rice wine (にほんしゅ) which is often referred to simply as おさけ even though さけ (酒) is really a generic term for alcoholic beverages. The next is しょうちゅう, a popular distilled spirit made from various grains or potatoes. The third one is a sweet liqueur made from しょうちゅう and plums うめ (ume). The last is a popular mix of whiskey and water.

■Conversation 15.4.1　かいわ　会話

At a liquor store　さかや　で　酒屋で

You are at a liquor store さかや buying supplies for a party.

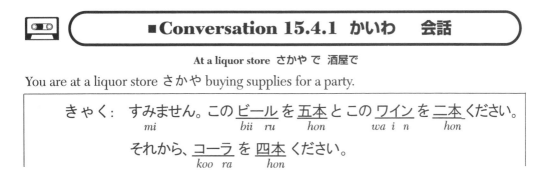

きゃく： すみません。この ビール を 五本 とこの ワイン を 二本 ください。
mi　　　　　 *bii ru*　*hon*　　　*wa i n*　*hon*

それから、コーラ を 四本 ください。
koo ra　*hon*

てんいん: すみません、<u>コーラ</u> を なん本 ですか。
　　　　　　　_{mi}　　　　_{koo ra}　　　_{bon}

きゃく: <u>四本</u> です。
　　　　　_{hon}

てんいん: はい、わかりました。ほかには....。

きゃく: それだけ です。

Notes:

ほかに は is an unfinished question meaning: "Anything else...?"
それだけ means "only that." だけ means 'only'.
コーラ (koora) is cola.
Practice the above かいわ substituting the drinks and numbers of bottles.

■**Conversation 15.4.2　かいわ　会話**

What did you buy?

When you (A) get home home from the さかや, your roommate (B) asks you what you have bought.

A: なに を かいましたか。

B: <u>ビール</u> と <u>ワイン</u> を かいました。
　　_{bii ru}　　_{wa i n}

A: <u>コーラ</u> も かいましたか。
　　_{koo ra}

B: ええ、<u>四本</u> かいました。
　　　　　_{hon}

A: <u>にほんしゅ</u> は 。
　　　　　_{shu}

B: あ、わすれました。

Note:

わすれました means "(I) forgot." The dictionary form of the verb is わすれる.
Practice the above かいわ substituting underlined parts.

■Language pattern 15.4　ぶんけい　文型

Q:にほんしゅ を なん本 かいましたか。　Q:How many bottles of **nihonshu**
　　 shu　　　 *bon*　　　　　　　　　　　did you buy.

A:(にほんしゅ を) 四本 かいました。　　A: (I) bought four bottles.
　　 shu　　　 *hon*

The pattern is: **thing** を **number verb**. The number or amount comes after the thing it refers to, but the object marker を follows directly after the thing. This is because the number is not the object of "bought," it is the にほんしゅ which is bought.

15.5 Colors　いろ　色

Here are a number of colors. Use the じしょ at the back of this text to find out the えいご for them.

あかい　赤い _____		あおい　　青い _____	
しろい　白い _____		きいろい　黄色い _____	
ro		*ro*	

These colors are adjectives and in 日本ご adjectives go in front of the noun they refer to: あかい はな red flower. The pattern is: **adjective + noun**.

■Conversation 15.5　かいわ　会話

At a florist　はなや で　花屋で

When you (A) go to a はなや (flowershop) in 日本 you will buy はな by the stalk. Since はなや are often small and full of many different はな, the てんいん (B) may have trouble working out which you want. Listen to the tape and fill in the blanks.

A: すみません、あの はな を _____。
　　　　　　　　　　　　 mi

B: _____ですか。

A: あの _____ はな です。

B: これ ですか。

A: はい、_____ です。いくら ですか。

B: 一本 _____ 円 です。
　　 pon

A: ＿＿＿＿＿＿、七本 ください。
     hon

B: はい。 あのう、 おくりもの ですか。

A: ええ、 そう です。

Notes:

どれ is the question word "which?" See below.

おくりもの means "gift." When you buy things you will often be asked this, so that the て
んいん will know whether or not to gift-wrap the item.

Practice the above かいわ substituting the number of stems, the price, and the color.

15.6 どれ and どの

We have already learned the pronouns "this" and "that." In えいご the question word
referring to such words is "which." We saw that in 日本ご "this" varies according to
whether it stands alone, i.e. これ or whether it precedes a noun, i.e. この はな. The same
goes for "which": by itself it is どれ while before a noun it is どの.

📼	1. Q: どれ ですか。	Q: Which is it?
	A: それ です。	A: It's that one.
	2. Q: どの はな ですか。	Q: Which flower is it?
	A: その あかい はな です。	A: It's that red flower.

However, どれ and どの cannot be used as "which" when the choice is only between two
alternatives. In this case different question words are used: どれ becomes どちら or どっ
ち (どちら is the politer version) and どの becomes どちらの or どっちの.

どれ	which (of more than two possibilities)
どっち (docchi)	which (of the two)
どの はな	which flower (of more than two flowers)
どっちの はな (docchino hana)	which flower (of the two flowers)

It may simplify the matter to use the politer version of the pronouns. We came across こちら (kochira) when introducing a person and also when indicating a direction. In these cases it meant either "this person" or "this way." In fact, こちら is a polite version of これ and can be used to replace これ in many instances. On top of that, こちら is also the polite version of ここ (here). All the pronouns along with the "whichs" have extra-polite versions. These double up on their meaning and can replace any of the more common forms as follows:

こちら	can replace	これ	or	この人	or	ここ
そちら	can replace	それ	or	その人	or	そこ
あちら	can replace	あれ	or	あの人	or	あそこ
どちら	can replace	どれ	or	どの人	or	どこ
どちら	can replace	どっち				

In front of a noun:

こちらの	can replace	この	or	ここの
そちらの	can replace	その	or	そこの
あちらの	can replace	あの	or	あそこの
どちらの	can replace	どの	or	どこの
どちらの	can replace	どっちの		

The どれ / どっち distinction is not made when the polite version どちら (dochira) is used. These polite pronouns are rather vague. In fact vagueness tends to be a feature of most polite language. Depending upon the context, こちら could mean "here," "this way," "this (thing)," "this person" or, by extension, "I," "me," "myself," or "us." In the same way, そちら (sochira) could mean "there (where you are)," "that (near you)," "that person (you referred to)" or "you." With such words the context is all important.

15.7 You and I

The use of こちら to mean "I" or "us" and of そちら to mean "you" is something you will often encounter. At this stage, it is better for you to use わたし since こちら can be confusing. However, when you can't remember a person's name and you need a word for "you" then そちら is a good choice in formal situations.

In 日本ご there is no general equivalent to the えいご "you." There are a number of words which can replace another person's name but they all carry extra meaning, and depend on relationship and context. Many textbooks give あなた as a general version of "you," but it is best to avoid this word because it is very often not appropriate. In 日本ご you can usually get away without using "you," just by using the person's name or title instead.

15.8 Asking age　ねんれい を たずねる　年齢を尋ねる

1. When asking the age of a child the 一つ, 二つ system is used for 1 through 9 years.

Q: いくつ ですか。	Q: How old are you?
A: 七つ です。	A: (I) am seven.

2. Generally, you won't ask adults their age, but you may be asked by officials, doctors, etc. To give your age you add the suffix さい (才) to the number.
An exception is twenty years old which is はたち (hatachi) (二十才).

Q: なんさい ですか。	Q: How old are you?
Or おいくつ ですか。	
A: 三十二才 です。	A: (I) am thirty two years old.
sai	

A common time to talk about people's ages is when talking about birthdays. In 日本ご this word is たんじょうび (誕生日).

■Conversation 15.8　かいわ　　会話

At the company　かいしゃ で　会社で

Johnson (B), an American, is leaving the office while others are still working overtime. As he is packing up to leave, a colleague (A) begins talking to him.

A: あ、ジョンソンさん、かえりますか。
jo n so n
B: はい、これから デパート へ いきます。
de paa to
むすこ の たんじょう日 の プレゼント を かいます。
mu　　　　　　　　　　*pu re ze n to*
A: ああ、そう ですか。 むすこさん は いくつ ですか。
mu
B: 五つ です。 (Shows photo of his son) むすこ の トミー です。
mu　　　*to mii*

A: ああ、かわいい ですね。じゃ、また あした。

B: ええ、おさき に しつれい します。

Notes

1. これから means "after this" and precedes talk about your next activity.

2. しつれい します (失礼します): We have seen しつれい as meaning "rude." When followed by します, it means "I'm going to be rude." This expression is often used when leaving a group or interrupting. It is like "excuse me."

3. おさき に (お先に): さき means "previous," in this expression it indicates that the speaker is going to leave the group or the office before the other people. It is often followed by しつれい します to form: おさき に しつれい します (お先に失礼します) which is an expression commonly used by people who are leaving before others. You should always use this expression when leaving the office earlier than others, as it indicates you are aware of the implicit rudeness of leaving before something is finished. In 日本 the smooth functioning of human relationships is highly valued, so expressions of awareness of the effect of one's own actions upon others are common.

4. おさき に どうぞ is said when allowing another person to go before you. It is like "After you." Don't confuse this expression with the one above. In this case it is the other person who is "previous" ie. さき, not yourself.

5. かわいい means "cute" so かわいい ですね。 means "(someone or something) is cute, isn't he/it etc." This is an almost mandatory comment about other people's children.

Practice the above かいわ substituting son/daughter, name, and age.

15.9 The year とし 年

When saying the year in 日本ご, you just read it out as a number and add the suffix ねん (年) which means "year." Try saying these years and writing them in ひらがな:

📼	1991	せん きゅうひゃく きゅうじゅう いち ねん	1991年
	1985	_____	1985年
	1996	_____	1996年
	2000	_____	2000年

However, it isn't quite that simple. In 日本 another system of counting years is also used. This system counts the years of the reigning emperor and has been used since the seventh century. Each time an emperor dies and another succeeds, the year reverts to one. Each reign is named after the emperor, the current one being へいせい. The word for the monarch of 日本 is てんのう (天皇) which is usually translated as "emperor." The current てんのう is called あきひと but this is his personal name and it is not generally used. He is always referred to simply as てんのう. The Japanese imperial family has no family name and to distinguish between the various てんのう of the past the name of the reign is used. The current てんのう's father ひろひと was referred to as しょうわ てんのう (昭和天皇) because the name of his reign was しょうわ (昭和). He died in 1989 and the reign changed to へいせい (平成).

1900 was めいじ 32 ねん	明治三十二年
1913 was たいしょう 2 ねん	大正二年
1988 was しょうわ 63 ねん	昭和六十三年
1989 was both しょうわ 64 ねん and へいせいがんねん	昭和六十四年 and 平成元年
1990 was へいせい 2 ねん	平成二年

What are the following in Japanese years? 1910, 1939, 1950, 1964, 1973, 1997.

15.10 The date ひづけ　日付

In えいご the date is always written with the day first then the month and year. In 日本ご the order is reversed. Since you will often need to write the date on forms, it is worth learning how to recognize the かんじ for day, month, and year. Dates are written as follows:

_____年 _____月 _____日   e.g.   1996年 11月 23日
　　year　　month　　day

Note: When writing horizontally, Arabic rather than かんじ numbers are used.

Date of birth is せいねんがっぴ. On forms you can tell your date of birth is required because the かんじ for date will be preceded by 生, i.e. 生年月日.
The space for your age will be followed by 才.

Filling out a form ようし に かきこむ　用紙に書き込む

Here is the same form（ようし）in both えいご and 日本ご.Try filling in the Japanese ようし below with your personal details.

name: _____　sex: M F

date of birth: _____　age: ___

address: _____

_____

Tel. No: (____) _____

名前: _____　　　性別: 男 女

生年月日: ____ 年 ____ 月 ____ 日　___ 才

住所: _____

_____

電話: (____) _____

Answers こたえ　答え

Conversation 15.5 ください; どれ; あかい; そう; 200; じゃ.

15.9 めいじ 43 ねん; しょうわ 14 ねん; しょうわ 25 ねん;. しょうわ 39 ねん;

しょうわ 48 ねん; へいせい 9 ねん;

The next ひらがな is mu む. It is written in three strokes. Be careful not to confuse it with す.

With this next ひらがな me め you are able to write the seventh line of the ひらがな chart as follows: ま、み、む、め、も. It is written with two strokes.

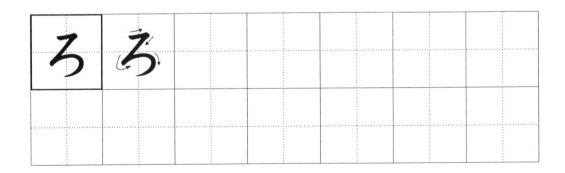

The ひらがな ro ろ is written in one stroke. Be careful not to confuse it with る. You can now write the ninth line of the ひらがな chart: ら、り、る、れ、ろ. When using some word processors you can also type this in as "lo."

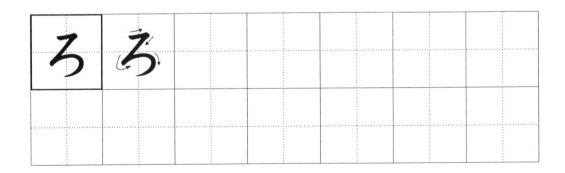

The last ひらがな to learn is nu ぬ . It is written in two strokes. Now you can write the fifth line of the ひらがな chart: な、に、ぬ 、ね、の. Be careful not to confuse it with め.

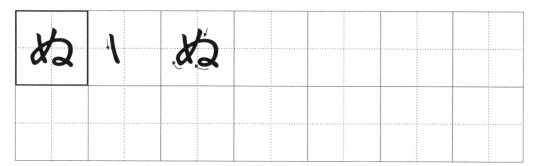

This next かんじ follows people's ages. It is pronounced さい and means "years old." It is written with three strokes.

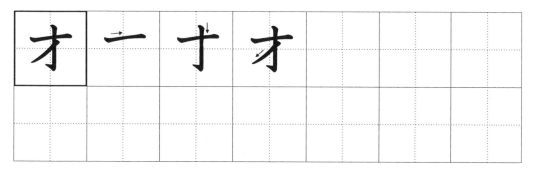

This かんじ means "years." When written alone it is pronounced とし but when it follows a year it is pronounced ねん. It is written with six strokes.

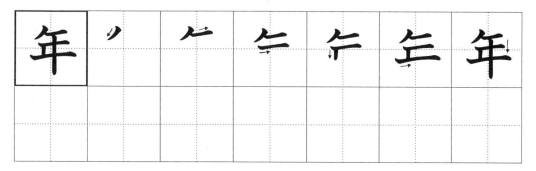

1. Choose the correct one.

1) はがき を （五つ、 五まい、 五本） ください。

2) みかん を （七つ、 七まい、 七本） かいました。
  mi

3) A: （いくら、 いくつ、 なに を） かいましたか。
  B: 八つ かいました。

4) A: あの はな を ください。
  B: （どれ、 どの、 どちら） はな ですか。
    chi

5) ともだちのたんじょうびの （プレゼント、 おみやげ） を かいました。
        pu re ze n to　　*mi　ge*

6) すみません、（これ、 この、 ここ） を ください。

7) A: きって を かいましたか。
  B: あ、（わかりました、 わすれました）。 かいませんでした。

2. Translate the following sentences into 日本ご.

1) I'd like three bottles of beer and two bottles of wine please.

_____

2) I'd like six 60-yen stamps please.

_____

3) How many apples did you buy?

_____

4) A: How old is your younger sister?

_____

  B: (She is) 18 years old.

_____

5) How much is that yellow flower over there?

_____

3. Answer the following questions in 日本ご.

1) 1996 is what year in the Japanese calendar?

_____

2) What do you say when you leave the office earlier than the other people?

_____

3) Write your date of birth in Japanese using Japanese order.

_____

4. Read the following passage aloud and then answer the questions in 日本ご.

あさって は ひろこさん の 二十才 の たんじょう日 です。ひろこさん は わたし
の だいがく の ともだち です。しゅみ は りょうり と どくしょ です。きょう、わた
し は でんしゃ で かんだ へ いきました。そして、ひろこさん の たんじょう日 の
プレゼント を かいました。イタリアりょうりの 本 です。
pu re ze n to　　　　　*i ta ri a*
それから、かわいい カード も かいました。
　　　　　　　　kaa do

1) いま、ひろこさん は なん才 ですか。

2) ひろこさん の しゅみ は なん ですか。

3) 「わたし」 は どこ で イタリアりょうり の 本 を かいましたか。
　　　　　　　i ta ri a

5. Write the following words in 日本ご. Write 1) and 2) in ひらがな and 3) in かんじ。

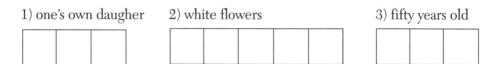

1) one's own daugher　　2) white flowers　　　　　　　3) fifty years old

第十六課

In this lesson the ローマ字 for all the ひらがな and for the following かんじhas been removed: 月一二三四五六七八九十千円日火水木金人土本.

16.1 あります

In Lesson 14 we learned to use the verb います when referring to the existence of people and animals. However, when we refer to the existance of things such as, items of furniture, plants, we have to use the verb あります. Since the sentence patterns are basically the same you should be able to look at the picture below and work out the sentence:

きょうしつ に つくえ が あります。

This sentence could be translated into えいご as: "There is a desk in the classroom." "There are desks in the classroom." or as "The classroom has desks (in it)." The point is that it is simply a statement of what exists in the classroom.

To make the question "What is in the room?" all you do is substitute なに for つくえ.

■Practice 16.1　れんしゅう　　練習

What's in the classroom?

In the picture below there are the following items. Look up the じしょ at the back of the text to work out what they are and write the えいご in the blanks.

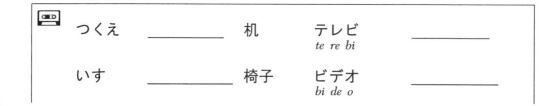

| つくえ | _____ | 机 | テレビ
te re bi | _____ |
| いす | _____ | 椅子 | ビデオ
bi de o | _____ |

242

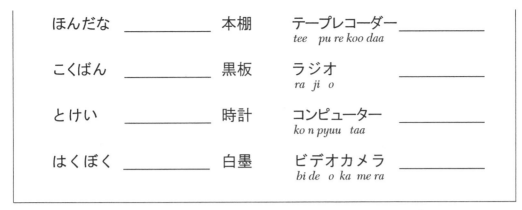

ほんだな	_____ 本棚	テープレコーダー	_____
		tee pu re koo daa	
こくばん	_____ 黒板	ラジオ	_____
		ra ji o	
とけい	_____ 時計	コンピューター	_____
		ko n pyuu taa	
はくぼく	_____ 白墨	ビデオカメラ	_____
		bi de o ka me ra	

Looking at the picture of a きょうしつ we can ask the following question.

> Q: きょうしつ に なに が ありますか。
> A: (きょうしつ に) <u>つくえ</u> が あります。

Practice this short dialogue by substituting the underlined word.

16.2 The conjunction や "and so on"

In the above きょうしつ there are quite a number of things. We can combine a number of them in the same sentence by joining them with the conjunction や. For example:

きょうしつ に つくえ **や** いす **や** テレビ が あります。
te re bi

や means "and" but can only be used to join items on a list which is not complete. In the above example there are more things in the きょうしつ besides つくえ, いす, and テレビ These are just examples of the things in the classroom. Therefore や is like "and so on" or "etc." in えいご.

When all things are listed と must be used. For example, if we were talking about electrical equipment and the きょうしつ had a テレビ and a ビデオ only, we would say:

きょうしつ に テレビ と ビデオ が あります。
　　　　　　　te re bi　　*bi de o*

▪Conversation 16.2　かいわ　　会話

Hakone is a nice place はこね は いい ところ です 箱根はいい所です

Smith スミス is going to はこね for the first time. Yamada やまだ knows はこね well and tells him about what things are there.

> やまだ: スミスさん は もう <u>はこね</u> に いきましたか。
>
> スミス:　いいえ まだ です。でも こんしゅう の 土よう日 に <u>すずき</u>さん といきます。
>
> やまだ: それ は いい です ね。<u>はこね</u> は いい ところ です よ。
>
> スミス:　そう です か。<u>はこね</u> に なに が あります か。
>
> やまだ: いろいろ あります よ。<u>おんせん</u> や <u>びじゅつかん</u> や <u>みずうみ</u> があります。
>
> スミス:　そう です か。

Notes:
はこね（箱根）is a region near とうきょう known for its tourist attractions (see Lesson 12).
それ は いい です ね。 means something like "Oh that's good."
ところ tokoro（所）means "place."
いろいろ iroiro（色々）means "various."
みずうみ（湖）means "lake."

Imagine you are talking to a Japanese visitor to your country who is going to a famous place. Practice the above かいわ substituting the place name and attractions.

16.3 Japanese Housing 日本 の じゅうたく　日本の住宅

In the large cities in 日本 it is getting more difficult for people to afford to live in an individual house いっこだて (一戸建て), so many people live in apartment buildings or in large housing complexes called だんち (団地), usually run by government or large corporations. Older style apartments are referred to as アパート (apaato). This word used to sound modern but now it sounds rather old fashioned so more modern ferrocement apartment blocks are called マンション (manshon). These buildings often have fancy sounding names such as メゾン・ロイヤル (mezon roiyaru) or カサ・ルネッサンス (kasa runessansu) which are also written on the buildings in roman letters, i.e. Maison Royale, Casa Renaissance.

In general, individual apartments are fairly small. For example an アパート described as "2DK" would have two rooms and a small dining kitchen. The size of rooms is given in じょう (畳) which is the size of a tatami (about 180cm x 90 cm). Typical room sizes are よじょうはん (四畳半), ろくじょう (六畳) and はちじょう (八畳).
Apartments vary in style with some having Japanese-style rooms わしつ, some Western style rooms ようしつ and others a mixture of styles.

■Conversation 16.3　かいわ　　会話

Have you got a video ?

In the following かいわ person A is asking person B about the equipment they have in their room (へや) at home.

A:　へや に テレビ が ありますか。
　　　　　　te re bi

B:　はい、あります。

A:　ビデオ も ありますか。
　　　bi de o

B:　いいえ、ビデオ は ありません。
　　　　　　bi de o

　　　　または (Or)

B:　はい、ビデオ も あります。
　　　　　bi de o

Note:
The particle が changes to も when the meaning is "also." This particle also undergoes change in the negative reply. This time が changes to は. This generally happens when the reply to a question is in the negative (see notes at end of lesson).

1.　Q: place に なに が ありますか。　Q: What is in the place.
　　A: (place に)thing が あります。　　A: There is a thing (in the place).

2.　Q: place に thingが ありますか。　Q: Is there a thing in the place.?
　　A: はい、 (thing が) あります。　　A: Yes, there is (a thing).

The use of は in the negative reply serves to highlight the non-existence of the thing that was asked about. If there is no reason for wishing to emphasize the lack of the thing, the short answer いいえ、 ありません is sufficient.

■**Practice 16.3**　れんしゅう　　練習

Imagine you live in either the へや in Picture A or the one in Picture B at the end of this lesson, and your あいて lives in the other へや. Each of these rooms has some of the modern items listed below. Practice variations on かいわ 16.3 with one of you looking at Picture A below and the other looking at Picture B. Tick off the items in your partner's room.

でんわ	テレビ *te re bi*	ビデオ *bi de o*	ステレオ *su te re o*	ラジオ *ra ji o*	コンピューター *ko n pyuu taa*
ファックス *fa kku su*	CDプレイヤー *pu re i yaa*	ワープロ *waa pu ro*	エアコン *e a ko n*	カラオケ・セット *ka ra o ke se tto*	

Picture A

LESSON 16 第十六課

16.4 Reading comprehension
どっかい 読解　わしつ と ようしつ　和室と洋室

Japanese-style rooms (わしつ) and Western-style rooms (ようしつ) are different in a number of ways. Read the following passage to find out about わしつ. Then write the answers to the しつもん in 日本ご.

わしつ には カーペット が ありません。でも たたみ が あります。ドア が ありません。
　　　　　　kaa　pe tto　　　　　　　　　　　　　　　　　　　　　　*do a*

でも しょうじ が あります。そして とこのま が あります。とこのま に はな と かけじく が

あります。いす は ありません。でも ざぶとん が あります。おしいれ が あります。おしいれ

に ふとん や ざぶとん が あります。ベッド は ありません。 ふとん に ねます。
　　　　　　　　　　　　　　　　　　be ddo

Questions　しつもん　質問 ─────────────────────

1. わしつ に たたみ が ありますか。　　　＿＿＿＿＿＿＿＿＿＿＿

2. わしつ に ドア が ありますか。　　　　＿＿＿＿＿＿＿＿＿＿＿

3. どこ に はな と かけじく が ありますか。　＿＿＿＿＿＿＿＿＿＿＿

4. おしいれ に なに が ありますか。　　　　＿＿＿＿＿＿＿＿＿＿＿

Notes:

には	は can follow に to make the place the topic of the sentence.
たたみ	(畳) is a thick, finely-woven straw matting floor.
おしいれ	(押し入れ) is a built-in wall closet for storing ふとん and other things.
ふとん	(布団) is a padded mat for sleeping on.
ざぶとん	(座布団) is a cushion for sitting on.
しょうじ	(障子) are paper-fitted sliding doors.
とこのま	(床の間) is a small alcove in which pictures are hung and ornaments placed.
かけじく	(掛軸) is a hanging scroll of calligraphy or a painting.
ベッド	(beddo) means bed.
カーペット	(kaapetto) means carpet.
ドア	(doa) is a hinged door.

place に ねます　　the particle に follows the place where you lie down.

■Practice 16.4 れんしゅう   練習

The two rooms in pictures A and B above are quite different in style and contain different items. Picture A is of a わしつ while picture B is of a ようしつ. With each of you looking at different pictures, ask whether you have various items in your rooms using questions and answers like the following:

Q: name さん の へや に いす が ありますか。

A: いいえ、ありません。でも、ざぶとん が あります。　Or　はい、あります。

Note: the conjunction でも was introduced in Lesson 13.

16.5 Apologizing for lack of goods

When you are shopping you often have to ask whether the store has what you are looking for. In such cases the item is the topic and the following pattern is used:
Q: thing は ありますか。
If they have the item, the てんいん will reply: はい、あります。
or more formally: はい、ございます。

However, if the store doesn't have any in stock, the てんいん will have to apologize using the phrase: もうしわけ ありません (申し訳ありません) which is a more polite version of すみません. This phrase is like the えいご "I'm terribly sorry." but translates literally as "there is no excuse."

■Conversation 16.5 かいわ   会話

At the hotel shop ホテル の ばいてん で ホテルの売店で

You are working as a てんいん in a ばいてん in a ホテル (hoteru) outside Japan. A Japanese visitor (日本人のきゃく) wants something that you don't have.

てんいん：　いらっしゃいませ。

きゃく：　　あのう、日本 の しんぶん は ありますか。

てんいん：　もうしわけ ありません。日本 の しんぶん は ありません。

きゃく：　　ああ、そうですか。

Note: People working in the service industry use a more formal style of speech, called け
いご , when speaking with customers. Many verbs have a けいご version. We have seen two of these so far:

です	becomes	でございます	あります	becomes	ございます
ではありません	becomes	ではございません	ありません	becomes	ございません

Practice the かいわ substituting the underlined words. You can also substitute the けいご for あります. Remember, the customer doesn't use けいご, only the てんいん.

📖 ■Language pattern 16.5 ぶんけい   文型

When you are asking about something which hasn't yet been referred to, you can make it the topic of the sentence using は.

Q: thing は ありますか。	Q: Do you have a thing?
A1: はい、あります。	A1: Yes, I do (have it).
A2: いいえ、ありません。	A2: No, I don't (have it).

16.6 Counting nights accommodation

When you stay at ホテル (hoteru), りょかん, or みんしゅく you need to be able to say how many nights you wish to stay. The method of counting nights is rather like that we learned for bottles. You just add the counter はく to a number.
The question is なんぱく.

いっぱく	一泊	ごはく	五泊
にはく	二泊	ろっぱく	六泊
さんぱく	三泊	ななはく	七泊
よんはく	四泊	はっぱく	八泊

At a hotel ホテル で

When you (A) go to a ホテル (hoteru) to get a room for the night, the person at the front desk フロント (furonto) (B) will ask you whether you want a single シングル (shinguru) or a double ダブル (daburu) room, and for how many nights. You could also ask the price and about the へや and ホテル facilities.

A: すみません、へや は あります か。

B: はい、あります。シングル ですか、ダブル ですか。

A: シングル です。いくら ですか。

B: いっぱく 6500円 です。

A: へや に シャワー が あります か。

B: はい、あります。

A: れいぞうこ も あります か。

B: いいえ、れいぞうこ は ありません。

A: ホテル に プール は あります か。

B: はい、あります。

A: サウナ も あります か。

B: いいえ、サウナ は ありません。

■Practice 16.6 れんしゅう　練習

Write the えいご in the blanks and then practice the above かいわ with an あいて substituting the type of room, the price, and the facilities below. You can also make the role of the person on the front desk more realistic by using けいご.

れいぞうこ	_____	きっさてん	_____
でんわ	_____	サウナ *sa u na*	_____
おふろ	_____	プール *puu ru*	_____
シャワー *sha waa*	_____	レストラン *re su to ra n*	_____

エアコン *e a ko n*	_____	テニスコート *te ni su koo to*	_____
アイロン *a i ro n*	_____	ファックス *fa kkusu*	_____

16.7 Asking where　どこ に ありますか。

📼　We have learned to ask where something is by using the pattern:

thing は　　どこ　　　ですか。

The same type of question can be asked another way:

thing は　　どこ に　　ありますか。

Both of these questions have the same meaning and are interchangeable.

You can ask すずき where his company is located using the following question:

Q:　　すずきさん の <u>かいしゃ</u> は どこ に ありますか。

A:　　<u>しんじゅく</u> に あります。

From this we can make the following statement:

すずきさん の かいしゃ は しんじゅく に あります。

In this sentence Suzuki's company is the topic.

■Practice 16.7　れんしゅう　　練習

📼　　　**Rail Map** でんしゃろせんず　電車路線図

Below is a greatly simplified rail map (でんしゃろせんず) of central Tokyo which shows the main overground rail lines. The circular line is called the Yamanote Line やまのてせん. The line that passes through the middle is the Chuo Line ちゅうおうせん. These lines are operated by Japan Rail (JR), often referred to as JR (せん). Under this area is a complex network of underground lines referred to as ちかてつ which means "underground line."

Below is a list of stations on these two lines written in ひらがな and かんじ. These are also the names of suburbs. On the map, these station names are only given in かんじ.

First work out which station is which and draw lines to them.

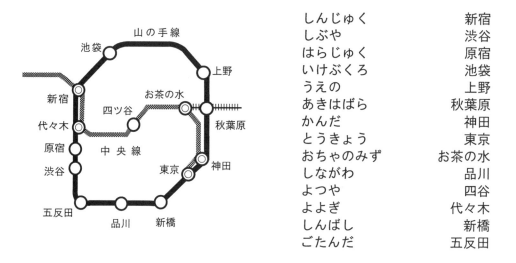

しんじゅく	新宿		
しぶや	渋谷		
はらじゅく	原宿		
いけぶくろ	池袋		
うえの	上野		
あきはばら	秋葉原		
かんだ	神田		
とうきょう	東京		
おちゃのみず	お茶の水		
しながわ	品川		
よつや	四谷		
よよぎ	代々木		
しんばし	新橋		
ごたんだ	五反田		

Write the えいご for the following places and then practice asking where they are using the question and answer introduced in 16.7. Use the suburbs of central Tokyo in your replies.

がっこう	学校 _____	じむしょ	事務所	_____
だいがく	大学 _____	みせ	店	_____
いえ	家 _____	こうじょう	工場	_____

📖 ■**Language pattern 16.7** ぶんけい 文型

thing は place に あります。

Q: thing は どこ に ありますか。 Q: Where is **the thing**?
A: place に あります。 A: (It) is in **place**.

In this pattern the thing has become the topic of conversation so it is followed by は. This is in contrast to the **place** に **thing** が あります pattern which is simply a description of what there is in a place.

ビデオ は へや に あります。

Here the video is the topic so this sentence translates as: "The video is in the room."
When the place comes first, the previous sentence is transformed into:

へや に ビデオ が あります。

This sentence translates as "There is a video in the room."
The difference between these two sentences is rather like the difference between "a video" and "the video" in えいご.

16.8 Listening comprehension
ききとり れんしゅう 聞き取り練習

Listen to the following passage and identify what is in each place. Write your answers in the blanks in 日本ご.

やまのてせん には、ぜんぶ で えきが ＿＿＿＿＿ あります。やまのてせん の まわり には、いろいろな おもしろい ところ が あります。しぶや と しんじゅ く と いけぶくろ には デパート が たくさん あります。うえの には、どうぶつ えん や、びじゅつかん が あります。あきはばら には、＿＿＿＿＿ や、コン ピューター の みせ が たくさん あります。かんだ には、＿＿＿＿＿ が たくさ ん あります。はらじゅく には おおきい じんじゃ が あります。レストラン や ＿＿＿＿＿ も たくさん あります。しながわ には、大きい ホテル が 四つ あり ます。よよぎには 大きい こうえん が あります。

Notes:
In this passage は is often used after the **place** に pattern which we learned earlier. The function of this は is to make the place the topic about which some information will be given.

まわり (回り) means "around," "surrounding," or "in the vicinity of."

おもしろい (面白い) is an adjective meaning "interesting" or "entertaining."

たくさん (沢山) means "much," "many," or "a lot." Since it is an amount, it is not followed by a particle and comes immediately before the verb.

じんじゃ (神社) is the word for "Shinto shrine." Here it refers to the very large national shrine called "Meiji Jingu" めいじじんぐう (明治神宮).

When an amount or number referring to a thing is placed in a sentence it usually comes before the verb and is not followed by a particle. Here are some examples:

1. へや に おとこ の 人 が 三人 います。

2. やまださん は にほんしゅを 四本 かいました。

3. きって が にまい あります。

4. たなかさん は おさけを たくさん のみました。

> topic は thing を amount / number のみます/かいます etc。
>
> place に thing が amount/ number あります/います。

16.3 Picture B

ラジオ	ステレオ	CDプレイヤー	ワープロ	でんわ
ra ji o	*su te re o*	*pu re i yaa*	*waa pu ro*	

ファックス	エアコン	テレビ	ビデオ	カラオケ・セット
fa kku su	*e a ko n*	*te re bi*	*bi de o*	*ka ra o ke se tto*

Answers こたえ 答え

16.8: 29; でんきや; 本や; きっさてん

1. Write either います **or** あります **in the blanks as appropriate.**

1) きょうしつ に がくせい が 八人 （　　　　　　　　　）。

2) あそこ に でんわ が （　　　　　　　）。

3) ゆうびんきょく は どこ に （　　　　　　　） か。

4) いま、もりさん は とうきょう に （　　　　　　　　　）。

2. Write なに, どこ, **or** いくら **in the blanks as appropriate.**

1) やまださん の いえ は （　　　　　　　　　） ですか。

2) かまくら に （　　　　　　　） が ありますか。

3) Q: へや は 一ぱく （　　　　　　　） ですか。
　 A: 九千円 です。

3. Write one ひらがな **in each blank.**

A: へや （　　　　　　　　　） でんわ が ありますか。

B: はい、あります。

A: ファックス （　　　　　　　） ありますか。
　　 fa　　kku su

B: いいえ、ファックス （　　　　　　　　） ありません。
　　　 fa　　kku su

4. Translate the following English sentences into 日本ご **or vice versa.**

1) What things are there in Harajuku?

_____

2) Kamakura is a nice place.

_____

LESSON **16** 第十六課

3) There are desks, chairs, telephones, and so on in the office.

_____

4) きょねん.さとうさん はいろいろな えいが を みました。

_____

5) わたし はいつも くだもの を たくさん たべます。

_____

5. **Answer the following questions about yourself in** 日本ご.

1) へや に なに が ありますか。 _____

2) まち(town) には なに が ありますか。 _____

3) もう 日本 へ いきましたか。 _____

6. **What is the expression which is equivalent to, but more polite than** どうも
すみません? **(it is used in apologizing).**

7. ✍ **Let's write in Japanese! How do you write the English word in** ひらがな?

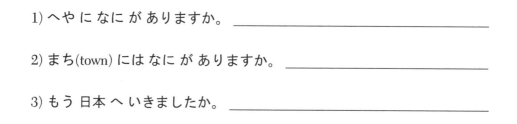

1) Japanese-style room   2) Western-style room   3) newspaper

4) this week

5) customer / guest   6) shop

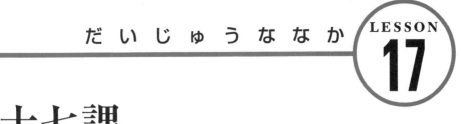

LESSON
17

第十七課

The ローマ字 for all the ひらがな and the following かんじ:月一二三四五六七八九十千 円日火水木金人土本口才 has been removed.

17.1 Where you live

When talking about living in a place we use the verb すんでいます.
As in あります the particle に follows the place. We can say that Tanaka lives in Tokyo like this:

たなかさん は とうきょう に すんでいます。

📖	**■Language pattern 17.1　ぶんけい　　文型**

Q: どこ　に　すんでいますか。	Q: Where do you live?
A: place　に　すんでいます。	A: I live in (place).

This question literally translates as "Where are you living?" since a person is considered to be "living" at their home all the time, regardless of whether they are there at the moment or not. You cannot use this question to refer to staying somewhere on a trip.

 ■Conversation 17.1　かいわ　　会話

My home town

An オーストラリア人 (oosutorariajin) called メイ (mei) and a 日本人 have just met and are talking about the small town まち of Ballina バリナ (barina) which is in the state of New South Wales. Listen to the かいわ and answer the しつもん. You'll need these words:

おおきい 大きい big / large　　ちいさい 小さい little / small

257

日本人:　<u>メイ</u>さん は どこ に すんでいますか。

メイ:　　<u>バリナ</u> に すんでいます。

日本人:　<u>バリナ</u> は どこ に ありますか。

メイ:　　<u>ニューサウスウエールズしゅう</u> に あります。
　　　　　nyuu　sa u su　u ee　ru　su

日本人:　そう ですか。<u>バリナ</u> は おおきい まち ですか。

メイ:　　いいえ、ちいさい まち です。人口 は <u>1まん7千人</u> です。

日本人:　そう ですか。<u>バリナ</u> に <u>くうこう</u> が ありますか。

メイ:　　はい、あります。

日本人:　<u>日本レストラン</u> は ありますか。
　　　　　re su　to ra n

メイ:　　いいえ、<u>日本レストラン</u> は ありません。

Questions　しつもん　質問 ───────────────

1. メイさん は どこ に すんでいますか。　　　　　_____

2. メイさん の まちは おおきい ですか、ちいさい ですか。　_____

3. 人口 は なん人 ですか。　　　　　　　　　　　_____

4. くうこう は ありますか。　　　　　　　　　　　_____

5. 日本 レストラン は ありますか。　　　　　　　　_____

Practice telling someone about your home town.

17.2 States, provinces, and counties　しゅう　州

The word しゅう (州) can be found as part of the names of some of the main islands of 日本. However, with regard to other countries, it refers to major administrative divisions, such as states, provinces, territories, and counties. Following are some names of such divisions in various countries. Since these are foreign place names they are written in **katakana** カタカナ.

■Practice 17.2　れんしゅう　練習

Look up the **katakana** カタカナ chart in this text to work out the names of the following.

アメリカ がっしゅうこく の しゅう　　　アメリカ合衆国の州

アリゾナしゅう　　　　　　アリゾナ州　　　　　　　_____

オハイオしゅう　　　　　　オハイオ州　　　　　　　_____

ユタしゅう　　　　　　　　ユタ州　　　　　　　　　_____

カリフォルニアしゅう　　　カリフォルニア州　　　　_____

オレゴンしゅう　　　　　　オレゴン州　　　　　　　_____

ニューヨークしゅう　　　　ニューヨーク州　　　　　_____

オーストラリア の しゅう　　　　　オーストラリアの州

ニューサウスウエールズしゅう　ニューサウスウエールズ州　_____

ビクトリアしゅう　　　　　ビクトリア州　　　　　　_____

クイーンズランドしゅう　　クイーンズランド州　　　_____

サウスオーストラリアしゅう　サウスオーストラリア州　_____

タスマニアしゅう　　　　　タスマニア州　　　　　　_____

ノーザンテリトリーしゅう　ノーザンテリトリー州　　_____

カナダ の しゅう　　　　　　　　カナダの州

オンタリオしゅう　　　　　オンタリオ州　　　　　　_____

ケベックしゅう　　　　　　ケベック州　　　　　　　_____

ブリティッシュコロンビアしゅう　ブリティッシュコロンビア州　_____

サスカチワンしゅう　　　　サスカチワン州　　　　　_____

イギリス の しゅう　　　　　　　イギリスの州

サフォークしゅう　　　　　サフォーク州　　　　　　_____

サマセットしゅう	サマセット州	_____
ダービーシャーしゅう	ダービシャー州	_____
デボン（シャー）しゅう	デボン（シャー）州	_____
ハンプシャーしゅう	ハンプシャー州	_____

17.3 Have you got...?

The verb あります is also used in the sense of "have," "possess," or "have available." For example we can make the following statements:

やまださん は おかね が たくさん あります。 Yamada has got lots of money.
わたし は おかね が ありません。 I don't have (any) money.

However, you will usually come across this kind of sentence in questions. When you want something from somebody you can ask a question of the type:

person さん は **thing** が ありますか。

The thing in this question could be an item or it could be time じかん. Here are two conversations to illustrate this usage of あります.

■Conversation 17.3.1　かいわ　会話

Do you have a moment? じかん が ありますか　時間がありますか

Yamamoto wants to talk to Ishizaki about Smith's (スミス) visit tomorrow.

やまもと: ちょっと、<u>いしざきさん</u>、いま じかん が ありますか。

いしざき: ええ、ありますよ。

やまもと: あのう、あした、<u>スミス</u>さん が <u>アメリカ</u> から きます。
　　　　　su mi su　　　　*a me ri ka*

いしざき: ああ そう ですか。

やまもと: ええ、<u>五じはん</u> ごろ かいしゃ に つきます。
　　　　　<u>いしざきさん</u>、<u>五じはん</u> ごろ かいしゃ に いますか。

いしざき: ええ、いますよ。

やまもと: それ は よかった です。

Practice this かいわ by substituting the underlined parts.

■Conversation 17.3.2 かいわ　会話

Do you have a 10 yen coin? じゅうえんだまが ありますか　十円玉 がありますか

Person A wants to make a local phone call but doesn't have any 10 yen coins. In this type of conversation the が is often dropped in the question.

A: すみません、十円だま (が) ありますか。
B: (has a look) いいえ、ぜんぜん ありません。
　でも、<u>テレホンカード</u> が ありますよ。どうぞ。
A: あ、すみません。

Note: テレホンカード (terehonkaado): telephone card

■Practice 17.3 れんしゅう　練習

Here are some pairs of things which have similar uses. Look up the じしょ to find the えいご.

えんぴつ	鉛筆	_____	ペン	(pen)	_____
ライター	(raitaa)	_____	マッチ	(macchi)	_____
こうちゃ	紅茶	_____	日本ちゃ	日本茶	_____
ウイスキー	(uisukii)	_____	ブランデー	(burandee)	_____
でんたく	電卓	_____	そろばん	算盤	_____

Practice the above かいわ and then substitute items from this list. You will have to drop ぜんぜん for the items which are objects because ぜんぜん refers to an amount of something.

Note:

でんたく (電卓) is an electronic calculator. These are common in 日本 but the traditional そろばん (算盤) (abacus) is still in use. The reason for this is that when used by a skilled person, the そろばん is faster at addition and subtraction than the でんたく. Also, no batteries are required.

📖 ■**Language pattern 17.3　ぶんけい　文型**

Q: (thing) が あります か。	Q: Have you got (a thing/anything)?
A: ええ、あります。	A: Yes, I have.
いいえ、ありません。	No, I haven't.

17.4 Self introduction letter
じこしょうかい の てがみ　自己紹介の手紙

Tamiko has written the the following letter introducing herself to a magazine for foreign students of Japanese in order to find a penfriend overseas.

はじめまして、わたし は うえの たみこ です。21才 です。だいがくせい です。いえ は とうきょう の すぎなみく に あります。かぞく と すんでいます。わたし は あに と いもうと が います。いもうと は 18才 です。かぞく と すんでいます。でも、あに は ほっかいどう に すんでいます。30才 です。まだ どくしん です。わたし の いえ には、いぬ と ねこ が います。いぬ の なまえ は しろ です。ねこ の なまえ は たま です。わたし の しゅみ は りょこう です。だいがく の やすみ に、よく ともだち と りょこう を します。きょねん の ふゆやすみ に きゅうしゅう へ いきました。ことし の なつやすみ に カナダ に いきます。カナダ の かた、
ka na da
てがみ を ください。どうぞ よろしく。

Notes:

1. Here are the relative time expressions referring to years:

おととし	一昨年	the year before last
きょねん	去年	last year
ことし	今年	this year
らいねん	来年	next year
さらいねん	再来年	the year after next

2. カナダ の かた has the same meaning as カナダ人. The word かた is a politer alternative of じん or ひと (人). This means that 日本人 can be replaced with 日本の かた when you wish to be more formal.

■Practice 17.4　れんしゅう　練習

Many 日本人 keep pet animals. They are regarded as members of the family. Look up the じしょ in the back of this text to find the えいご for these common pets (ペット).

ねこ	猫	_____	きんぎょ	金魚	_____
とり	鳥	_____	うさぎ	兎	_____
いぬ	犬	_____	モルモット *mo ru mo tto*		_____

Then try writing a similar self introduction letter for yourself. Include where you live, your age, your occupation, your family members, your pets, and interests.

17.5 The days of the month　ひにち　日にち

We have learned two sets of numbers ひとつ, ふたつ, and いち, に. When we count the days of the month we use both these methods with some variations°. Firstly, the name of the 1st day of the month doesn't fit either system, then, from the 2nd to the 10th the ひとつ, ふたつ system is used except that the つ is replaced by 日 which is pronounced か. From the 11th onwards the other system is used, the numbers being followed by 日 with its more usual pronunciation of にち. However, the number 4 keeps its earlier form in the 14th and the 24th and the 20th has a special name, just like the age twenty years did (see Lesson 15).

When writing the days, the かんじ is quite regular. It is when you say them that you have to be careful.

ついたち*	一日	じゅうろくにち	十六日
ふつか	二日	じゅうしちにち	十七日
みっか	三日	じゅうはちにち	十八日
よっか	四日	じゅうくにち	十九日
いつか	五日	はつか*	二十日
むいか	六日	にじゅういちにち	二十一日
なのか	七日	にじゅうににち	二十二日
ようか	八日	にじゅうさんにち	二十三日
ここのか	九日	にじゅうよっか*	二十四日
とおか	十日	にじゅうごにち	二十五日
じゅういちにち	十一日	にじゅうろくにち	二十六日
じゅうににち	十二日	にじゅうしちにち	二十七日
じゅうさんいち	十三日	にじゅうはちにち	二十八日
じゅうよっか*	十四日	にじゅうくにち	二十九日
じゅうごにち	十五日	さんじゅうにち	三十日

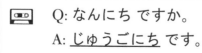

■Practice 17.5　れんしゅう　　練習

With your あいて, help each other learn the days of the month. Cover the ひらがな parts on the list above, and then point to the かんじ and ask:

Q: なんにち ですか。	Q: なん日ですか。
A: <u>じゅうごにち</u> です。	A: <u>十五日</u>です。

17.6 Birthday　　たんじょうび　誕生日

We know that "birthday" in 日本ご is たんじょうび. We have done one of the かんじ in this word so we will use it from now on. To ask someone when their birthday is, you can use the following question:

> Q: nameさん、たんじょう日 は いつ ですか。
> A: 十月三日 です。

Try asking various people their birthdays.

17.6 Listening Practice　　ききとりれんしゅう　聞き取り練習

Suzuki and Honda are taking about their ともだち の たんじょう日. Listen to the tape and fill in the missing information in the blanks.

すずき: ＿＿＿＿＿＿ さん の たんじょう日 は いつ ですか。

ほんだ: ＿＿＿＿＿＿です。

すずき: ああ そう ですか。らいしゅう の ＿＿＿＿＿＿ ですね。

ほんだ: ええ、そう ですね。

すずき: ほんださん は もう プレゼント を かいましたか。
　　　　　　　　　　　　 pu re ze n to

ほんだ: いいえ、＿＿＿＿＿＿ です。すずきさん は。

すずき: ええ、もう かいました。

ほんだ: なに を かいましたか。

すずき: ＿＿＿＿＿＿ の 本 を かいました。

17.7 Having an appointment
よてい が あります　予定があります

We have seen the verb あります used to refer to the existence of things and for having things. However, this verb can also be used for events, in the sense of having an appointment. To say that you have an appointment or plan (よてい) on a certain day you can use the following pattern:

十一日 に よてい が あります。　　I have an appointment on the 11th.

The word よてい is very useful since it is rather vague. However, you can also use this pattern to be specific:

十一日 に かいぎ が あります。　　　I have a meeting on the 11th.

■Conversation 17.7 かいわ　会話

Mr. Smith's welcome party
スミスさん の かんげいかい スミスさんの歓迎会

Suzuki and Yamada are trying to fit a welcome party (かんげいかい) for Smith (スミス) into Yamada's busy schedule.

> すずき: やまださん、あのう、<u>スミスさん の かんげいかい</u> の 日 ですが‥。
> 　　　　らいげつ の <u>三日</u> に よてい が ありますか。
>
> やまだ: ちょっと まってください。よていひょう を みます。
> 　　　　あ、五じから <u>かいぎ</u> が あります。
>
> すずき: ああ そう ですか。<u>六日</u> は いかが ですか。
>
> やまだ: <u>六日</u> も ちょっと。
>
> すずき: では、<u>九日</u> は。
>
> やまだ: <u>九日</u> は だいじょうぶ です。
>
> すずき: はい、わかりました。

Notes:

1. ちょっと まってください This is another version of しょうしょう おまちください which we learned in Lesson 8.

2. ちょっと means "a little," but in this situation it is used to indicate something is not convenient. This is an easy way of refusing a suggestion because you don't have to finish the sentence and say what is inconvenient about the suggestion. You can just leave it hanging with:
   (time/thing) は ちょっと ‥‥。

3. だいじょうぶ (大丈夫) means "all right."

Practice the above かいわ by substuting the dates and events.

Appointment Book よていひょう　予定表

This is a page from an appointment book (よていひょう). Person B is the ぶちょう of a company and has quite a lot of appointments. Person A is a ひしょ who is trying to arrange a number of events (see list below よていひょう). Use a conversation like the one below to arrange the events (you will have to extend it since there are three days to choose from). Then write them into the よていひょう.

A: ぶちょう、<u>event</u> の日です が。らうげつ の <u>date 1</u> は いかが ですか。

B: <u>date 1</u> ですか。ちょっと まって。<u>date 1</u> は ちょっと・・。

　　<u>then says the appointment that is on that day</u> (convert to **masu** form) 。

A: じゃ、<u>date 2</u> は いかが ですか。

B: ええ、だいじょうぶ ですよ。

Part A

Here are four events each with three possible dates which the ひしょ wishes to arrange.

Event		Possible dates
しゃいんりょこう	社員旅行	二日、八日、十二日
せったいゴルフ	接待ゴルフ	四日、十日、十一日
しゅっちょう	出張	十三日、十四日、十五日
はなみ	花見	二十七日、二十八日、三十日

Extend this れんしゅう by adding some more appointments.

Cultural Note せったい 接待

Japanese companies often invite their clients out to dinner, out for drinks, or for a game of golf, and foot the bill. This activity is called せったい. This is aimed a deepening the business relationship and is a very important aspect of Japanese corporate culture. People in the sales division of a company tend to spend a lot of time doing せったい.

time (に) event が あります。

Q: <u>十五日</u> に <u>よてい</u> が ありますか。   Q: Do you have an <u>appointment</u> on the <u>15th</u>?

A: はい、あります。   A: Yes, I do (have one).

    いいえ、ありません。   No, I don't (have one).

17.8 Japanese holidays 日本のしゅくじつ 日本の祝日

If you are going to 日本, it is advisable to avoid trying to book a ホテル (hoteru) during one of the main holiday periods. The most crowded times are New Year おしょうがつ, and Golden Week.

▭▭

おしょうがつ (お正月) Officially the only public holiday is Jan.1, but most people have four or five days off at this time.

ゴールデン ウィーク (gooruden uiiku) This is a popular name for a cluster of public holidays at the end of April and beginning of May. This gives people the chance to take about one week off. The official public holidays こくみん の しゅくじつ in this week are:

みどり の ひ	緑の日	Greenery Day	4月29日
けんぽう きねんび	憲法記念日	Constitution Day	5月3日
こども の ひ	子供の日	Children's Day	5月5日

Other こくみん の しゅくじつ (国民の祝日) are:

せいじん の ひ	成人の日	Coming-of-age Day	1月15日
けんこく きねんび	建国記念日	National Day	2月11日
しゅんぶん の ひ	春分の日	Spring Equinox Day	3月20日
けいろう の ひ	敬老の日	Respect the Elderly Day	9月15日
しゅうぶん の ひ	秋分の日	Autumn Equinox Day	9月23日
たいいく の ひ	体育の日	Sports Day	10月10日
ぶんか の ひ	文化の日	Culture Day	11月3日
きんろうかんしゃ の ひ	勤労感謝の日	Labor Day	11月23日
てんのうたんじょうび	天皇誕生日	Emperor's Birthday	12月23日

 ■Conversation 17.8 かいわ 会話

A public holiday

Two overseas students are talking. One of them doesn't know much about Japanese しゅくじつ.

A: 月よう日 に なに を しますか。
B: 月よう日 ですか。 もちろん、 がっこう へ いきます。
A: でも、 月よう日 は やすみ ですよ。
B: えっ、 ほんとう でうか。
A: ええ、 ほんとう ですよ。 月よう日 は しゅくじつ ですよ。
B: なんの日 ですか。
A: こどもの日 です。
B: そう ですか。 しりません でした。

Notes:

1. ほんとう (本当) means "really" or "truly." The expression ほんうとう ですか translates as "Do you mean that" or "You're not kidding." You use it when you are surprised at what someone has just told you.

2. なんの (何の) This is just the question word なん being attached to a noun with の. You use this type of question when you want to ask the name of something. For example:

なんの えいが　　What movie?
なんの 本　　　　What book?

3. しりません is the negative form of the verb しる (知る) which means "know." しりません でした means "I didn't know (that)."

Practice the above かいわ by substituting the days and しゅくじつ.

17.9 Cutural note: Children's Day こどものひ 子供の日

5月5日 was originally called たんご の せっく (端午の節句) and was for boys only. But in 1948 the day was designated a national holiday. Although it is called こども の 日 to wish all children steady growth and happiness, the festival is still aimed mainly at boys. (Girls have their own festival called ひなまつり.) The most obvious symbol of こども の 日 is the colourful cloth or paper carp streamers that families hoist up on poles outside their houses, topped with colored streamers called ふきながし (吹き流し). The carp streamers are called こいのぼり (鯉のぼり) and symbolize strength and determination. The carp is considered to be a strong, courageous fish since it is able to swim upstream and even up waterfalls. Parents hope that their sons will grow up strong and succeed in overcoming any obstacles in their life like the carp.
The こいのぼり are of different sizes and colors and represent the family members as follows:

—the largest black こいのぼり represents おとうさん.
—the large red こいのぼり represents おかあさん.
—the other smaller こいのぼり represent the こども.

On this day families with a young boy also display miniature suits of armor called よろいかぶと (鎧甲) and samurai dolls representing legendary heroes such as きんたろう (金太郎), the boy who defeated a bear, in the house. People also eat special foods such as rice dumplings wrapped in bamboo leaves called ちまき or a half-moon shaped, sweet rice cake which is wrapped in oak leaves and called かしわもち (柏餅).

Many people also take a special bath on this day—the leaves or roots of the iris しょうぶ (菖蒲) are put into the bath. This custom has a complex origin. On one hand, the word しょうぶ is a homonym for a word meaning "military spirit" (尚武). On the other, the old festival of たんご の せっく was associated with hunting and the gathering of medicinal herbs of which しょうぶ (菖蒲) is one. しょうぶ also has the reputation of being able to drive away evil spirits. I suspect that the use of this herb in the treatment of psychological disorders has something to do with this belief.

よろいかぶと

こいのぼり

しょうぶ

かしわもち

ちまき

Part B

四月	予定表	四月	予定表
1 木	しゅっちょう	16 金	
2 金	しゅっちょう	17 土	
3 土		18 日	せったいゴルフ
4 日	くうこう に いく	19 月	
5 月		20 火	
6 火		21 水	
7 水		22 木	
8 木	おおさか に いく	23 金	
9 金	おおさか から かえる	24 土	
10 土	むすこ の たんじょう日	25 日	

11 日		26 月	
12 月		27 火	4じ〜 かいぎ
13 火	5じ〜 かいぎ	28 水	しゃちょうと ばんごはん
14 水	かちょうと ばんごはん	29 木	みどりの日
15 木		30 金	

Answers こたえ 答え

Practice 17.2

Arizona, Ohio, Utah, California, Oregon, New York, New South Wales, Victoria, Queensland, South Australia, Tasmania, Northern Territory, Ontario, Quebec, British Columbia, Saskatchewan, Suffolk, Somerset, Derbyshire, Devon(shire), Hampshire.

Conversation 17.6

うえだ; 一月十五日; 金よう日; まだ りょこう.

1. Read the following dates aloud.

   1) 五月十日　　　2) 十月二十四日　　　3) 九月六日

   4) 二月二十日　　　5) 十二月十四日　　　6) 四月一日

2. Fill in the blanks with の, は, が, と, に, も or で. If no particle is needed, put an X.

   1) うえの さん は しぶや （　　） すんで います。

   2) わたし は あね （　　） すんで います。

   3) らいげつ （　　） 五日 に よてい が ありますか。

   4) ながさき は きゅうしゅう （　　） あります。

   5) あした は すずき さん （　　） かんげいかい （　　） 日です。

   6) 日本 （　　） かた、 てがみ （　　） ください。

3. Answer the following questions about yourself in 日本ご.

   1) あなた は どこ に すんで いますか。

   _____

   2) あなた の まち は おおきい ですか、 ちいさい ですか。

   _____

   3) あなた の いえ に いぬ が いますか。

   _____

   4) あなた の たんじょう日 は いつ ですか。

   _____

   5) つぎ の しゅくじつ は いつ ですか。 なん の 日 ですか。

   _____

4. Complete the dialogues using one of the words listed below.

1) かとう: おのさん、あした かいしゃ は やすみ ですよ。
   まつい: えっ、（　　　　　　　　　　）ですか。しりません でした。

2) おの: もりさん、しゃいんりょこう の 日 ですが・・。十日 は いかが ですか。
   もり: はい、十日 は （　　　　　　　　）です。

3) さとう: ほんださん、あした やまださん の かんげいかい に いきますか。
   ほんだ: ええ、（　　　　　　　　）いきます。

   だいじょうぶ　　　もちろん　　　ほんとう　　　よかった

5. Translate the following English sentences into 日本ご or vice versa.

1) Does Ms. Mori live in Japan?

_____

2) Do you have time now?

_____

3) I don't have (any) ten yen coins at all.

_____

4) My mother went to Hokkaido last year.

_____

5) Ms. Hayashi, do you have any plans on the fifteenth of next month?

_____

6) ともださん、あした の 五じごろ うち に いますか。

_____

7) わたし の うち に は いぬ と うさぎ が います。

_____

HIRAGANA ひらがな　（平仮名）

	Principal Syllables						Combined Syllables		
	a	i	u	e	o		(y)a	(y)u	(y)o
	あ	い	う	え	お	k	きゃ	きゅ	きょ
k	か	き	く	け	こ	g	ぎゃ	ぎゅ	ぎょ
g	が	ぎ	ぐ	げ	ご	sh	しゃ	しゅ	しょ
s	さ	し *shi*	す	せ	そ	j	じゃ	じゅ	じょ
z	ざ	じ *ji*	ず	ぜ	ぞ	ch	ちゃ	ちゅ	ちょ
t	た	ち *chi*	つ *tsu*	て	と	n	にゃ	にゅ	にょ
d	だ	ぢ *ji*	づ *zu*	で	ど	h	ひゃ	ひゅ	ひょ
n	な	に	ぬ	ね	の	b	びゃ	びゅ	びょ
h	は	ひ	ふ *fu*	へ	ほ	p	ぴゃ	ぴゅ	ぴょ
b	ば	び	ぶ	べ	ぼ	m	みゃ	みゅ	みょ
p	ぱ	ぴ	ぷ	ぺ	ぽ	l/r	りゃ	りゅ	りょ
m	ま	み	む	め	も				
y	や		ゆ		よ				
l/r	ら	り	る	れ	ろ				
w	わ				を *o/wo*				
	ん *n/m*								

Note: All of the above are single syllables. When pronounced they are short, lasting for only one beat. The vowel sounds can, however, be lengthened to two beats. In such cases they are written differently as follows:

aa	ああ	saa	さあ	chii	ちい
ii	いい	soo	そう	jii	じい
uu	うう	koo	こう	nee	ねえ
ee	ええ	shoo	しょう		
oo	おお or おう	shuu	しゅう		

When a syllable is not voiced and skipped over its position is filled by small つ e.g. **gakkoo** がっこう.

275

カタカナ　（片仮名）

	Principal Syllables						**Combined Syllables**		
	a	i	u	e	o		(y)a	(y)u	(y)o
	ア	イ	ウ	エ	オ	k	キャ	キュ	キョ
k	カ	キ	ク	ケ	コ	g	ギャ	ギュ	ギョ
g	ガ	ギ	グ	ゲ	ゴ	sh	シャ	シュ	ショ
s	サ	シ *shi*	ス	セ	ソ	j	ジャ	ジュ	ジョ
z	ザ	ジ *ji*	ズ	ゼ	ゾ	ch	チャ	チュ	チョ
t	タ	チ *chi*	ツ *tsu*	テ	ト	n	ニャ	ニュ	ニョ
d	ダ	ヂ *ji*	ヅ *zu*	デ	ド	h	ヒャ	ヒュ	ヒョ
n	ナ	ニ	ヌ	ネ	ノ	b	ビャ	ビュ	ビョ
h	ハ	ヒ	フ *(fu)*	ヘ	ホ	p	ピャ	ピュ	ピョ
b	バ	ビ	ブ	ベ	ボ	m	ミャ	ミュ	ミョ
p	パ	ピ	プ	ペ	ポ	l/r	リャ	リュ	リョ
m	マ	ミ	ム	メ	モ				
y	ヤ		ユ		ヨ				
l/r	ラ	リ	ル	レ	ロ				
w	ワ				ヲ *o/wo*				
	ン *n/m*								

Other combined syllables

ヴァ *va*	クァ *kwa*	グァ *gwa*	ツァ *tsa*	ファ *fa*
ウィ *wi*	ヴィ *vi*	ティ *ti*	ディ *di*	フィ *fi*
ヴ *vu*	デュ *dyu*			

イェ *ye*	ウェ *we*	ヴェ *ve*	ジェ *je*	チェ *che*	ツェ *tse*	フェ *fe*
ヴォ *wo*	ヴォ *vo*	クォ *kwo*	グォ *gwo*	ツォ *tso*	フォ *fo*	

Note: All of the above are single syllables. When pronounced they are short, lasting for only one beat. The vowel sounds can, however, be lengthened to two beats. In such cases they are followed by a dash as follows: aa ア— ; ii イ— ; uu ウ— ; ee エ— ; oo オ—. This dash is referred to as "ぼう." Here are some examples: コーヒー、 パーティー、ビール、ケーキ 。
When a syllable is not voiced and skipped over, its position is filled by small ツ.
eg. koppu コップ、macchi マッチ、chekku チェック。

276

How to use a Japanese dictionary 日本語の辞書の使い方

The word for "dictionary" is じしょ (辞書) or じてん (辞典). There are a number of types of Japanese dictionaries but they are generally arranged either by かんじ or by かな（ひらがな、カタカナ）. The following vocabulary index is arranged in the order of the ひらがな chart. Since this is the way most Japanese-English わえい (和英) dictionaries are arranged, it is worth getting used to. The logic of the arrangement is the same as for an English dictionary. It starts with the first character in the ひらがな chart i.e. あ and ends with the last one ん. However, there are a number of points to remember when looking up a word in a わえい じてん（和英辞典）.

1. The dictionary is arranged according to the main syllables i.e. those without superscripts. The arrangement is a combination of the vowel sounds あ い う え お and the consonant sounds か さ た な は ま や ら わ such that かい will precede かう and こ precedes さ.

2. Characters with superscripts i.e.てんてん or まる follow directly the same unsuperscripted character e.g. が follows か but precedes き. The supersript てんてん precedes まる e.g. ば follows は but precedes ぱ.

3. ひらがな precedes カタカナ so カコ follows かこ but precedes かさ.

4. Words with combined syllables follow those in which the same two characters are written separately e.g. きょ follows きよ.

5. Words which contain a skipped over syllable which is filled by a small つ（ちいさい つ）are entered in the じしょ as if the つ were pronounced, but they follow entries which have a large つ (pronounced) e.g. がっ follows がつ.

6. In カタカナ lengthened syllables are written with a dash ー. This can represent any vowel sound e.g. カー (**kaa**),キー、クー、ケー、コー. When such words are entered in the じしょ they are ordered as if the vowel sound were written as a character, e.g. カー precedes カイ, and ウイ precedes ウー.

VOCABULARY INDEX さくいん 索引

Following are all the vocabulary items that appear in this textbook. The left hand column gives the word in かな (ひらがな or カタカナ) and the next column shows how the word can be written in かんじ (漢字). In some cases the かんじ may not be in common use but has been included to give you exposure to the form of an authentic わえいじてん that will include かんじ even if it is obscure. Since some personal names can be written using a number of different かんじ only two common possibilities have been included. The third column gives the えいご (英語) for the entry based on the meaning it has in this textbook. The fourth column gives the section (かしょ) where the word first appears.

Key to column 4: k (**kaiwa**), kr (**kikitori renshuu**), r (**renshuu**), re (**rei**), s (**shukudai**), and d (**dokkai**).

仮名 かな *kana*	漢字 かんじ *kanji*	英語 えいご *English*	箇所 かしょ *section*
[あ]			
ああ		oh (F)	k1.3
あいきどう	合気道	aikido	14.9
あいさつ	挨拶	greeting	6.7
アイス		ice (coffee)	11.2
あいづち	相槌	expression showing interest	k1.3
あいて	相手	partner	k6.9
アイロン		an iron	r16.6
あおい	青い	blue	15.5
あかい	赤い	red	15.5
アカイ		Akai (BN)	r9.7
あき	秋	Autumn	5.3
あきはばら	秋葉原	Akihabara (PN)	r16.7
あきら	明	Akira (GN)	1.5
あさ	朝	morning	3.1
あさくさ	浅草	Asakusa (PN)	k6.7
あさごはん	朝ご飯	breakfast	3.2
あさって	明後日	day after tomorrow	6.9
あした	明日	tomorrow	6.6
あしのこ	芦ノ湖	Lake Ashino	4.6
あす	明日	tomorrow	6.9
あそさん	阿蘇山	Mt. Aso (PN)	4.6
あそこ		(over) there	k4.2
あちら		(over) there (pol)	15.6
あつい	暑い	hot (weather)	3.6
あと		later, after	k7.3
あなた		you	15.7
あに	兄	(my) elder brother	14.5
あね	姉	(my) elder sister	14.5
あの		that (thing)	11.3
あのう		um, er (F)	kr7.7
アパート		apartment (older style)	16.3
あまり		not so (+neg. verb)	13.6
アメリカ		America	1.3
アメリカン		American style coffee	11.2
ありがとう		thank you	k3.4
アリゾナしゅう	アリゾナ州	Arizona	r17.2
あります		exist, be, have (things,plants) (masu f)	16.1
あれ		that one (over there)	4.4
アンケート		questionnaire	13.6
[い]			
いい		good, OK, pleasant	3.6
いいえ		no, not at all	2.4
いえ	家	home, house	s2
いかが		How?, How about? (pol.)	k9.6
いきさき	行き先	destination	12.3
いきます	行きます	go (masu f.)	6.1
イギリス		England	1.3
いく	行く	go (dict. f.)	6.8
いくつ		how many? how old?	15.1
いくら		How much (price)?	9.4
いけだ	池田	Ikeda (FN)	8.6.1
いけぶくろ	池袋	Ikebukuro (PN)	r16.7
いしゃ	医者	doctor (medical)	1.4
いしかりがわ	石狩川	Ishikari River (PN)	4.6
いしざき	石崎	Ishizaki (FN)	1.5
いしだ	石田	Ishida (FN)	1.5
いす	椅子	chair	b4.3
いせたんデパート	伊勢丹デパート	Isetan Store Department (BN)	10.2
いただきます	頂きます	(said before eating)	k3.4
イタリア		Italy	1.3
いち	一	1	5.1
いちがつ	一月	January	5.2
いちまん	一万	10,000	9.1
いちろう	一郎	Ichiro (GN)	1.5
いつ		When?	5.4

仮名 かな kana	漢字 かんじ kanji	英語 えいご English	箇所 かしょ section
いっこだて	一戸建て	free standing house	16.3
いつつ	五つ	5 (things), 5 years old	15.1
いってきます	行って来ます	(said when leaving house)	6.7
いってください	言って ください	please say	k4.3
いってらっしゃい	行って らっしゃい	(said to person leaving)	6.7
いつも		always	13.6
いま	今	now	k7.1
います		be,exist (people, animals) (masu f)	14.6
いみんきょく	移民局	immigration office	r5.6
いもうと	妹	(my) younger sister	14.5
いもうとさん	妹さん	(your) younger sister	14.5
いやな	嫌(な)	unpleasant, nasty	3.6
いらっしゃいませ		Welcome (SI)	k11.2
いる		be,exist (people, animals) (dict f)	b14.6
いろ	色	color	15.5
いろいろ(な)	色々(な)	various	d12.8
インド		India	1.3
インドネシア		Indonesia	1.3

[う]

仮名	漢字	英語	箇所
ウイスキー		whiskey	15.4
ウイリアムス		Williams (FN)	r4.1
うえだ	上田	Ueda (FN)	1.5
うえの	上野	Ueno (PN)	k6.7
うえの	上野	Ueno (FN)	d7.4
うきよえ	浮世絵	Ukiyo picture	k10.5
うける	受ける	receive, get (dict. f.)	8.1
うさぎ	兎	rabbit	r17.4
うし	牛	cow, ox	s3
うち	家	home, my place	k5.5
うめしゅ	梅酒	plum liqueur	15.4
うめぼし	梅干し	preserved plum	k11.4

[え]

仮名	漢字	英語	箇所
え (with rising intonation)		What! (F)	k4.2
エアコン		air conditioner	r16.3
えいが	映画	film, movie	kr7.7
えいがかん	映画館	cinema	kr7.7
えいが かんしょう	映画観賞	cinema going, film appreciation	14.9
えいご	英語	English language	r2.3
ええ		yes	k3.6
ええと		er, um (F)	14.11
えき	駅	train station	4.2
えきいん	駅員	station attendant	k7.5

仮名 かな kana	漢字 かんじ kanji	英語 えいご English	箇所 かしょ section
えきべん	駅弁	station bento	k11.4
えど	江戸	Edo (PN)	k6.7
えみ	恵美	Emi (GN)	1.5
えん	円	yen	9.2
えんぴつ	鉛筆	pencil	r17.3

[お]

仮名	漢字	英語	箇所
お	御	honorific prefix	k1.3
おおきい	大きい	big, large	k17.1
オークランド		Auckland (PN)	r14.3
おおさか	大阪	Osaka (PN)	6.4
オーストラリア		Australia (PN)	1.3
おかあさん	お母さん	(another's) mother	14.5
おかえりなさい	お帰りなさい	welcome home!	6.7
おかね	お金	money	9.2
おきなわ	沖縄	Okinawa (PN)	1.8
おきます	起きます	get up (out of bed) (masu f)	13.3
おきゃくさん	お客さん	customer, client, guest (pol.)	14.7
おく	億	hundred million unit	9.1
おくさん	奥さん	(another's) wife	14.10
おくりもの	贈り物	gift	k15.5
おこさん	お子さん	(another's) child	14.10
おさきに	お先に	before you, after you	k15.8
おさけ	お酒	alcoholic drinks	13.6
おしいれ	押し入れ	built in closet in Japanese room	d16.4
おじぎ	お辞儀	bow	1.2
おしぼり	お絞り	small wet towel, washer	11.2
おしょうがつ	お正月	New Year	17.8
おしんこう	お新香	pickled cucumber	k11.4
おそまつさま でした	お粗末様 でした	(polite phrase)	3.5
おちゃ	お茶	Japanese tea	r3.4
おちゃのみず	お茶ノ水	Ochanomizu (PN)	r16.7
おてあらい	御手洗い	toilet, washroom	4.2
おとうさん	お父さん	(another's) father	14.5
おとうと	弟	(own) younger brother	14.5
おとうとさん	弟さん	(another's) younger brother	14.5
おとこ	男	man, male (not polite)	k12.6
おとこのひと	男の人	man, male	k12.6
おととい	一昨日	day before yesterday	6.10
おととし	一昨年	the year before last	17.4
おなじ	同じ	same	5.4
おにいさん	お兄さん	(another's) elder brother	14.5
おにぎり	お握り	compressed rice cake	k11.2

279

仮名 かな *kana*	漢字 かんじ *kanji*	英語 えいご *English*	箇所 かしょ *section*
カンタスこうくう	カンタス航空	Qantas Airlines	r5.6
かんだ	神田	Kanda (PN)	k6.1
がんねん	元年	first year of reign	15.9

[き]

きいろい	黄色い	yellow	15.5
ききます	聞きます	listen (masu f)	13.1
ききとり	聞き取り	listening comprehension	kr3.8
きく	聞く	listen, ask (dict f)	9.4
きくのはな	菊の花	chrysanthemum flower	2.12
きこう	気候	climate	5.7
きせつ	季節	season	5.3
きただけ	北岳	Kitadake (PN)	4.6
きたはんきゅう	北半球	Northern Hemisphere	5.4
きっさてん	喫茶店	coffee shop	11.2
きって	切手	postage stamp	k15.3.1
きってあつめ	切手集め	stamp collecting	14.9
きてください	来てください	please come (this way)	k4.2
きのう	昨日	yesterday	6.10
きます	来ます	come (masu f)	8.4
きみ	君	you (familiar)	k11.3
きみがよ	君が代	Japanese National Anthem	2.13
きゃく	客	customer, guest	k9.5
キャノン		Canon (BN)	9.5
きゅう	九	9	5.5
きゅうしゅう	九州	Kyushu (PN)	1.8
ぎゅうにゅう	牛乳	cows' milk	k11.4
きょう	今日	today	6.9
きょうかしょ	教科書	textbook	r11.3
きょうこ	京子、恭子	Kyoko (GN)	k13.5
きょうし	教師	teacher, instructor	1.4
きょうしつ	教室	classroom	4.5
きょうだい	兄弟	brothers and sisters, siblings	14.6
きょうと	京都	Kyoto (PN)	6.4
きょねん	去年	last year	17.4
ギルダー		guilder	r9.8
キン		Kim (FN)	r4.1
きんぎょ	金魚	gold fish	r17.4
ぎんこう	銀行	bank	4.2
ぎんこういん	銀行員	bank employee	r4.1
ぎんざ	銀座	Ginza (PN)	kr7.7
きんたろう	金太郎	Kintaro (GN)	17.9
きんようび	金曜日	Friday	10.1
きんろうかんしゃのひ	勤労感謝の日	Labor Day	17.8

[く]

く	九	9	5.1
く	区	municipality	14.12
クイーンズランドしゅう	クイーンズランド州	Queensland (PN)	r17.2
くうこう	空港	airport	r10.3
くがつ	九月	September	5.2
くし	櫛	comb	s1
ください	下さい	please	k4.2
くだもの	果物	fruit	15.2
くち	口	mouth, entrance	14.13
くつ	靴	shoes	s5
くっしゃろこ	屈斜路湖	Lake Kussharo (PN)	4.6
くに	国	country, nation	1.3
くまがいぐみ	熊谷組	Kumagai Constructions (BN)	r8.1
クラス		class	14.7
くる	来る	come (dict. f.)	8.4
くるま	車	car	k11.5
くん	君	Mr., Ms. (suf.)	k11.3

[け]

けいさつ	警察	police	r5.6
けいろうのひ	敬老の日	Respect for the Elderly Day	17.8
ゲーム		game	r13.5
けさ	今朝	this morning	6.9
けしゴム	消ゴム	eraser	r11.3
げつようび	月曜日	Monday	10.1
ケベックしゅう	ケベック州	Quebec (PN)	r17.2
けん	県	prefecture	14.12
げん	元	yuan	r9.8
げんかん	玄関	entrance hall	k8.6.3
げんき	元気	healthy, well	2.2
けんこくきねんび	建国記念日	National Day	17.8
けんじ	健次、賢治	Kenji (GN)	1.5
けんぽうきねんび	憲法記念日	Constitution Day	17.8

[こ]

ご	五	5	5.1
ご	御	honorific prefix	8.6
ご	語	language (suf.)	2.3
こいのぼり	鯉のぼり	carp streamer	17.9
ごう	号	number, No.	14.12
こうえん	公園	park	k6.7
こうかんする	交換する	exchange (dict. f.)	8.7
こうじょう	工場	factory	r16.7
こうちゃ	紅茶	tea	11.2
こうつう	交通	transportation	7.10

281

仮名 かな *kana*	漢字 かんじ *kanji*	英語 えいご *English*	箇所 かしょ *section*
こうばん	交番	police box	4.2
こうべ	神戸	Kobe (PN)	6.4
こうむいん	公務員	public servant	1.4
こうよう	紅葉	autumn leaves	5.7
コーヒー		coffee	11.2
コーディネーター		coordinator	k14.7
コーラ		cola	k15.4.1
ゴールデンウィーク		Golden Week	17.8
ゴールドコースト		Gold Coast (PN)	r10.3
ごがつ	五月	May	5.2
こくせき	国籍	nationality	2.3
こくばん	黒板	blackboard	4.5
こくみん	国民	citizens, the public	17.8
ここ		here	6.3
ごご	午後	p.m.	7.7
ここのつ	九つ	nine (things)	15.1
ごしゅじん	ご主人	your husband	14.10
こしょう	胡椒	pepper	s4
ごしょうかい します	ご紹介します	I'll introduce you.	8.6
ゴジラ		Godzilla	kr7.7
ごぜん	午前	a.m.	7.7
ごたんだ	五反田	Gotanda (PN)	r16.7
ごちそうさま でした	ご馳走様 でした	(said after a meal)	3.5
こちら		this, here, I	8.6
こちらこそ		It is I who should...	k8.6.1
ことし	今年	this year	17.4
ことば	言葉	word, language	2.3
こども	子供	child(ren)	14.10
こどものひ	子供の日	Children's Day	17.8
この		this (thing)	11.3
ごはん	ご飯	meal, cooked rice	3.2
こまつ	小松	Komatsu (FN)	k8.6.1
ゴルフ		golf	r10.3
これ		this	k3.4
これから		after this	k15.8
ごろ	頃	about,around (suf.)	8.4
こんしゅう	今週	this week	10.4
こんにちは	今日は	Good Afternoon	2.1
こんばん	今晩	this evening	6.9
こんばんは	今晩は	Good Evening	2.1
コンピューター		computer	r16.1

[さ]

仮名	漢字	英語	箇所
さあ		mm, well (F)	k8.6.3
サーフィン		surfing	14.9
サーブ		SAAB (BN)	r11.5
さい	才、歳	years old (suf.)	15.8

仮名 かな *kana*	漢字 かんじ *kanji*	英語 えいご *English*	箇所 かしょ *section*
サウズオースト ラリアしゅう	サウズオース トラリア州	South Australia (PN)	r17.2
サウナ		sauna	k16.6
さかな	魚	fish	k3.4
さかや	酒屋	liquor store	k15.4.1
さき	先	previous	k15.8
さくばん	昨晩	last night	6.10
さくら	桜	cherry blossom	2.12
サクラ		Sakura (BN)	9.5
さくらぎんこう	さくら銀行	Sakura Bank (BN)	r8.1
さくらじま	桜島	Sakurajima (PN)	4.6
さけ	鮭	salmon	k11.4
さけ	酒	alcoholic beverage	13.6
サスカチワン しゅう	サスカチワン 州	Saskatchewan (PN)	r17.2
さとう	佐藤	Sato (FN)	8.2
さつ	札	note, bill (suf.)	9.3
サッカー		soccer	14.9
ざっし	雑誌	magazine	11.4
さっぽろ	札幌	Sapporo	6.4
サハリン		Sahalin (PN)	1.8
サフォーク しゅう	サフォーク 州	Suffolk (PN)	r17.2
ざぶとん	座布団	kind of cushion	d16.4
さま	様	Mrs., Ms., Mr. (suf.)(pol.)	14.2
サマセット しゅう	サマセット 州	Somerset (PN)	r17.2
さむい	寒い	cold (weather)	3.6
さようなら		Good bye	3.7
さらいしゅう	再来週	the week after next	10.4
さらいねん	再来年	the year after next	17.4
サラダ		salad	k11.2
さん	三	3	5.1
さん		Mrs., Ms., Mr.(suf.)	k1.3
さんがつ	三月	March	5.2
サンドイッチ		sandwich	k11.4
さんぽ	散歩	stroll	r6.2
サンヨー	三洋	Sanyo (BN)	k9.6

[し]

仮名	漢字	英語	箇所
し	四	4	5.1
し	市	city (suf.)	14.12
じ	時	o'clock (suf.)	7.1
CD プレイヤー		CD player	r16.3
しお	塩	salt	s1
しがいきょく ばん	市外局番	area code	k5.5
しがつ	四月	April	5.2
じかん	時間	time, hours(suf.)	7.1

仮名 かな kana	漢字 かんじ kanji	英語 えいご English	箇所 かしょ section
じこしょうかい	自己紹介	self introduction	17.4
しこく	四国	Shikoku (PN)	1.8
しごと	仕事	job, occupation	1.4
じしょ	辞書	dictionary	s4
じしん	地震	earthquake	s3
しせいどう	資生堂	Shiseido (BN)	r8.1
したまち	下町	Shitamachi	k6.7
しち	七	seven	5.1
しちがつ	七月	July	5.2
しつもん	質問	question	kr3.8
しつれい	失礼	rudeness	14.10
しでん	市電	tram, streetcar	12.5
じてんしゃ	自転車	bicycle	12.5
じどうし	自動詞	transitive verb	13.3
シドニー		Sydney (PN)	r14.3
しながわ	品川	Shinagawa (PN)	r16.7
しなもの	品物	merchandise, goods	k11.4
シネマ		cinema	kr7.7
しぶや	渋谷	Shibuya (PN)	r16.7
じぶん	自分	oneself	14.5
します		do (masu f)	13.2
ジム		Jim (GN)	r2.9
じむしょ	事務所	office	r16.7
じゃ		well, in that case	k4.2
しゃいん	社員	employee (of a company)	r14.7
シャープ		Sharp (BN)	r9.7
ジャガー		Jaguar (BN)	r11.5
ジャクソン		Jackson (FN)	r4.1
しゃしょう	車掌	(transport) conductor	k7.3
しゃしん	写真	photograph	k12.6
しゃちょう	社長	CEO of a company	8.6
じゃ、また		Bye, See you later	3.7
シャワー		shower	k16.6
しゅう	週	week	10.3
しゅう	州	state, province, county	17.2
じゅう	十	ten	5.1
じゅういちがつ	十一月	November	5.2
じゅうがつ	十月	October	5.2
じゅうぎょういん	従業員	employee	r14.7
じゅうしょ	住所	address	14.11
ジュース		juice	k11.4
じゅうたく	住宅	housing	16.3
じゅうどう	柔道	judo	14.9
じゅうにがつ	十二月	December	5.2
しゅうぶんのひ	秋分の日	Autumn Equinox Day	17.8
じゅうろくべん	十六弁	16 petals	2.12
じゅぎょう	授業	lesson	r7.7
しゅくじつ	祝日	public holiday	17.8
しゅくだい	宿題	homework	s1
しゅくはく	宿泊	accommodation	3.3
しゅじん	主人	husband	12.4
しゅっちょう	出張	business trip	r6.2
しゅみ	趣味	hobby, interest	14.8
じゅわき	受話器	receiver (of phone)	8.1
じゅん	純、淳	Jun (GN)	1.5
しゅんぶんのひ	春分の日	Spring Equinox Day	17.8
じょう	畳	tatami (suf.)	16.3
しょうかいします	紹介します	introduce (masu f.)	8.6
じょうぎ	定規	ruler	r11.3
じょうきゃく	乗客	passenger	k7.3
しょうしょう	少々	a little	8.2
しょうじ	障子	Japanese sliding door	d16.4
じょうず	上手	good at	k8.6.3
しょうちゅう	焼酎	type of distilled spirit	15.4
しょうぶ	菖蒲	iris	17.9
しょうぼうしょ	消防署	fire station	r5.6
しょうゆ	醤油	soy sauce	r3.4
しょうわ	昭和	Showa Period	15.9
ジョギング		jogging	13.6
じょし	助詞	particle	12.7
ジョン		John (GN)	2.5
しる	知る	know (dict. f.)	k17.8
しろい	白い	white	15.5
シンガポール		Singapore (PN)	r9.8
しんかんせん	新幹線	Shinkansen	r7.2
シングル		single	k16.6
じん	人	person, people (suf.)	2.3
じんこう	人口	population	14.3
じんじゃ	神社	Shinto shrine	kr16.8
しんじゅく	新宿	Shinjuku (PN)	k3.7
しんばし	新橋	Shinbashi (PN)	r16.7
しんぶん	新聞	newspaper	11.4

[す]

仮名	漢字	英語	箇所
すいえい	水泳	swimming	s3
スイス		Switzerland (PN)	r9.8
すいようび	水曜日	Wednesday	10.1
スケジュール		schedule	r10.3
すし	寿司	sushi	s3
すずき	鈴木	Suzuki (FN)	k1.1
スズキ		Suzuki (BN)	r11.5
ステレオ		stereo	r16.3
スバル		Subaru (BN)	r11.5
スペイン		Spain (PN)	r9.8
スポーツ		sports	13.2
スミス		Smith (FN)	k1.3

283

仮名 かな kana	漢字 かんじ kanji	英語 えいご English	箇所 かしょ section
すみだがわ	隅田川	Sumida River (PN)	4.6
すみません		excuse me, sorry	k2.4
すもう	相撲	sumo wrestling	14.9
する		do (dict. f)	13.8
すわります	座ります	sit down (masu f)	k3.4
すんでいます	住んでいます	live (masu f)	17.1

[せ]

仮名	漢字	英語	箇所
せいかつ	生活	life	13.4
せいじんのひ	成人の日	Coming-of-Age Day	17.8
せいねんがっぴ	生年月日	date of birth	15.10
せいひん	製品	product, goods	9.7
せいぶデパート	西武デパート	Seibu Department Store (BN)	10.2
せいべつ	性別	gender	r15.10
せつぞくし	接続詞	conjunction	13.4
せったい	接待	entertaining clients	r17.7
セット		set	11.2
せとないかい	瀬戸内海	Inland Sea (PN)	1.8
ゼロ		zero	5.5
せん	線	line	7.5
せん	千	a thousand	9.1
せんしゅう	先週	last week	10.4
せんせい	先生	(polite title), teacher	2.8
せんせんしゅう	先々週	the week before last	10.4
ぜんぜん	全然	not at all, never	13.6
せんそうじ	浅草寺	Senso Temple (PN)	k6.7
せんだい	仙台	Sendai (PN)	6.4
ぜんぶで	全部で	all together	k11.4

[そ]

仮名	漢字	英語	箇所
そうですか		really, is that so?	k1.3
そこ		there	6.3
そして		and, then	13.4
そちら		that, there, you	15.6
ソニー		Sony (BN)	r9.7
その		that (thing)	11.3
それ		that	k3.4
それから		and then, after that	13.4
それだけ		only that, that's all	k15.4.1
そろばん	算盤	abacus	r17.3

[た]

仮名	漢字	英語	箇所
ダービーシャーしゅう	ダービーシャー州	Derbyshire (PN)	r17.2
タイ		Thailand	1.3
たいいくのひ	体育の日	Sports Day	17.8
だいがく	大学	university	k5.5
だいがくせい	大学生	university student	r14.7

仮名 かな kana	漢字 かんじ kanji	英語 えいご English	箇所 かしょ section
たいしかん	大使館	embassy	5.6
たいしょう	大正	Taisho Period	15.9
だいじょうぶ	大丈夫	all right, fine	k17.7
だいすけ	大助	Daisuke (GN)	1.5
たいせつな	大切(な)	important	5.6
ダイハツ		Daihatsu (BN)	r11.5
たいふう	台風	typhoon	5.7
だいぶつ	大仏	Big Buddha statue	12.2
たいへいよう	太平洋	Pacific Ocean	1.8
だいまるデパート	大丸デパート	Daimaru Department Store (BN)	r8.1
ダイヤモンドヘッド		Diamond Head (PN)	d12.8
たいわん	台湾	Taiwan (PN)	1.3
たかい	高い	expensive, high	k9.6
たかこ	孝子, 多香子	Takako	k13.5
たくさん	沢山	much, many, a lot	kr16.8
タクシー		taxi	12.5
だけ		only	k15.4.1
たずねる	尋ねる	ask (dict. f.)	15.8
タスマニア		Tasmania (PN)	re2.6
タスマニアしゅう	タスマニア州	Tasmania (PN)	r17.2
ただいま	ただ今	I'm home!	6.7
たたみ	畳	matting floor	d16.4
たち	達	(plural suffix)	k12.6
たどうし	他動詞	transitive verb	13.2
たなか	田中	Tanaka (FN)	k1.1
たべもの	食べ物	food	3.9
たばこ	煙草	cigarette	k11.4
ダブル		double (room)	k16.6
たべます	食べます	eat	13.1
だま	玉	coin (suf.)	9.3
たまご	卵	egg	r3.4
たみこ	民子	Tamiko (GN)	k8.6.3
だれ	誰	Who?	k11.3
だれの	誰の	whose?	k11.3
たろう	太郎	Taro (GN)	1.5
たんじょうび	誕生日	birthday	15.8
ダンス		dancing	14.9
だんち	団地	housing complex	16.3

[ち]

仮名	漢字	英語	箇所
ちいさい	小さい	small	k17.1
チーズ		cheese	k3.4
チェン		Chen (FN)	r4.1
ちがいます	違います	not correct, different	2.4
ちかてつ	地下鉄	subway, underground railway	12.5
ちず	地図	map	1.8

仮名 かな *kana*	漢字 かんじ *kanji*	英語 えいご *English*	箇所 かしょ *section*
ちち	父	(own) father	14.5
ちまき		kind of rice dumpling	17.9
チャック		Chuck (GN)	re2.6
ちゅうおうせん	中央線	Chuo Line	r16.7
ちゅうごく	中国	China	1.3
ちゅうもん	注文	order	k11.2
ちょうめ	丁目	division of a suburb	14.12
ちょっと		a little	k17.7
ちり	地理	geography	4.6

[つ]

ツアー		tour	r10.3
つうか	通貨	currency	9.3
つかいかた	使い方	way of using	10.6
つき	月	moon, month	5.2
つぎ	次	next	k7.2
つく	着く	arrive (dict f.)	7.3
つくえ	机	desk	4.5
つくります	作ります	make (masu f.)	13.1
つくる	作る	make (dict. f.)	12.1
つけもの	漬物	pickles	r3.4
つとめさき	勤め先	place of employment	k5.5
つゆ	梅雨	wet season	5.3
つり	釣	fishing	14.9

[て]

で		by, in (method) (p.)	4.3
で		by, at (place) (p.)	13.5
ティー		tea	k11.2
ティッシュ		tissue	k11.4
テープレコーダー		tape recorder	r16.1
てがみ	手紙	letter	13.1
でございます		humble form of desu (pol.)	8.1
です		is, am, are	k1.1
テニス		tennis	13.6
テニスコート		tennis court	r16.6
では		well (then)	k3.7
デパート		department store	r7.7
デボン(シャー) しゅう	デボン (シャー)州	Devon(shire)	r17.2
でる	出る	depart, leave (dict. form)	7.3
でも		but	k13.6
テレビ		television	9.7
テレホンカード		telephone card	k17.3.2
てるてる ぼうず	照る照る 坊主	kind of doll	k4.4
てん		comma	1.9
てんいん	店員	shop assistant	s3

仮名 かな *kana*	漢字 かんじ *kanji*	英語 えいご *English*	箇所 かしょ *section*
てんき	天気	weather	3.6
でんきや	電気屋	electrical goods shop	k9.6
でんしゃ	電車	electric train	r7.2
てんじょう	天井	ceiling	4.5
でんたく	電卓	electronic calculator	r17.3
てんてん		ditto mark, superscript	3.10
てんのう	天皇	monarch of Japan	15.9
てんのうけ	天皇家	Imperial family	2.12
てんのう たんじょうび	天皇誕生日	Emperor's Birthday	17.8
でんわ	電話	telephone	4.2
でんわばんごう	電話番号	telephone number	5.5

[と]

と		and, with (p.)	k6.5
ドア		door (hinged)	4.5
ドイツ		Germany	1.3
トイレ		toilet	4.2
どういたしまして		you're welcome	kr7.7
とうきょう	東京	Tokyo (PN)	1.8
どうこうしゃ	同行者	companion (on a trip)	12.4
とうしばでんき	東芝電気	Toshiba Electric (BN)	r8.1
どうぞ		"go ahead", "here you are"	k1.1
とうふ	豆腐	tofu, bean curd	k3.4
どうぶつえん	動物園	zoo	10.2
どうも		"thanks"	1.7
とお	十	10 (objects)	15.1
トースト		toast	k11.2
とき	時	time	6.6
ときどき	時々	sometimes	13.6
どくしょ	読書	reading	14.9
どくしん	独身	single, unmarried	14.10
とけい	時計	clock, watch	k7.1
どこ		Where?	4.1
どこか		somewhere/anywhere	10.5
とこのま	床の間	alcove (in Japanese room)	d16.4
どこへも		nowhere (plus neg. verb)	10.5
ところ	所	place	k16.2
とし	年	year	15.9
としょかん	図書館	library	10.2
どちら		Who, Which, Where? (pol.)	15.6
どっかい	読解	reading compre- hension	d7.4
どっち		Which?	15.6
とても		very	k3.6
とねがわ	利根川	Tone River (PN)	4.6

仮名 かな *kana*	漢字 かんじ *kanji*	英語 えいご *English*	箇所 かしょ *section*
どの		Which (thing)?	11.5
ともこ	友子	Tomoko (GN)	1.5
ともだ	友田	Tomoda (FN)	kr3.8
ともだち	友達	friend(s)	12.4
どようび	土曜日	Saturday	10.1
トヨタ		Toyota (BN)	k11.5
とり	鳥	bird	r17.4
どれ		Which?	11.5
ドレス		dress	k13.5
ドル		dollar	9.8

[な]

ながさき	長崎	Nagasaki (PN)	6.4
なかたに	中谷	Nakatani (FN)	k8.4
なごや	名古屋	Nagoya (PN)	6.4
なし	梨	nashi, type of pear	s4
なつ	夏	summer	5.3
なな	七	7	5.5
ななつ	七つ	seven (things)	15.1
なに	何	What?	b13.5
なは	那覇	Naha (PN)	6.4
なまえ	名前	name	1.5
なん	何	What?	k3.4
なんがつ	何月	What month?	r5.2
なんさい	何才	How old?, What age?	15.8
なんじ	何時	What time?	7.1
なんで	何で	By what? How?	12.3
なんにん	何人	How many people?	14.1
なんばん	何番	What number?	5.5
なんようび	何曜日	What day (of the week)?	10.1

[に]

に		to (p.)	6.1
に	二	2	5.1
にいがた	新潟	Niigata (PN)	6.4
にがつ	二月	February	5.2
にく	肉	meat	s1
ニコン		Nikon (BN)	9.5
にし	西	west	s1
にち	日	day of month (suf.)	17.5
にちようび	日曜日	Sunday	10.1
ニッサン	日産	Nissan (BN)	r11.5
にっしょうき	日章旗	Japanese national flag	2.10
にっぽん	日本	Japan	2.11
にほん	日本	Japan	1.3
にほんえん	日本円	Japanese yen	9.8
にほんかい	日本海	Japan Sea (PN)	1.8
にほんこうくう	日本航空	Japan Airlines, JAL (BN)	r5.6

仮名 かな *kana*	漢字 かんじ *kanji*	英語 えいご *English*	箇所 かしょ *section*
にほんこうつう こうしゃ	日本交通 公社	Japan Travel Bureau, JTB (BN)	r8.1
にほんしき	日本式	Japanese-style	3.3
にほんしゅ	日本酒	Japanese rice wine	15.4
にほんちゃ	日本茶	Japanese tea	r17.3
にほんでんき	日本電気	Nippon Electric NEC (BN)	r9.7
ニューサウス ウエールズしゅう	ニューサウス ウエールズ州	New South Wales (PN)	k17.1
ニュージ-ランド		New Zealand (PN)	1.3
ニューヨーク		New York (PN)	r14.3
ニューヨーク しゅう	ニューヨーク 州	New York State (PN)	r17.2
にん	人	people (suf.)	14.1

[ぬ]

[ね]

ね		isn't it, aren't they etc. (p.)	k3.6
ねこ	猫	cat	s10
ねだん	値段	price	9.2
ねます	寝ます	go to bed, sleep (masu f)	13.3
ねる	寝る	go to bed, sleep (dict. f)	13.8
ねん	年	year (suf.)	15.9
ねんれい	年齢	age	15.8

[の]

の		of, 's (p)	2.7
ノーザンテリ トリーしゅう	ノーザンテリ トリー州	Northern Territory (PN)	r17.2
ノート		note book	r11.3
のみます	飲みます	drink (masu f.)	13.1
のむ	飲む	drink (dict. f.)	13.8
のり	海苔	nori (type of sea vegetable)	k3.4

[は]

は		wa (p.)	k1.3
は		tooth	s1
バーツ		baht	r9.8
パーティー		party	r6.2
バーベキュー		barbecue	r10.3
はい		yes, I hear you	2.2
ハイキング		hiking	14.9
ばいてん	売店	small shop, kiosk	11.4
はえ	蝿	a fly	s2
はがき	葉書	postcard	d8.5
はかた	博多	Hakata (PN)	7.10
はく、ぱく	泊	nights (suf.)	16.6

仮名 かな *kana*	漢字 かんじ *kanji*	英語 えいご *English*	箇所 かしょ *section*
はくばん	白板	white board	4.5
はくぶつかん	博物館	museum	10.2
はくぼく	白墨	chalk	r16.1
はこね	箱根	Hakone (PN)	k12.6
はし	箸	chopsticks/bridge	s1
はじめまして		"Pleased to meet you"	k1.1
ばしょ	場所	place	r5.6
バス		bus	k7.2
バスてい	バス停	bus stop	4.2
はた	旗	flag	2.10
はたち	二十(才)	20 years old	15.8
はち	八	8	5.1
はちがつ	八月	August	5.2
はつおん	発音	pronunciation	1.6
はな	花	flower	s4
ハナウマ ベイ		Hanauma Bay (PN)	d12.8
はなこ	花子	Hanako (GN)	1.5
はなみ	花見	flower viewing	5.7
はは	母	(own) mother	14.5
はらじゅく	原宿	Harajuku (PN)	r16.7
バリナ		Ballina (PN)	k17.1
はる	春	Spring	5.3
パルシ ステム		PAL system	9.7
はん	半	half (suf.)	7.1
ばん	晩	evening	3.1
ばん	番	number (suf.)	7.5
パン		bread	k11.4
ハンカチ		handkerchief	k11.4
はんが	版画	wood block print	k10.5
バンクーバー		Vancouver (PN)	r14.3
ばんごう	番号	number	5.5
ばんごうあんない	番号案内	directory assistance	r5.6
ばんごはん	晩ご飯	evening meal	3.2
ばんち	番地	banchi (division of land)	14.12
ハンドバッグ		handbag	k13.5
ハンプシャー しゅう	ハンプ シャー州	Hampshire (PN)	r17.2

[ひ]

ひ	日	day	10.7
ビーエム		BMW (BN)	r11.5
ビーチ		beach	b13.5
ビール		beer	13.1
ビクトリア しゅう	ビクトリア 州	Victoria (PN)	r17.2
ひこうき	飛行機	airplane	kr3.8
びじゅつかん	美術館	art gallery	10.2
ひしょ	秘書	secretary	1.4
ひたち	日立	Hitachi (BN)	k9.6

仮名 かな *kana*	漢字 かんじ *kanji*	英語 えいご *English*	箇所 かしょ *section*
ひづけ	日付	date	15.10
ビデオ		video	k9.6
ビデオカメラ		video camera	r16.1
ひと	人	person	12.2
ひとつ	一つ	1 (object)	15.1
ひとり	一人	one person, alone	14.1
ひとりで	一人で	alone, by oneself	12.4
ひなまつり	雛祭	doll festival	17.9
ひのまる	日の丸	Japanese flag	2.10
ひゃく	百	100	9.1
ヒュンダイ		Hyundai (BN)	r11.5
びょういん	病院	hospital	r14.7
ひょうげん	表現	expression	6.6
ひらがな	平仮名	hiragana	1.6
ひる	昼	middle part of day	3.1
ビル		Bill (GN)	r2.9
ひるごはん	昼ご飯	lunch	3.2
ヒルダ		Hilda (GN)	r2.9
ひろし	弘、浩	Hiroshi (GN)	1.5
ひろしま	広島	Hiroshima (PN)	6.4
びわ	枇杷	loquat	15.2
びわこ	琵琶湖	Lake Biwa (PN)	4.6
ひんど	頻度	frequency	13.6

[ふ]

ふ	府	administrative division (suf.)	14.12
ファックス		fax	r16.3
フィアット		Fiat (BN)	r11.5
フィリピン		Philippines (PN)	r4.1
フイルム		photographic film	k11.4
プール		swimming pool	k16.6
フェリー		ferry	r7.2
フォード		Ford (BN)	r11.5
ふくおか	福岡	Fukuoka (PN)	6.4
フジ		Fuji (BN)	9.5
ふじごこ	富士五湖	Fuji Five Lakes (PN)	4.6
ふじさん	富士山	Mt. Fuji (PN)	4.6
ふたつ	二つ	2 (objects)	15.1
ふたり	二人	two people	14.1
ふつう	普通	usual, normal	13.4
ふとん	布団	mat for sleeping on	d16.4
ふね	船	boat, ship	12.5
ぶちょう	部長	department head	8.6
ふゆ	冬	winter	5.3
ブライアン		Brian (GN)	2.9
ブラウン		Brown (FN)	r4.1
ブラジル		Brazil (PN)	k4.1
フラン		franc	r9.8

仮名 かな *kana*	漢字 かんじ *kanji*	英語 えいご *English*	箇所 かしょ *section*
フランス		France (PN)	1.3
ブランデー		brandy	15.4
ブリチッシュ コロンビアしゅう	ブリチッシュ コロンビア州	British Colombia (PN)	r17.2
プレゼント		a present	kr17.6
ブレンド		blend (coffee)	11.2
フロント		front desk (of hotel)	k16.6
ふん	分	minutes (suf.)	7.2
ぶん	文	sentence	12.1
ぶんかのひ	文化の日	Culture Day	17.8
ぶんけい	文型	language (sentence) pattern	b1.1

[へ]

へ		to (p.)	k6.5
へいせい	平成	Heisei Period	15.9
へいわきねん こうえん	平和記念 公園	Peace Memorial Park (PN)	d8.5
ペセタ		peseta	r9.8
ベッド		bed	d16.4
へや	部屋	room	16.3
ヘラ		Heller (FN)	r4.1
べんごし	弁護士	solicitor, lawyer	1.4
ペン		pen	4.5
ベンツ		Mercedes-Benz (BN)	r11.5
べんきょう	勉強	study	13.2
べんとう	弁当	packed meal	k11.4
べんとうばこ	弁当箱	lunch box	k11.4
ペンフレンド		pen friend	14.11

[ほ]

ぼうし	帽子	hat	s3
ホール		Hall (FN)	r4.1
ホールデン		Holden (BN)	r11.5
ほか	他	other, else	14.5
ぼく	僕	I (informal, male use)	8.2
ほっかいどう	北海道	Hokkaido (PN)	1.8
ホット		hot coffee	11.2
ホテル		hotel	3.3
ホノルル		Honolulu (PN)	d12.8
ボルト		volt	9.7
ボルボ		Volvo (BN)	r11.5
ほん	本	book`	s2
ほん	本	(counter) (suf.)	15.3.2
ホンコン	香港	Hong Kong	r9.8
ほんしゅう	本州	Honshu (PN)	1.8
ほんだ	本田	Honda (FN)	1.5
ホンダ		Honda (BN)	r11.5
ほんたな	本柵	bookshelf	r16.1
ポンド		pound	r9.8

仮名 かな *kana*	漢字 かんじ *kanji*	英語 えいご *English*	箇所 かしょ *section*
ほんとう	本当	really, truly	k17.8

[ま]

まあ		Ah! (surprise, female use) (F)	k8.6.3
まい	枚	(counter) (suf.)	15.3.1
まいあさ	毎朝	every morning	13.6
まいしゅう	毎週	every week	13.6
まいにち	毎日	every day	13.6
まいばん	毎晩	every evening	13.6
マウイとう	マウイ島	Maui Island (PN)	d12.8
まさこ	正子、雅子	Masako (GN)	1.5
また		again	8.2
まだ		not yet, still	13.7
まだまだです		not really, not yet	k8.6.3
または	又は	or	13.4
まち	町	city, town	6.4
まつい	松井	Matsui (FN)	k1.3
マツダ		Mazda (BN)	r11.5
マッチ		match, matches	r17.3
まって ください	待って ください	please wait	k17.7
まで		till, as far as	5.4
マテロ		Matello (FN)	r4.1
まど	窓	window	4.5
マリア		Maria (GN)	4.1
マリーン		Marlene (GN)	r2.9
まる	丸	circle, period, superscript	1.9
マレーシア		Malaysia (PN)	1.3
まわり(に)	回り(に)	surrounding, in the vicinity	kr16.8
まん	万	10,000	9.1
マンション		apartment (newer style)	16.3
まんが	漫画	comic	11.4

[み]

みかん	蜜柑	mandarin orange	15.2
みき	三木	Miki (FN)	k8.6.2
みずうみ	湖	lake	k16.2
みずわり	水割り	whisky and water	15.4
みそしる	味噌汁	miso soup	r3.4
みちお	道夫	Michio (GN)	1.5
みちこ	道子、美知子	Michiko (GN)	1.5
みつこしデパート	三越デパート	Mitsukoshi Department store(BN)	10.2
みっつ	三つ	3 (objects)	15.1
みつびし じどうしゃ (BN)	三菱自動車	Mitsubishi Motors	r8.1
みどりのひ	緑の日	Greenery Day	17.8

仮名 かな *kana*	漢字 かんじ *kanji*	英語 えいご *English*	箇所 かしょ *section*
みな	皆	everybody	d12.8
みなみはんきゅう	南半球	Southern Hemisphere	5.4
ミノルタ		Minolta (BN)	9.5
みます	見ます	see, look (masu f)	13.1
みやげもの	土産物	gift item	14.8
みゆき	美由紀	Miyuki (GN)	1.5
みる	見る	see, look (dict f)	k13.6
ミルク		milk	11.2
みんしゅく	民宿	Japanese guest house	3.3

[む]

仮名	漢字	英語	箇所
むすこ	息子	son	14.10
むすこさん	息子さん	(another's) son (pol.)	14.10
むすめ	娘	daughter	14.10
むすめさん	娘さん	(another's) daughter (pol.)	14.10
むっつ	六つ	6 (objects)	15.1

[め]

仮名	漢字	英語	箇所
メイ		May (FN)	2.9
めいし	名刺	name card, business card	kr3.8
めいじ	明治	Meiji Period	15.9
メーカー		manufacturer, make	9.5
めがね	眼鏡	glasses, spectacles	k11.3
メニュー		menu	k11.2
メリー		Mary (GN)	k2.4

[も]

仮名	漢字	英語	箇所
も		also, too (p)	6.2
もう		already	12.6
もういちど	もう一度	once again	k4.3
もうしわけありません	申し訳ありません	terribly sorry (pol.)	16.5
モーニングセット		morning set, set breakfast	k11.2
もくようび	木曜日	Thursday	10.1
もしもし		Hello (on the phone)	8.1
もちろん	勿論	of course	k13.5
もの	物	thing	15.1
もも	桃	peach	15.2
もり	森	Mori (FN)	k12.6
もりおか	盛岡	Morioka (PN)	7.10
モルモット		guinea pig	r17.4

[や]

仮名	漢字	英語	箇所
や		and (so on)	16.2
や	屋	shop (suf.)	k9.5
やあ		Ah! (m)	k8.6.3
やく	約	approximately	14.3

仮名 かな *kana*	漢字 かんじ *kanji*	英語 えいご *English*	箇所 かしょ *section*
やきゅう	野球	baseball	14.9
やすい	安い	cheap	k9.6
やすだ	安田	Yasuda (FN)	k6.1
やすみ	休み	break, rest, holiday	10.2
やっつ	八つ	8 (objects)	15.1
やまぐち	山口	Yamaguchi (FN)	k14.9
やまだ	山田	Yamada (FN)	1.5
やまのてせん	山の手線	Yamanote Line	r16.7
やまもと	山本	Yamamoto (FN)	1.5

[ゆ]

仮名	漢字	英語	箇所
ゆうびんきょく	郵便局	post office	4.2
ゆうびんばんごう	郵便番号	zip code	14.12
ゆか	床	floor	4.5
ゆき	行	bound for (suf.)	7.5
ゆきお	幸男	Yukio (GN)	1.5
ゆきこ	雪子、幸子	Yukiko (GN)	1.5
ユタしゅう	ユタしゅう	Utah (PN)	r17.2
ゆでたまご	ゆで卵	boiled egg	k11.2
ゆみ	由美	Yumi (GN)	1.5
ゆみこ	由美子	Yumiko (GN)	k2.4

[よ]

仮名	漢字	英語	箇所
よ		emphatic sentence ending	8.2
ようし	用紙	a form	r15.10
ようしつ	洋室	Western style room	16.3
ようび	曜日	day of week (suf.)	10.1
よかったですね		"that was good, wasn't it."	k10.5
よく		often	13.6
よこはま	横浜	Yokohama (PN)	14.11
よしだ	吉田	Yoshida (FN)	12.2
よっつ	四つ	4 (objects)	15.1
よつや	四谷	Yotsuya (PN)	r16.7
よてい	予定	plan, schedule	10.3
よていひょう	予定表	appointment book	r17.7
よみます	読みます	read (masu f)	13.1
よむ	読む	read (dict f)	13.8
よよぎ	代々木	Yoyogi (PN)	r16.7
よる	夜	night	3.1
よろいかぶと	鎧甲	armor and helmet	17.9
よろしい		all right (pol.)	d12.8
よろしく		(formal expression)	k1.1
よん	四	4	5.5

[ら]

仮名	漢字	英語	箇所
ライ		Lai (FN)	r4.1
らいげつ	来月	next month	10.4

仮名 かな *kana*	漢字 かんじ *kanji*	英語 えいご *English*	箇所 かしょ *section*	仮名 かな *kana*	漢字 かんじ *kanji*	英語 えいご *English*	箇所 かしょ *section*
らいしゅう	来週	next week	10.4	レストラン		restaurant	r7.7
らいねん	来年	next year	17.4	れっしゃ	列車	train	r7.2
ライター		cigarette lighter	k11.4	れっとう	列島	archipelago	1.8
ラグビー		rugby	14.9	レモン		lemon	11.2
ラジオ		radio	r16.1	れんしゅう	練習	practice	r2.3
ラジカセ		radio cassette player	r9.7				

[り]　　　　　　　　　　　　　　　　　**[ろ]**

仮名	漢字	英語	箇所	仮名	漢字	英語	箇所
りえ	理恵	Rie (GN)	1.5	ローマじ	ローマ字	Roman characters	1.6
リコー		Ricoh (BN)	9.5	ろく	六	6	5.1
リサ		Lisa (GN)	d12.8	ろくがつ	六月	June	5.2
りょうり	料理	cuisine, food	13.1	ロス		Ross (FN)	k8.6.2
りょかん	旅館	Japanese-style hotel	3.3	ロビー		hotel lobby	d12.8
りょこう	旅行	travel, trip	14.9	ロペス		Lopez (FN)	k4.1
りょこうがいしゃ	旅行会社	travel company	k10.3	ロレン		Loren (FN)	r4.1
リラ		lire	r9.8	ロンドン		London (PN)	r14.3
りんご	林檎	apple	15.2				
リンギ		ringit	r9.8				
リンダ		Linda (GN)	k6.7				

[る]　　　　　　　　　　　　　　　　　**[わ]**

仮名	漢字	英語	箇所	仮名	漢字	英語	箇所
ルノー		Renault (BN)	r11.5	ワープロ		word processor	r9.7
ルピー		rupee	r9.8	ワイン		wine	15.4
				わかりません	分かりません	don't understand	k4.2
				わしつ	和室	Japanese-style room	16.3

[れ]

仮名	漢字	英語	箇所
れい	例	example	2.6
れい	零	zero	5.5
れいぞうこ	冷蔵庫	refrigerator	k16.6

わすれました	忘れました	forgot (masu f.)	k15.4.2
わすれもの	忘れ物	lost thing	k11.3
わたし	私	I, me	2.9
わたしの	私の	my, mine	2.9

[を]

| を | | (p.) after object of verb | 9.6 |

Abbreviations

PN	place name		masu f	*masu* form of verb
FN	family name		dict f	dictionary form of verb
GN	given name		pol.	polite form
BN	brand or business name		suf.	suffix
SI	used by service industry workers		p.	particle
F	filler word: to indicate emotion, hesitation, etc.			

Index to Structures

The sections refer to the first occurrence of the grammatical point. Sections with more extensive notes are also referenced in some cases.

Grammatical Point	Section	Illustrative function or situation	Grammatical Point	Section	Illustrative function or situation
6. Affixes　せつじ　接辞			かわいい	15.8	At the company
			きいろい	15.5	Colors
honorific お	1.3-4	Asking country, job	この、その、あの	11.3	note
くん	11.3	Lost things	さむい	3.6	The weather
honorific ご	8.6.1	A formal introduction	しろい	15.5	Colors
ごろ	8.4	note	たかい	11.2	At a coffee shop
name さま	14.12	note	ちいさい	17.1	My home town
name さん	1.3	note	よかった	10.5	A day off
じ	7.1	Time			
たち　（達）	12.6	Flower viewing in Hakone	**10. Adverbs　ふくし　副詞**		
まい　（毎）	13.6	note	あまり	13.6	note
よう日	10.1	Days of the week	いつも	13.6	note
			いろいろ	16.2	Hakone is a nice place
7. Counters　すうし　数詞			ぜんぜん	13.6	note
			ときどき	13.6	note
円	9.3	Japanese currency	また	8.2	Making a phone call
才	15.7	Asking age	まだ	13.7	note
つ	15.1	Counting objects	もう	4.3	Asking the Japanese name of something
日	17.5	The days of the month		12.6	Flower viewing in Hakone
人	14.1	Counting people		13.7	note
はく　（泊）	16.5	Counting nights accommodation	よく	13.6	note
ばん　（番）	7.5	Finding the right train			
ふん、ぶん　（分）	7.2	Fractions of an hour	**11. Verbs　どうし　動詞**		
本	15.4.1	At a liquor store	あります	16.1	What's in the classroom?
まい　（枚）	15.3.1	At a post office	いきます	6.1	Going places
年	15.9	The year	いってください	4.3	Asking the Japanese name of something
			います	14.6	Asking about brothers and sisters
8. Conjunctions　せつぞくし　接続詞			おきます	13.3	note
これから	15.8	At the company	かいます	13.1	Everyday actions
じゃ	4.2	Looking for a toilet	かえります	8.4	note
そして	13.4	note	かきます	13.1	Everyday actions
それから	13.4	note	ききます	13.1	Everyday actions
でも	13.6	Seeing movies	きてください	4.2	Looking for a toilet
と(and)	6.5	A trip to Japan	きます	8.4	note
または	13.4	note	ください	9.6	Shopping
や	16.2	note	ございます	16.5	Apologizing for lack of goods
			します	13.2	note
9. Adjectives　けいようし　形容詞			すんでいます	17.1	Asking where someone lives
あおい	15.5	Colors	たべます	13.1	Everyday actions
あかい	15.5	Colors	ちがいます	5.4	Seasonal differences
あつい	3.6	The weather	つきます	7.3	Arrival and departure times
いい	3.6	The weather	つくります	13.1	Everyday actions
いやな	3.6	The weather			
いろいろな	12.8	Aloha Tours			
おおきい	17.1	My home town			
おもしろい	16.8	note			

Grammatical Point	Section	Illustrative function or situation	Grammatical Point	Section	Illustrative function or situation
でます	7.3	Arrival and departure times	おやすみなさい	3.7	Finishing a conversation
ねます	13.3	note	かしこまりました	11.2	At a coffee shop
のみます	13.1	Everyday actions	こんにちは	2.1	Greeting someone you know
みます	13.1	Everyday actions	こんばんは	2.1	Greeting someone you know
よみます	13.1	Everyday actions			
わすれました	15.4.2	What did you buy?	こちらこそ	8.6.1	A formal introduction
			ごちそうさまでした	3.5	Finishing a meal

12. Fillers　かんどうし　感動詞

			さようなら	3.7	Finishing a conversation
			しつれいします	3.7	Finishing a conversation
あ	2.2	Meeting by chance		15.8	At the company
ああ	3.6	Talking about the weather	しつれいですが	14.10	note
あのう	7.8	Tonight's movie	じゃ、また	3.7	Finishing a conversation
え	4.2	Looking for a toilet	しょうしょうおまち ください	8.2	Making a phone call
ええと	14.11	My penfriend's address	すみません	2.4	Meeting someone at the airport
さあ	8.6.3	At the front door			
まあ	8.6.3	At the front door	だいじょぶ	17.7	Mr. Smith's welcome party
やあ	8.6.3	At the front door	ただいま	6.7	Greetings used in the home

13. Expressions　ひょうげん　表現

			ちょっと	17.3.1	Do you have a minute?
ありがとうございます	3.4	Breakfast at a minshuku	ちょっとまって	17.7	Mr. Smith's welcome party
いいですね	6.5	A trip to Japan	どういたしまして	7.8	Tonight's movie
いただきます	3.4	Breakfast at a minshuku	どうぞよろしく	1.1	Introducing oneself
いってきます	6.7	Greetings used in the home	どうも、どうぞ	1.7	note
いってらっしゃい	6.7	Greetings used in the home	どうもすみません	4.2	Looking for a toilet
いらっしゃいませ	11.2	At a coffee shop	はじめまして	1.1	Introducing oneself
おかえりなさい	6.7	Greetings used in the home	ほかには	15.4.1	At a liquor store
			ほんとうですか	17.8	A public holiday
おさきに	15.8	At the company	まだまだです	8.6.3	At the front door
おそまつさまでした	3.5	Finishing a meal	もうしわけありません	16.5	Apologizing for lack of goods
おねがいします	2.4	Meeting someone at the airport			
			もちろん	13.5	Shopping in Ginza
おはようございます	2.1	Greeting someone you know	わかりません	4.2	Looking for a toilet

Answers こたえ 答え

HW 1

1.1) oshigoto おしごと; 2) okuni おくに; soo desu そう です.

2.1) hajimemashite, (your family name) desu. doozo yoroshiku はじめまして、(your family name) です。どうぞ よろしく. 2) the family name; 3) doozo どうぞ.

3. Honshu ほんしゅう; Hokkaido ほっかいどう; Kyushuu きゅうしゅう; Shikoku しこく; Tokyo とうきょう.

4. くに; おくに.

HW 2

1.1) は; 2) の; 3) か; はい; 4) chigaimasu ちがいます; 5) そう です.

2.1) chuugokugo ちゅうごくご; 2) sensei せんせい; 3) Kimigayo きみがよ.

3.1) sumimasen, Hanako san desu ka. すみません、はなこ さん です か.; 2) watashi wa Oosutorariajin desu. わたし は オーストラリアじん です.; 3) ohayoo gozaimasu おはよう ございます.; 4) watashi no eigo no sensei no namae wa Biru desu. わたし の えいご の せんせい の なまえ は ビル です.; 5) konbanwa こんばんは.

4. にほん; いいえ; はい.

HW 3

2.1) nan なん; 2) dewa arimasen では ありません; 3) soo そう.

3.1) sore wa nan desu ka. それ は なん です か.; 2) itadakimasu いただきます.; 3) gochisoosama deshita. ごちそう さまでした。.

4.1) ii tenki desu ne. いい てんき です ね。; 2) doomo arigatoo. どうも ありがとう.; iie いいえ。; 3) sayoonara さよ うなら。.

5. にほんじん; ばん; いい.

HW 4

2.1) の; は; 2) で; 3) どこ.

3.1) Sumisu san no kuni ha doko desu ka. スミスさん の くに は どこ です か.; 2) kite kudasai. きて ください.; 3) ginkoo wa eigo de "bank" desu. ぎんこう は えいご で "bank" です.; 4) moo ichido itte kudasai. もう いちど いって ください.; 5) wakarimasen. わかりません.。.

4. Fuji san; Tonegawa; 70%.

5. どこ; なん; しごと; こうばん.

HW 5

2.1) いつ; から; まで; 2) は; と; 3) なんばん; の; は; の.

3.1) なつ; samui さむい; 2) haru はる; 3) aki あき; 4) kisetsu きせつ.

4.1) tsuyu wa eigo de "wet season" desu. つゆ は えいごで "wet season" です.;2) nihon no fuyu wa 12 gatsu kara 2 gatsu made desu. にほん の ふゆ は じゅうに月 から に月 まで です. 3) nihontaishikan no denwabangoo wa nanban desu ka. にほんたいしかん の でんわばんごう は なんばん です か。.

5. いつ; なんばん; なつ; に月（二月）.

HW 6

1.1) に; に; にも; には;2) に; も; に;3) いつ; に;4) の; に; に.

2.1) いきます; いきません; 2) いきました; いきませんでした.

3.1) いってらっしゃい itterasshai; 2) おかえりなさい okaerinasai; 3) ここ.

4.1) A:（わたし は）あした の あさ ながさきに いきます。 B: いい です ね。

2)たなかさん は 三月 に おおさか と きょうと へ いきました。

5. いってきます; きせつ; べんごし. shopping, a walk, a wall.

HW 7

2.1) の; は; 2) は; に; 3) の; は; から; まで.

3.1) どこ; 2) なんじ; 3) なんばんせん.

4.1) すみません。いまなんじですか。 2) つぎのバスは五じはんにでます。 3) えいがは四じから六じはんまでです。

5.1) さようなら; 2) さくら .一月、四月、二月、三月

6.1) Ms. Sato is going to Ginza with Ms. Ono this evening.; 2) The banks are open from 9 to 3 o'clock. (or similar)

HW 8

1. 1)はい、ですが、おねがいします、おまちください 2)ごしょうかい、こちら、こちら、はじめまして、こちらこそ

2. 1)A:きます B:いきます B:いいですよ 2)B:いいえ、まだまだです

3. 1)わたし は 五ごろ ぎんさ に つきます。 2)うえのさん は きのう わたし の うち に きませんでした。 3)（わたしは）あした の ごご おおさか から きょうと まで いきます。
4)（わたしは）七じ ごろ （うち へ/に）かえります。 5)また でんわ します。

HW 9
3.1)いくら 2)どこ 3)どこの
4 1)も は 2)か よ ね を 3)と 4)で
5. おかえりなさい; をください; 五十円; 七千円; 八千円.

HW 10
1.1)なんじ 2)なんようび 3)いつ 4)なん月
2.1)に,に 2)の,と 3)か
3.1)ぎんこう は 月よう日 から きんよう日 まで です。 2)さとうさん は きのう どこへも いきません でした。 3)やすみ は らいしゅう の すいよう日 です。
4.1)どうぞ 2)おかね 3)ひこうき 4) Monday

HW 11
1.ごちゅうもん; をください; ですか; ですか; をください; かしこまりました
2.1)どこ 2)これ 3)どれ 4)この
3.1)の 2)で 3)は,も
4.1)A:このかさは1500円です。そのかさは1300円です。B:じゃ、これをください。
　2)これはだれのきょうかしょですか。　3)それはわたしのではありません。
5.1) I go to the library on Tuesdays and Wednesdays./ I am going to the library on Tuesday and Wednesday.
2) Excuse me, I don't understand. I'll call again. 3) This is the thing (that) Tanaka forgot.

HW 12
1.1) X, で, に/へ　2) に, に　3) の, の　4) の, と
2.1) どこか、なんで　2) だれと　3) だれ, 4) いつ
3.1)Q:かとうさんはもうかまくらに／へいきましたか。A:ええ、せんしゅうの日よう日にいきました。2)（わたしは）一人でくるまでくうこうへ／にいきました。3)あした（わたしは）かないとともだちのいえへ／にいきます。4)これはわたしのかいしゃのしゃしんです。
4. 1) 木よう日; 金よう日 2)a)かいしゃいん　b)でんしゃ　c)でんわばんごう　d)あした　e)やすい　f)たかい

HW 13
1.えいがをみます、ビールをのみます、おんがくをききます、ごはんをたべます、しんぶんをよみます／かいます、かいものをします、くつをかいます
2.1)X、に　2)と、で、を　3)に、を、で、へ／に　4) で、を 5) X、で、を
3.1)もりさんはときどききっさてんでてがみをかきます。2)かないはあまりりょうりをつくりません。3)たなかさんはせんしゅうの日よう日にぎんざでかいものをしました。4)わたしはまいにち五じごろともだちとテニスをします。
4.1)わたし は ぜんぜん こうちゃ （おちゃ）を のみません。 2)（わたし は）ほん を よみました。そして／それから、１１じ ごろ ねました。 3) 土よう日 に うえのさん は よく テニス を します。または、ゴルフ を します。 4) けさ （わたしは）あさ ごはん を たべませんでした。 5)Q:たなかさんは もう （うちへ）かえりましたか。A: いいえ、まだです。
6) 日本人; 日本円; 土よう日

HW 14
1.いちまんごせん、さんじゅうななまん、よんひゃくはちじゅうまん、ごせんまん、ななおく、はっぴゃくにじゅうおく
2.1)は、が、が、と、が　2)に、が、X　3)に、も、に
4.1)このツアーにおきゃくさんが七人います。2)日本の人口はやくいちおくにせんまん人です。3)しつれいですが、どくしんですか。4)（わたしの）ちちはかいしゃいんです。5)すずきさんのおとうさんはおおさかにすんでいます。
5.つま、あね、ごしゅじん、おこさん
6) かぞく; ともだち; おみやげ; じゅうしょ; しゅみ; 人口

HW 15
1.1)五まい　2)七つ　3)いくつ　4)どの　5)プレゼント　6)これ　7)わすれました
2.1)ビールを三本とワインを二本ください。　2)六十円きってを六まいください。3)りんごをいくつかいましたか。
4)A:いもうとさんはなんさい／おいくつですか。B:十八さいです。　5)あのきいろいはなはいくらですか。
3.1)へいせい八ねんです。　2)おさきにしつれいします。3)年　月　日
4.1) 十九さい です。　2)りょうり と どくしょ です。　3)かんだ で かいました。
5. むすめ; しろいはな; 五十才

HW 16

1.1)います　2)あります　3)あります　4)います

2.1)どこ　2)なに　3)いくら

3.に、も、は

4.1)はらじゅくになにがありますか。　2)かまくらはいいところです。　3)じむしょに（は）つくえやいすやでんわがあります。　4)Mr.Sato watched various (a variety of) movies last year.　5)I always eat a lot of fruit.

6.もうしわけありません or もうしわけございません

7.1) わしつ;2) ようしつ;3) しんぶん;4) こんしゅう;5) きゃく;6) みせ

HW17

2.1)に　2)と　3)の　4)に　5)の、の　6)の、を

4.1)ほんとう　2)だいじょうぶ　3)もちろん

5.1)もりさんは日本にすんでいますか。　2)いま　じかんがありますか。3)（わたしは）十円だまがぜんぜんありません。

4)ははきょねんほっかいどうへ／にいきました。　5)はやしさん、らい月の十五日によていがありますか。

6) Ms. Tomoda, will you be home around 5 o'clock tomorrow?

7) I've got a dog and a rabbit at my house.

インタラクティブ・ジャパニーズ 1
INTERACTIVE JAPANESE 1

1996年 7 月26日　第 1 刷発行

著　者　　友田多香子
　　　　　ブライアン・メイ
発行者　　野間佐和子
発行所　　講談社インターナショナル株式会社
　　　　　〒112 東京都文京区音羽 1-17-14
　　　　　電話：03-3944-6493

印刷所　　株式会社　平河工業社
製本所　　株式会社　国宝社

KODANSHA INTERNATIONAL DICTIONARIES
Easy-to-use dictionaries designed for non-native learners of Japanese.

ふりがな和英辞典
KODANSHA'S FURIGANA
JAPANESE-ENGLISH DICTIONARY
The essential dictionary for all students of Japanese.
  • Furigana readings added to all Kanji • Comprehensive 16,000-word basic vocabulary
Vinyl binding, 592 pages, ISBN 4-7700-1983-1

ふりがな英和辞典
KODANSHA'S FURIGANA
ENGLISH-JAPANESE DICTIONARY
The essential dictionary for all students of Japanese.
  • Furigana readings added to all Kanji • Comprehensive 14,000-word basic vocabulary
Vinyl binding, 728 pages, ISBN 4-7700-2055-4

ポケット版　ローマ字和英辞典
KODANSHA'S POCKET ROMANIZED
JAPANESE-ENGLISH DICTIONARY
Easy-to-use and convenient, an ideal pocket reference for beginning and intermediate students, travelers, and business people.
  • 10,000-word vocabulary. • Numerous example sentences.
Paperback, 480 pages, ISBN 4-7700-1800-2

ローマ字和英辞典
KODANSHA'S ROMANIZED JAPANESE-ENGLISH DICTIONARY
A portable reference written for beginning and intermediate students of Japanese.
  • 16,000-word vocabulary. • No knowledge of *kanji* necessary.
Vinyl binding, 688 pages, ISBN 4-7700-1603-4

ポケット版　教育漢英熟語辞典
KODANSHA'S POCKET KANJI GUIDE
A handy, pocket-sized character dictionary designed for ease of use.
  • 1,006 *shin-kyoiku kanji*. • 10,000 common compounds.
  • Stroke order for individual characters.
Paperback, 576 pages, ISBN 4-7700-1801-0

常用漢英熟語辞典
KODANSHA'S COMPACT KANJI GUIDE
A functional character dictionary that is both compact and comprehensive.
  • 1,945 essential *joyo kanji*. • 20,000 common compounds.
  • Three indexes for finding *kanji*.
Vinyl binding, 928 pages, ISBN 4-7700-1553-4

日本語学習使い分け辞典
EFFECTIVE JAPANESE USAGE GUIDE
A concise, bilingual dictionary which clarifies the usage of frequently confused Japanese words and phrases.
  • Explanations of 708 synonymous terms. • Numerous example sentences.
Paperback, 768 pages, ISBN 4-7700-1919-X